Seasoned
with
Sun

A Blending of Cultures

Published by the Junior League of El Paso, Inc.

EL PASO, TEXAS

ABOUT THE ARTISTS

The Junior League of El Paso is grateful to Mr. Russell Waterhouse for the cover of this cookbook.

Mr. Waterhouse, a native southwesterner, was born in El Paso and spent his boyhood summers as a working cowboy on New Mexico ranches. After graduation from college he decided that he would some-day paint the raw mountains and endlessly changing desert of the Southwest.

Mr. Waterhouse's paintings and drawings have been shown at numerous museums, and are a part of the permanent collection of the West Texas Museum of Art at Texas Tech University. His work has been represented by Baker's Collector's Gallery of Lubbock, Texas, and by Doug Jones Gallery, La Jolla, California. He has illustrated several books with southwestern themes published by Alfred A. Knopf, Inc., New York, and the Texas Western Press of the University of Texas at El Paso. In 1970 he was appointed by the Governor of Texas to the Texas Commission on the Arts and Humanities for a five-year term.

His knowledge of the Southwest has enabled him to impart a sense of truth to his work and this has made him a favorite of ranchers and cowboys, as well as museum directors and collectors.

The drawings inside this book were done by Miss Charlotte Hays. A native El Pasoan, Charlotte has studied art since she was fourteen. She attended the University of Texas at El Paso and the University of New Mexico and studied extensively with many local outstanding artists.

Charlotte teaches oil painting and drawing. Her work is displayed in several galleries in Texas, New Mexico and California. Art patrons throughout the United States, Mexico and Europe collect her paintings and drawings; she is represented in the collections of the State National Bank of El Paso and the Roswell Savings and Loan Association, Roswell, New Mexico.

Working with oil and pen and ink primarily, she is also proficient in watercolors, acrylics and graphics, as well as photography. Versatility and imagination make her work unique and mark her as a truly talented artist.

ISBN 0-9607974-0-8
Copyright © 1974
by
Junior League of El Paso, Inc.
All Rights Reserved

First Printing	15,000 copies
Second Printing	15,000 copies
Third Printing	10,000 copies
Fourth Printing	20,000 copies
Fifth Printing	20,000 copies

Printed by
S. C. Toof & Co.
Memphis, Tennessee

INTRODUCTION

There's a world of difference in Southwestern cookery; it is distinguished by the spicy tang of traditional dishes and by the informal atmosphere in which they are usually enjoyed. And it is served with a regard for hospitality that is as real now as it was in the old days, when ranch families left their doors unlocked, with a pot of beans simmering on a back burner for any traveler who might happen by.

Yet Southwestern favorites are as American as apple pie — more so, even, because such vital ingredients as chiles, tomatoes, corn, and certain beans are native American foods, cultivated by Indians long before the arrival of Europeans.

Many of today's most popular Southwestern dishes can be traced to the cook pots of the Pueblo Indians, who have farmed the Rio Grande Valley for centuries. The Spaniards elaborated on these native American dishes when they followed the Rio Grande north during the 17th and 18th centuries, bringing with them Old World recipes and New World ideas picked up from the Mexican Indians.

When the American cowboys and traders came to the Southwest in great numbers during the 19th century, they introduced their distinctive chuckwagon chow, featuring fresh meat cooked over open mesquite fires. This tradition of trail life is continued in today's casual cook-out and in the more elaborate barbecue, in which whole steers or regional game may be roasted and served with a welcome as big as all outdoors.

So the recipes collected here represent a rich heritage, indeed. Some have the spice of Indian life, often with a Spanish accent. Others have the flavor of the Old West. But all are American classics. Enjoy!

PREFACE

Perhaps the most successful blending of cultures and cuisine in the world is demonstrated on the tables of El Paso's cooks. The casual and gracious attitude of our neighbors to the south has combined with the innovative spirit of the pioneers to convince everyone that there are few set rules for planning any meal. A barbecued brisket can be served with a mango salad for a delicious treat and Huevos Rancheros is a perfect way to start the day.

Of the thousands of recipes contributed by members of this Junior League, each was graded on quality and uniqueness and each was tested and retested before acceptance for the book. It is our hope that it is enjoyed from the Río Grande to the Amazon and from Maine to California. It has been planned for the unfortunate one who might never have the opportunity to visit the Southwest with its purple mountains and orange sunsets; its irrigated fields of onions grown in warm sunlight and its adobe walls adorned with freshly picked red chiles set out to dry. Truly, this cookbook has been Seasoned With Sun.

TABLE OF CONTENTS

SPECIALTY OF SEASONED WITH SUN

ENGLISH MENU

BARBECUE

Grilled Steak Southwestern
Rajas
Ranchero Beans
Country Cole Slaw
Vegetable Trio
Sour Dough Biscuits
Pink Adobe Apple Pie

INDOOR BUFFET

Standing Rib Roast
Chile Cheese Rice
Molded Gazpacho Salad
Fresh Buttered Asparagus
French Bread
Pecan Tarts

LUNCHEON

Chicken Crepes
Wine Marinated Artichoke
   Hearts
Mango Salad
Almond Empanaditas
Spanish Cream

DINNER PARTY

Pheasant
Exotic Rice
Canlis' Salad
Zucchini Slippers
Butterhorn Rolls
Angel Mango Pie
Pinot Noir Wine

At Sunset

APPETIZERS

HINTS FOR APPETIZERS

Mexican recipes prepared in miniature (little tacos, tamales, quesadillas, etc.) make excellent appetizers.

To keep olives shiny, roll them in a few drops of salad oil.

Sour cream will keep longer in the refrigerator if stored upside down so that air cannot enter the container.

Appetizers are called **antojos** (whims) or **antojitos** (little whims) in Spanish.

Try serving pepitas (toasted, salted pumpkin seeds) in place of potato chips or nuts.

Caviar should be served ice cold with hot buttered melba toast or crackers.

Instead of a bowl, use a hollowed-out red cabbage as a "dish" for a dip.

Canapés are savory, bite-sized morsels served on a base of bread, crackers, or rich pastry. They may be hot or cold.

Sautéed bread is especially good as a canapé base.

To keep canapés fresh, wrap snugly in plastic wrap, sandwich bags, or foil and refrigerate until ready to serve.

Dips may be served with potato chips, corn chips, tostadas, pretzel sticks, assorted crackers, or raw vegetables.

For a decorative punch bowl, freeze pre-boiled water (to prevent cloudiness) in a mold or bundt pan with fresh fruit or plastic flowers, fruit, or leaves. Add a little water to the decorations in the bottom of the mold or pan and freeze until set; add remaining water and continue freezing.

When buying mushrooms, select whiter caps for freshness.

AVOCADO COCKTAIL

Serves: 12

4 small avocados, cut in
    small squares
1 cup chile catsup
1 cup celery, diced

2 tablespoons lemon juice
4 drops Tabasco
1 teaspoon salt
1 teaspoon sugar

Make a sauce by combining all ingredients except avocados in a bowl; mix well. Serve avocados in cocktail glasses and put 2 tablespoons of the prepared sauce over each serving.

ACEITUNAS RELLENAS A LA ELENA
(ELENA'S STUFFED OLIVES)

1 7½-ounce can pitted
    green olives
1 ¾-ounce can anchovy fillets,
    cut in small pieces
1 can pimentos, chopped

1 clove garlic, pressed
⅓ cup wine vinegar
1 tablespoon olive oil
Oil from anchovies
¼ cup minced parsley

Drain olives and stuff with anchovy fillets. Combine the other ingredients, except parsley. Pour over the olives and marinate overnight. Mix in parsley 30 minutes before serving. These will keep for a week or more if parsley is added just before serving. Serve with toothpicks.

ARTICHOKE NIBBLES

Yield: 6 dozen   Oven: 325°

2 6-ounce jars marinated
    artichoke hearts
1 small onion, finely chopped
1 clove garlic, minced
4 eggs
¼ cup fine, dry bread crumbs
¼ teaspoon salt

⅛ teaspoon pepper
⅛ teaspoon oregano
⅛ teaspoon Tabasco
½ pound sharp Cheddar
    cheese, shredded
2 tablespoons minced parsley

Drain marinade from 1 jar of artichokes into skillet. Drain the other jar and chop all artichokes. Add onion and garlic to marinade and cook about 5 minutes until onion is soft. Beat eggs with a fork; add bread crumbs and seasonings. Stir in cheese, parsley, artichokes and onion mixture. Turn into greased 7x11-inch baking pan and cook 30-35 minutes. Cool 5 minutes and cut into small squares.

ARTICHOKE APPETIZERS

4-6 artichokes, cooked and chilled
1 8-ounce package cream cheese,
   softened
2 cups Kraft mayonnaise (has
   lemon juice)

2-3 teaspoons dried parsley flakes
1 small onion, grated
2 tablespoons anchovy paste

Cream mayonnaise with cream cheese. This mixture should taste more of mayonnaise than cream cheese; if necessary add more mayonnaise until it does. Add parsley flakes for color. Add anchovy paste, according to taste. Add grated onion. Chill. Remove cheese mixture from refrigerator 1-2 hours before serving. This mixture is used as a dip for artichoke leaves and heart. If time permits, separate leaves and cut heart into bite-sized pieces on toothpicks. This recipe can be prepared the day before serving and refrigerated.

WATER CHESTNUTS AND BACON

Serves: 24-30   Oven: 350°

1 8½-ounce can water
   chestnuts
½ cup soy sauce

¼ cup brown sugar
8-10 strips bacon

Cut water chestnuts into thirds or fourths. Soak in soy sauce for 30 minutes; drain. Dip lightly in brown sugar. Fry strips of bacon until half-done; cut into thirds and wrap around chestnuts. Secure with toothpick. Bake for 20 minutes. These may be wrapped in foil and reheated at serving time.

Variation: In place of water chestnuts, shrimp or stuffed green olives may be used.

HOT PEPPER PECANS

Yield: 1 cup   Oven: 300°

1 cup large pecan halves
2 tablespoons butter
2 teaspoons soy sauce

½ teaspoon salt
2-3 dashes Tabasco

Melt butter in shallow pan and spread pecans evenly in one layer. Bake for 30 minutes or until nuts begin to brown. Stir several times; do not overcook. Mix soy sauce, salt and Tabasco and stir into toasted pecans, turning them so the seasonings will be evenly distributed. Spread on a double thickness of paper towels to cool. Pack in jars with tight-fitting lids.

NACHOS

Serves: 6

6 tortillas	3 pickled jalapeño chiles,
6 tablespoons refried beans	cut into eights
6 tablespoons grated Cheddar or Longhorn cheese	

Slice tortillas into quarters. Fry in hot grease until crisp. Spread with refried beans; sprinkle with grated cheese and top each with a jalapeño chile. Broil until cheese melts. Serve hot.

ONION RYE PUFFS

Serves: 24   Oven: Broil

1 loaf party rye bread (1½ inches in diameter)	1 cup mayonnaise
4 medium Bermuda onions, thinly sliced	5 tablespoons Parmesan cheese

Toast bread on one side. Turn, place slice of onion on bread. Mix mayonnaise and cheese; spread on top of each slice. Broil approximately 10 minutes or until top puffs and browns.

STUFFED MUSHROOMS TARRAGON

Serves: 6

1 pound large mushrooms	½ cup dry bread crumbs
5 tablespoons butter	2 teaspoons brandy or sherry
2 tablespoons chopped chives	1 teaspoon chopped tarragon
1 egg, beaten	Salt and pepper to taste

Wash mushrooms and remove the stems. Chop stems and sauté with the chopped chives in butter. Add beaten egg, bread crumbs, brandy, herbs, salt and pepper to the stem mixture. Sauté the mushroom caps in butter and stuff them with the herb and stem mixture. Dot with butter and broil until brown. Prepare the recipe no more than a day ahead; cover and refrigerate. Broil minutes before serving.

Variation: Shrimp, turkey or chicken mixed with mayonnaise and slivered almonds may be used as stuffing.

MARINATED MUSHROOMS

Yield: 2 cups

⅔ cup olive oil
½ cup water
Juice of 2 lemons
1 bay leaf
6 whole peppercorns

2 cloves garlic, bruised
½ teaspoon salt
1 pound small, whole fresh
   mushrooms

Combine all ingredients except mushrooms in a 10-inch enameled or stainless steel skillet; bring to boil over moderate heat. Reduce heat, cover and simmer for 15 minutes. Strain marinade through a sieve. Return to skillet and simmer over low heat. Drop the mushrooms into the marinade and cook for 5 minutes, turning from time to time. Let cool and drain before serving. These mushrooms will keep in the refrigerator at least two days. Serve at room temperature or serve cold.

HOT MUSHROOM TURNOVERS

Yield: 50 appetizers   Oven: 450°

3 3-ounce packages cream
   cheese
½ cup butter or margarine,
   softened
1½ cups sifted all purpose
   flour
½ pound fresh mushrooms,
   minced

1 large onion, minced
3 tablespoons butter or
   margarine
1 teaspoon salt
¼ tablespoon thyme
2 tablespoons all-purpose flour
¼ cup sour cream
1 egg, beaten

In a large bowl beat cream cheese, ½ cup butter, and 1½ cups flour until soft dough forms. Wrap dough in wax paper and refrigerate several hours or overnight. In medium-sized skillet over medium heat, cook mushrooms and onion in 3 tablespoons butter or margarine until tender. Add salt, thyme, and 2 tablespoons flour; stir in sour cream. On floured board, thinly roll out about one-fourth of dough. Cut into circles with a 2¾-inch cookie cutter. Roll dough scraps into ball and refrigerate. On half of each circle, place a teaspoonful of mushroom mixture; brush edges with egg. Fold pastry over filling and press edges together with fork; prick tops to let out steam. Repeat with remaining dough and filling. Place turnovers on ungreased cookie sheet, brush with egg, and bake for 12-15 minutes.

STUFFED MUSHROOMS

½ cup Swiss cheese,
    shredded
1 hard cooked egg,
    finely chopped
3 tablespoons fine,
    dry bread crumbs
½ clove garlic, minced

2 tablespoons butter or
    margarine, softened
1 pound small fresh
    mushrooms, washed
    and stemmed
4 tablespoons butter or
    margarine, melted

In mixing bowl combine cheese, egg, crumbs, garlic and softened butter; blend thoroughly. Place unfilled mushrooms rounded side up on baking sheet. Brush with melted butter. Broil three inches from heat for 2-3 minutes. Remove when lightly browned. Turn over mushrooms; fill each with cheese mixture. Return filled mushrooms to broiler; broil 1-2 minutes more.

COCKTAIL CARROTS A LA JALAPEÑO

8 thin carrots, peeled
1 4-ounce can button
    mushrooms
1 4-ounce can mild jalapeños

1 package Good Seasons
    Garlic salad dressing,
    mixed as directed

Slice and boil carrots 8-10 minutes until tender but still firm; drain. Mix salad dressing. Drain mushrooms; mix with carrots in a jar. Add dressing and half of the juice from the can of jalapeños. Slice finely 1 or 2 jalapeños (no seeds) and place in jar. Cover jar and keep in refrigerator at least one week before using, turning jar daily to thoroughly marinate carrots. Serve as an hors d'oeuvre or as accompaniment for roast beef.

JICAMA EN ESCABECHE

Yield: 2½ quarts

3-4 carrots
1 cup vinegar
1 cup water
½ cup oil
3 onions, sliced
6 cloves garlic

1 teaspoon salt
2 teaspoons oregano
3-4 bay leaves
1 4-ounce can jalapeño chiles
2 large peeled, sliced jícamas

Cut carrots into small chunks; cook in salted water until tender. Drain and cool. In a large pan combine vinegar, water, oil, onions, garlic and salt and cook until onions are tender. Add oregano and bay leaves. Boil and let cool. Add jalapeños, carrots and jícamas; let sit for several hours. Store in refrigerator. Serve as a salad or appetizer with crackers.

STUFFED JALAPEÑOS

11-ounce can pickled jalapeño
    chiles

1 8-ounce package cream cheese
Onion salt

Drain chiles; slit each down one side and remove seeds. Soften cream cheese (with a little sour cream if needed) and season to taste with onion salt. Stuff each chile with the cheese; press closed and chill until firm. Slice stuffed chiles into bite-sized pieces to serve.

Variation: Jalapeños are delicious stuffed with Shrimp Paste (see Index), salmon, tuna, or sardines mixed with a little sour cream. Any good seasoned softened cheese may also be used.

STUFFED JALAPEÑOS CON HUEVOS

1 pound can jalapeño chiles
1 8-ounce package cream
    cheese, softened
2 hard cooked eggs, mashed
½ teaspoon garlic salt

¼ cup chopped pecans
    (optional)
Mayonnaise
1 teaspoon salad seasoning
    or paprika

Halve chiles lengthwise and devein. Soak at least overnight in ice water in refrigerator. Beat cream cheese with mashed eggs, garlic salt, pecans and salad seasoning. Add mayonnaise to consistency of paste. Fill chiles, mounding stuffing slightly. Sprinkle tops with paprika or salad seasoning. Do not freeze. Can be made a day ahead and covered with plastic wrap. Refrigerate.

JALAPEÑO BEAN DIP

16-ounce can mashed refried
    beans
¼-½ pound Cheddar cheese,
    grated

1 small onion, chopped
1 4-ounce can jalapeño chiles,
    drained and chopped
Salt and pepper to taste

Sauté onions in butter; add other ingredients and stir over low heat. Thin with milk if desired. Serve warm with chips, tostados or Fritos.

JERKY
Oven: 140°-170°

Meat (any of the less tender cuts,
    beef or game)

Smoked seasoned salt
Ground pepper

Trim meat of any fat. Slice as thin as possible (partially frozen meat slices best). Season with smoked seasoned salt and pepper. Place on oven racks. Let dry in oven, but leave the door open so the meat will dry without cooking. Leave in oven overnight.

COLD CHILE CON QUESO

Serves: 8 - 10

1 pint carton large curd
    creamed cottage cheese
1 4-ounce can jalapeño relish

1 avocado, cut in small chunks
Tostados

Mix the first three ingredients together. Serve as a dip with tostados. Can be served in small bowls with spoons and tostados. This recipe cannot be prepared ahead and cannot be frozen.

CHILE CON QUESO

3 tablespoons butter or oil
3 tablespoons flour
1 cup milk
2 pounds brick or Monterrey
    Jack cheese, cubed or
    grated
10-ounce can tomatoes and green
    chile

2 4-ounce cans chopped green
    chile, drained
1 small onion, chopped
Salt and pepper
Tabasco or Worcestershire
    sauce
Garlic salt

In a double boiler combine butter or oil, flour and milk to make cream sauce. Add cheese and cook over slow heat until melted. Add chile and onion. Season to taste with remaining ingredients. If too dry, add tomato juice or milk.

CHILE CON QUESO MEXICANO

6 fresh green chiles, roasted,
    peeled and cut in length-
    wise slices
1 onion, chopped
2 tablespoons bacon grease
1 clove garlic, minced

2 large fresh tomatoes,
    peeled and finely
    chopped
2½ cups grated Jack or
    Longhorn cheese
Salt to taste

Sauté chiles and onion in bacon grease. Add garlic and cook until soft. Add tomatoes, cheese and salt. Heat until cheese melts.

El Paso Daily Times   Sunday May 26, 1895
Star Grocer Co.
219 San Antonio St.
20 lbs. of sugar for $1.00
10 lb. pail of pure lard $1.00
6 bars of White Star Soap 25¢

SALSA DE QUESO

6-8 fresh green chiles
1 onion
½ cup butter
14½-ounce can tomatoes

⅓ cup milk
1 8-ounce package Old
   English cheese
1 8-ounce package Velveeta
   cheese

Peel chiles and chop into large pieces; chop onion fine. Sauté both in butter in iron skillet. Mash tomatoes well; add to skillet. Add milk; stir in cheese, cut in cubes, until melted. Add salt and garlic to taste. This is delicious as a dip or over cold turkey sandwich. If used as a dip, a little flour for thickening may be needed. Chopped raw jalapeño adds zip; a little grated Cheddar cheese adds to the texture.

GUACAMOLE DIP OR SALAD

Serves: 8 as dip
        4 as salad

2 ripe avocados
1 tablespoon lime juice
4 canned green chiles, rinsed,
   seeded and chopped
1 clove garlic, minced
½ teaspoon ground coriander

2 tablespoons grated onion
½ teaspoon salt
Pepper to taste
1 large ripe tomato, skinned
   and finely chopped

Mash avocados to a smooth pulp. Add remaining ingredients and serve accompanied by tostados as a dip or on lettuce leaf as a salad.

CREAMY GUACAMOLE

Serves: 10 for salad
        30 - 40 for dip

8 large ripe avocados
1 3-ounce package cream cheese
   (optional)
Juice of 4-5 limes
½-1 teaspoon garlic powder

1 teaspoon salt
1 small onion, grated
2 small tomatoes, finely chopped
6 tablespoons picante sauce†

Mash avocados and cream cheese with fork. Add all other ingredients. Blend well with wooden spoon or hand mixer. For hotter flavor, chopped jalapeño chile may be added.

†See Glossary.

BROCCOLI DIP

1 package frozen chopped
   broccoli
½ large onion, chopped
2-3 stalks celery, chopped
2 tablespoons butter or
   margarine
1 4-ounce can chopped
   mushrooms

1 roll Kraft Garlic cheese
1 can cream of mushroom
   soup
Dash of Tabasco
Dash of A-1 sauce

Cook broccoli as directed, but do not cook until completely tender. Drain well. Sauté onion, celery and mushrooms in butter or margarine. Melt cheese in mushroom soup in double boiler. Add other ingredients and season with Tabasco and A-1 sauce.

CREAM CHEESE DIP AND CAVIAR

1 8-ounce package cream cheese
1 package Lipton Onion Soup Mix
1 8-ounce can minced clams,
   drained
Salt to taste

⅛ teaspoon lemon juice
1 tablespoon milk or sour cream
2 2-ounce jars red caviar
1 box Ritz crackers

Mix cream cheese, dry onion soup, clams, salt and lemon juice. Add only enough sour cream or milk to make a smooth consistency. Cream cheese needs to be thick but smooth. Put in a bowl and mash until smooth. Spread red caviar on top. Caviar should be placed so that the cream cheese is partially visible. Surround by Ritz crackers. This recipe can be prepared ahead but cannot be frozen.

ROQUEFORT DIP

1 8-ounce carton sour cream
1 tablespoon mayonnaise
¼ teaspoon Worcestershire
   sauce
2 teaspoons onion, grated
2 teaspoons chopped parsley

1½ teaspoons lemon juice
¼ teaspoon salt
3 drops Tabasco
1 4-ounce package Roquefort
   cheese, mashed

Combine all ingredients except Roquefort cheese. When well blended, add mashed Roquefort. A good dip with fresh vegetables: celery, carrots, green onions, cauliflower, cucumber slices and cherry tomatoes. Also excellent with apples! This recipe can be prepared ahead but it cannot be frozen.

PAT'S CHIPPED BEEF DIP

Serves: 6   Oven: 350°

1 2½-ounce package dried   ½ teaspoon garlic salt
   beef   2 tablespoons minced onion
1 8-ounce package cream   ½ bell pepper, minced*
   cheese, softened   ¼ cup pecans, chopped
2 tablespoons milk   1 teaspoon horseradish
½ pint sour cream   (optional)

Mix cream cheese with milk until soft; add sour cream and stir until well blended. Cut dried beef into tiny pieces and add to cheese mixture. Add remaining ingredients except pecans. Put in small casserole and sprinkle pecans on top. Bake 20-30 minutes. Serve with crackers or buffet rye slices.

Variations: For leftover dip or supper size sandwiches, mix pecans with cheese mixture and spread on toasted bread. Put a few green chile strips on toast first. Put under broiler to brown.

*One small can chopped green chile may be substituted for bell pepper.

PICKLED SHRIMP

Serves: 8 - 10

2½ pounds cleaned, raw shrimp   2 large onions, sliced
1 bag shrimp spice   7-8 bay leaves
3½ teaspoons salt

Pour boiling water over shrimp to cover. Add shrimp spice (or other seafood seasoning) and salt. Let water come to a boil; boil 5 minutes. Let shrimp cool in water. Alternate cleaned shrimp and sliced onions in shallow pyrex dish with bay leaves.

MARINADE:

1¼ cups salad oil   2½ tablespoons capers and
¾ cup white vinegar   juice
1½ teaspoons salt   Dash Tabasco sauce
2½ teaspoons celery seed

Mix all ingredients and pour over shrimp. Cover with foil and refrigerate 24-48 hours (flavor of shrimp improves when marinated longer). Sauce should be spooned over shrimp several times. Serve as appetizer or side dish.

PICKLED GARLIC SHRIMP

2 pounds raw shrimp, cooked
    and shelled, or 1½ pounds
    frozen shrimp, cooked
¾ cup oil
½ cup cider vinegar
2 tablespoons Worchestershire
    sauce
⅓ cup catsup

6 dashes Tabasco
½ teaspoon salt
½ teaspoon dry mustard
⅛ teaspoon garlic powder
¼ teaspoon pepper
2 large onions, sliced in
    thin rings

Blend all ingredients except shrimp and onions in blender until creamy. Layer shrimp and onions alternately in a large jar and pour sauce over all. Marinate at least one day before using. Serve with toothpicks.

SMOKED OYSTER DIP

Serves: 18-20

2 cans smoked oysters, crushed
2 tins smoked Kraft's Bacon and
    Horseradish dip

2 8-ounce packages cream cheese
½ cup sour cream
Smoked mustard to taste

Combine all ingredients. Melt slowly over low heat. Keep warm in chafing dish. Serve with Fritos or crackers.

CAVIAR RING

Serves: 40

1 cup sour cream
1 pound cottage cheese
½-1 teaspoon garlic powder
1 teaspoon Worcestershire
    sauce
½ teaspoon seasoned salt

1 tablespoon unflavored
    gelatine
¼ cup sherry
2 4-ounce jars black caviar
Juice of ½ lemon

Blend first five ingredients in blender. Soften gelatine in sherry. Place over hot water to melt. Add to cream mixture and blend. Pour into lightly greased 8-inch ring mold. Refrigerate 24 hours. Unmold. Frost with caviar mixed with lemon juice. Serve with Melba rounds.

El Paso Herald   September 28, 1881

Mr. Haas, the well known grocer, has received a fine assortment of goods. He sells at reasonable prices, and is extremely accommodating to his patrons, which accounts for his having so many of them.

CRABMEAT BACON ROLLS

Yield: 3 dozen

½ cup tomato juice
1 egg, well beaten
1 cup dry bread crumbs
Dash salt
Dash pepper

½ teaspoon chopped parsley
½ teaspoon chopped celery
    leaves
1 6½-ounce can crabmeat, flaked
12 slices bacon, cut in thirds

Mix tomato juice and egg. Add remaining ingredients except bacon and mix thoroughly. Roll into finger-sized rolls about 1½-inches long. Wrap each roll in a third of a slice of bacon and fasten with toothpick. Broil, turning frequently to brown evenly. Serve hot. These can be made ahead and frozen or refrigerated until broiled.

CRABMEAT COCKTAIL RING

Serves 15 - 20

1 envelope gelatine
½ cup cold water
1 cup cream (half-and-half and
    whipping cream mixed
    equally)
1 cup mayonnaise
3 7½-ounce cans crabmeat

1 teaspoon onion salt
1 teaspoon Worcestershire sauce
1 2½-ounce bottle capers,
    drained
Parsley flakes for color
Salt and pepper to taste

Dissolve gelatine in ½ cup cold water. Heat cream and add to gelatine. Add mayonnaise and combine this mixture with the rest of the ingredients. Pour into a greased mold. Mold size can be 9 inches in diameter with a 4-inch hollow center, 2½-3-inches deep. Prepare one day in advance. To remove from mold, place bottom of mold in warm water to loosen. Serve with soda crackers on flat dish or tray with spreader. This recipe can be prepared ahead but cannot be frozen.

LIVERWURST LOG

1 8-ounce package cream cheese
1-2 teaspoons lemon juice
1 teaspoon minced onion
Tabasco
Garlic salt

1 package liverwurst or
    Braunschwieger
Minced parsley flakes or
    paprika

Soften cream cheese and thin with lemon juice to consistency of icing. Add minced onion. Add Tabasco and garlic salt to taste. Place liverwurst on serving tray and press down until slightly flat on bottom. Frost with cream cheese mixture. Sprinkle parsley flakes or paprika on top for garnish. Surround with crackers and serve with a cheese or butter knife. It is best to prepare and refrigerate several hours before serving.

CEVICHE

Serves: 8

1 **pound white fish***	1 **tablespoon parsley**
1 **cup lemon juice**	¼ **teaspoon marjoram**
5 **large tomatoes**	¼ **teaspoon thyme**
1 **large onion**	½ **teaspoon sage**
1 **tablespoon oil**	2 **4-ounce cans chopped green**
15 **stuffed green olives**	**chile**

Cut fish in bite-sized pieces; cover with lemon juice. Leave in refrigerator at least 4 hours or overnight. Stir occasionally. Chop tomatoes, onions, and olives and combine with fish. Add all other ingredients. Let stand at least 4-6 hours. Serve well-chilled as an appetizer with saltines, tostados, or as a seafood cocktail.

*Frozen thawed fillet of sole can be used. Never use mackerel.

CEVICHE SABROSO

Serves: 8 - 10

2 **pounds any good firm fish***	1 **2½-ounce jar capers**
Lemon juice to cover fish	4 **tablespoons cilantro**
½ **cup olive oil**	**Salt to taste**
1 **large onion**	1 **fresh manzano (yellow**
2 **peeled ripe tomatoes**	**banana chile)**
10-15 **stuffed green olives**	2 **medium avocados, cubed**

Bone fish and chop into ½-inch cubes. Cover fish with lemon juice; let stand for 20 minutes or more turning so that juice permeates all parts. When acid has cooked fish, pour off juice. Add olive oil and all other ingredients, which have been chopped. Add avocados last. Devein and chop hot chile; place over fish (gives an excellent flavor even for those who cannot take much chile). Serve with crackers for dip.

*If frozen fish is used, use cod.

PATE MOLD

Serves: 12

1 8-ounce package cream cheese
1 tablespoon mayonnaise
1 4-ounce can liver paste
Salt and pepper to taste
1 can consommé

1 envelope unflavored
   gelatine, dissolved in
   2 tablespoons water
1 jigger bourbon

Mix together cream cheese, mayonnaise, and liver paste and season with salt and pepper. Mix and beat together the consommé and the gelatine dissolved in water. When cold, add bourbon. Cover the bottom of a one-pint mold with half the gelatine mixture and set in refrigerator for 15 minutes. Pour in paste and press on top of gelatine. Pour remaining gelatine over the top and allow to set. Unmold, slice and serve with crackers. The mold may be stored in refrigerator for up to three days.

HAM PASTRIES

Yield: 2 - 3 dozen   Oven: 400°

1 4-ounce package cream cheese
½ cup butter
1 cup flour
½ pound ground smoked ham

Durkee's mustard to taste
1 egg white
Caraway seed

Let cheese and butter stand at room temperature. Cream thoroughly; add flour and mix well. Wrap in wax paper and foil and refrigerate for 24 hours. When ready to use, let stand at room temperature 30 minutes for easy handling. Roll out very thin. Cut into squares a little over 2 inches. Mix ham and mustard and put 1 teaspoon of mixture in center of each square. Fold corners to center and press down. Brush with slightly beaten egg white. Sprinkle with caraway seed. Place on cookie sheet and bake about 20 minutes. Loosen from pan immediately with spatula. To serve after freezing, let stand to near room temperature; place in hot oven for short time to heat through. *Fun to eat with copitas!*

CHEESE AND SAUSAGE ROLLS

Yield: 4 dozen   Oven: 400°

16 sausage links
16 slices bread, crusts removed

1 cup American cheese, shredded
4 tablespoons butter

Cook sausage links; drain. Roll bread flat. Mix cheese and butter and spread on both sides of bread. Roll 1 sausage into each slice. Bake on greased cookie sheet 10-12 minutes. Slice into thirds.

CHEESE POCKETBOOKS

Yield: 96 pocketbooks or   Oven: 400°
       2 quarts cheese spread

2 pounds Cheddar cheese, grated
½ pound Bleu cheese
2 8-ounce packages cream cheese
2 tablespoons Worcestershire
     sauce
¼ teaspoon Tabasco
1 clove garlic, crushed

Salt, red pepper and paprika to
     taste
2-3 tablespoons fresh lemon juice
1-2 tablespoons mayonnaise
4 loaves extra-thin sliced bread
     (Pepperidge Farm)
Butter

Soften cheese and combine with all ingredients except bread and butter. Cut crusts from bread; butter one side. Flip over and place a spoonful of cheese mixture in center of bread slice and either roll the bread or fold the four corners to the center to form a pillow-shaped "pocketbook." These may need to be secured with a toothpick. Bake 12-15 minutes. These may be frozen and baked straight from the freezer. If so, add 5-10 minutes to baking time. Serve hot. Delicious accompaniment for a fruit plate or for a bowl of soup as a light meal. The cheese mixture alone may be used as a sandwich spread.

CHEESE TARTS

Serves: 24   Oven: 400°

CRUST:

1½ cups all-purpose flour
¾ teaspoon salt

½ cup shortening
5-6 tablespoons cold water

Make pie crust. Fit into 24 2-inch tart pans.

FILLING:

¼ cup grated onion
½ pound Swiss cheese, grated
2 tablespoons butter
⅛ teaspoon dry mustard
1 teaspoon salt

Ground black pepper
3 eggs
¾ cup whipping cream
¾ cup half-and-half

Sauté onion in butter for 5 minutes; add cheese and seasonings. Toss to mix well. In a separate bowl, beat eggs until foamy and add creams. Cover the bottom of each pastry with a portion of the cheese mixture. Follow by covering cheese mixture with a portion of egg mixture. Bake for 18 minutes. This recipe can be prepared ahead and frozen. When ready to serve, bake frozen tarts for 10 minutes.

FANTASTIC CHEESE BALL

Yield: 50 servings

1 ounce Roquefort cheese,
   or Bleu cheese
4 ounces Cheddar cheese
1 8-ounce package cream cheese
1 clove garlic, minced
¼ medium onion, minced

Dash Tabasco or Worcestershire
   sauce
½ cup pecans, chopped
Paprika
2 tablespoons sherry (optional)

Soften cheeses. Cut Cheddar cheese in small chunks. Mix together all ingredients except nuts and paprika. Form into ball. Roll in chopped pecans and sprinkle with paprika. This is better made the day before. It can be frozen. Set out at room temperature until thawed. Serve on Ritz crackers.

BLACK OLIVE-CHEDDAR CHEESE SPREAD

1 cup chopped black olives
1½ cups sharp Cheddar cheese,
   grated

½ cup mayonnaise
¼ teaspoon salt
¼ teaspoon curry powder

Mix together all of the ingredients. Chill or freeze until needed. Mound on Triskets or other cocktail crackers. Broil and serve at once.

CHEESE STRAWS OR BISCUITS

Yield: 2 dozen   Oven: 350°

½ teaspoon salt
2 cups flour, sifted
½ cup margarine

1 pound Cheddar cheese, grated
¼ teaspoon cayenne

Sift salt with flour. Cream margarine by hand. Gradually add grated cheese and flour. When well mixed, add cayenne. Knead thoroughly. Divide dough and flatten out. Cut into straws with knife or roll in small balls and flatten for biscuits. Bake on ungreased cookie sheet 10-15 minutes. These store well in a can.

Variations: Place 1 green olive, 1 pimento-stuffed olive, 1 onion-stuffed olive, 1 cocktail onion, or 1 jalapeño chile in center of cheese puff before cooking.

El Paso Herald   September 7, 1881

The milk dealers in this place are somewhat scarce. They charge 15¢ a quart for milk and it is said they may go higher. We suppose this is caused by the drug stores having raised the price of chalk on them.

From Adobe Ovens

BREADS

HINTS FOR BREADS

To knead dough, fold it toward you with a rolling motion, using the fingers of both hands; then push it away with the heels of both hands. Turn dough a quarter way around on board and repeat the folding and pushing. When dough has been kneaded sufficiently, bubbles will form and burst with a little smacking sound.

After adding yeast to warm water, let it sit for a few minutes before stirring. Then leave it in a warm spot for about 15 minutes until the mixture has risen with a fine froth. It must seethe and foam or it won't make bread.

To determine if baking powder is still active, mix a teaspoon in 1/3 cup hot water. Use the baking powder only if it bubbles.

Before scalding milk, rinse the pan with cold water to prevent sticking.

Place a small dish of water in the oven while bread is baking to keep the crust from getting too hard.

Fresh bread will keep its shape if cut with a hot knife.

If quick breads are sliced hot, they will crumble. Nut and fruit quick-breads should be baked the day before serving for easier slicing and a more mellow flavor.

To freshen bread or rolls, wrap in a damp cloth for 1 or 2 minutes or sprinkle the crust with cold water. Place in a pre-heated 350° oven 10 to 20 minutes and serve warm.

SOUR DOUGH STARTER

1 cup milk   **1 cup flour**

Place milk in a glass jar or crock (nothing metal) and allow to stand at room temperature for 24 hours. Stir in flour. (To speed process, cover jar with cheesecloth and place outside for several hours to expose dough to wild yeast cells floating in the wind.) Leave uncovered in a warm place (80°) for two to five days, depending on how long it takes to bubble and sour. (A good place is near the pilot light on a gas range.) If dough starts to dry out stir in enough tepid water to bring back to original consistency. When it has a good sour aroma and is full of bubbles, the mixture is ready to use. Try to maintain 1½ cups starter. Each time a part is used, replenish with a mixture of equal amounts of milk and flour. Leave at room temperature several hours or overnight, or until full of bubbles. Cover and store in refrigerator.

SOUR DOUGH BISCUITS

Yield: 2 dozen   Oven: 425°

1 cup flour   **¼ teaspoon baking soda**
1 teaspoon baking powder   **⅓ cup liquid shortening**
¼ teaspoon salt   **1¼ cups sour dough***

Thoroughly mix shortening and sour dough. Sift dry ingredients together and mix into liquid, stirring until well blended (dough may be very sticky). Fold onto floured board and knead, adding flour as needed until dough can be rolled. Don't overwork. Roll ¾-inches thick and cut with biscuit cutter. Place on greased pan and bake 15-18 minutes. Freezes very well.

*See Index.

DELICIOUS SOUTHERN WHITE BREAD

Yield: 5 small loaves   Oven: 300°

1 pint milk, scalded
½ cup sugar
2 heaping tablespoons shortening
1½ teaspoons salt
2 egg yolks, beaten

1½ packages active dry yeast
¼-⅓ cup warm water
6½-7 cups sifted flour
2 egg whites, stiffly beaten

Pour milk over sugar, salt and shortening. Let cool. Add egg yolks. Meanwhile, dissolve yeast in water. When milk and egg mixture is cool to the touch, add the yeast and water mixture. Stir. Add 3 cups flour. Beat with electric mixer until smooth. Fold in stiffly beaten egg whites. Add remaining flour. Stir and mix thoroughly. Cover and let rise in a warm place until doubled in size (about 1 hour). Place on board and work in small amount of flour until dough is no longer sticky. Knead 8-10 minutes. Divide into five pieces and knead a little more. Place in five 3⅝x7½-inch pans that have 1 or 2 teaspoons melted shortening in them. Press the dough into the edges and corners, turn it over so that the oil will be on top and press down smoothly and evenly in pan. Let rise until double in size. Bake 45-60 minutes. Remove from pan and let cool on rack. While warm, brush with butter. After the bread has completely cooled, use a knife with a serrated edge and slice the bread thin (20-23 slices). Butter each slice with soft butter and wrap in aluminum foil. Place in plastic bags and freeze.

FRENCH BREAD

Yield: 1 loaf   Oven: 450°

1 package active dry yeast
2½ cups warm water
7 cups sifted flour
2 tablespoons sugar

1 tablespoon salt
Corn meal
Sesame seeds

Dissolve yeast in warm water. Stir in 2 cups flour, sugar and salt until mixture is smooth, gradually beating in remaining 5 cups flour to make stiff dough. Turn onto lightly floured board and knead 5 minutes. Return to bowl and brush top with shortening. Let rise until double in size (about 1½ hours). Punch down, cover, and let rise again for 1 hour. Shape into a long loaf. Place on a cooking sheet which has been covered with corn meal. Make several evenly spaced shallow cuts diagonally in top of loaf. Let rise 1½ hours. Place pan of water on lower rack of oven. Place bread on middle rack and bake 15 minutes. Lower oven to 350° and bake 30 minutes.

FRENCH BREAD WITH POPPY SEEDS

Yield: 3 small loaves   Oven: 425°

1 cup lukewarm water
1 package active dry yeast
1 tablespoon sugar
1½ teaspoons salt
2 tablespoons cooking oil
3 cups flour

Corn meal
1 egg white
1 tablespoon water
1 teaspoon salt
Poppy seeds

Mix water and yeast; let stand 5 minutes. In a large bowl add next three ingredients and stir well. Add 1 cup flour. Beat thoroughly with electric mixer. Add 2 cups flour, one at a time until dough is stiff enough to knead. Sprinkle board with flour. Let dough stand for 10 minutes on board. Knead well, about 5 minutes. Butter bowl and top of dough. Let rise about 2-2½ hours or until doubled in size. Punch down, let rise again for 1 hour. Turn dough onto floured surface and divide into three equal parts. Let stand 10 minutes. Roll into a ¼-inch thick rectangle. Roll each piece tightly, pinching while rolling. Press and seal edges. Sprinkle cookie sheet with corn meal. Separate loaves on sheet to brown evenly. Cut diagonal slashes in loaves with shears about one inch deep. Beat together egg white, water and salt. Brush over tops of loaves. Sprinkle with poppy seeds. Let rise uncovered until double in bulk, about 1 hour. Place a large pan of boiling water in the bottom rack of oven with the sheet of bread on a rack above. Bake for 10 minutes. Brush again with egg white mixture. Reduce heat to 375° and bake until bread sounds hollow inside when tapped (about 25 minutes). Cool on rack.

DILLY BREAD

Serves: 6   Oven: 350°

1 package active dry yeast
¼ cup water
1 tablespoon butter
1 8-ounce carton creamed
    cottage cheese
2 tablespoons sugar
1 tablespoon instant
    minced onion*

2 tablespoons dill seed
1 teaspoon salt
¼ teaspoon baking soda
1 egg, beaten
2½ cups flour

Dissolve yeast in water. Heat butter and cottage cheese until warm; add yeast and all remaining ingredients. Mix well and place in greased loaf pan or 8-inch round casserole. Let rise until double. Bake until done. This recipe can be prepared ahead.

*This is even better with chopped fresh onion.

HONEY-WHEAT BREAD

Yield: 2 loaves   Oven: 350°

1 package active dry yeast
1 cup warm water
½ cup honey
1 tablespoon salt
2 tablespoons oil

1 cup scalded milk
3 cups unbleached flour
1 cup wheat germ
1-2 cups whole wheat flour
Sesame seed

Dissolve yeast in water. In medium bowl combine honey, salt, oil and milk which has been cooled. Add to yeast mixture. Beat in 2 cups flour for 2 minutes; add 1 more cup flour, wheat germ and whole wheat flour. Knead on floured surface until smooth and satiny (8-10 minutes). Let rise in warm place for 2½ hours. Punch down dough and divide in half. Shape into two loaves. Place in two wax paper-lined 5x9x3-inch pans and sprinkle with sesame seed. Cover and let rise 2-2½ hours. Bake 50-60 minutes. Cool.

OATMEAL BREAD

Yield: 3 loaves   Oven: 400°

1 package active dry yeast
¼ cup lukewarm water
4 cups boiling skim milk
2 cups rolled oats

¼ cup butter
½ cup brown sugar
1 tablespoon salt
8 cups sifted flour

Dissolve yeast in warm water. Add skim milk to the oats and butter and let stand for 30 minutes. Add brown sugar, salt, dissolved yeast and flour. Place in a buttered bowl, cover and let rise until doubled (1½-2 hours). Turn onto floured board; knead for 10 minutes. Divide into three loaves. Place in buttered 9-inch loaf pans and let rise again. Brush with melted butter and bake for 45 minutes.

WEST TEXAS CORNBREAD

Serves: 12   Oven: 400°

2 eggs
½ cup salad oil
1 cup sour cream
1 cup yellow corn meal
1 cup cream-style corn

3 teaspoons baking powder
1 cup grated Cheddar cheese
1 4-ounce can chopped green
   chile*

Mix all ingredients. Bake in a well-greased bundt cake pan for 35-40 minutes or bake in one large, well-greased iron skillet for 30-40 minutes.

*Or 1 4-ounce can chopped hot jalapeños can be used.

SOUTHERN CORNBREAD

Yield: 12 medium muffins   Oven: 450°

1½ cups corn meal (yellow)
3 tablespoons flour
1 teaspoon salt
1 teaspoon baking soda

2 cups buttermilk
1 egg
2 tablespoons bacon drippings
   or melted butter

Sift dry ingredients into bowl. Add buttermilk, egg and drippings. Stir until combined. Fill greased muffin pan two-thirds full or pour into greased 10-inch iron skillet. Bake about 20 minutes or until brown.

CHUCKWAGON BREAD

Serves: 8   Oven: 375°

2 medium onions, chopped
3 tablespoons butter
1 package refrigerated
   home-style or buttermilk
   biscuits

1 egg
1 cup sour cream
½ teaspoon salt
1 teaspoon poppy seeds

Sauté onions slowly in butter until softened. Separate the biscuits; place in a single layer in an ungreased 8-inch layer cake pan, pressing together to cover bottom completely. Beat egg slightly in a small bowl; blend in sour cream and salt. Add to onion mixture and pour over biscuits. Sprinkle with poppy seeds. Bake 30 minutes or until topping is set. Slice in wedges; serve warm. *Good for late breakfast or supper hot bread.*

El Paso Herald   September 14, 1881
For an A 1 cook stove at less money than can be had anywhere else in town call on M. Schoenfeld.

BRAIDED EGG BREAD

Yield: 2-3 loaves   Oven: 350°

2 packages active dry yeast   ¼ cup melted butter
1¾ cups warm water   7 cups sifted flour
1 tablespoon salt   4 eggs, beaten
½ cup sugar

Dissolve yeast in water. After 5 minutes add salt, sugar and butter. Blend 3 cups of flour and the eggs. Beat. Add remaining flour. Mix with hands to blend thoroughly. On a floured board knead for 10 minutes. Place in a buttered bowl; cover with a towel and let rise until doubled (1½-2 hours). Punch down and turn onto floured board. Divide dough into two parts; divide each part into thirds and roll each piece into long strips. To make each braided loaf, braid three of the long strips together. Place the two loaves on greased cookie sheets. Cover and let rise again until doubled. Brush with melted butter. Bake 30-50 minutes.

Variation: Divide dough into three parts; place cach piece in a buttered loaf pan. Cover, let rise until doubled, and brush with melted butter. Bake as above.

BUTTER DIPS

Yield: 32 sticks   Oven: 450°

2¼ cups flour, sifted   3½ teaspoons baking powder
1 tablespoon sugar   1½ teaspoons salt
⅓ cup butter   1 cup milk

Melt butter in 13x9½-inch pan. Set aside. Sift flour, sugar, baking powder and salt. Slowly add milk, mixing with fork until dough just clings together. Turn onto well floured board. Roll over to coat with flour. Knead lightly about 10 times. Roll into 12x8-inch rectangle ½-inch thick. With floured knife cut dough in half lengthwise, then cut crosswise into 16 strips. Pick up cut strips in both hands and dip each strip on both sides in melted butter. Place strips close together in two rows in buttered pan. Bake 15-20 minutes until golden brown. This recipe can be frozen.

Variations:

Add ½ cup grated sharp American cheese to dry ingredients.
Add ½ clove of finely minced garlic to butter before melting.
Sprinkle paprika, celery seed or garlic salt over buttered dips before baking.
Add ¼ cup minced chives or parsley to flour mixture.

El Paso Herald   September 14, 1881
Fresh oysters at the Globe. The Globe Dining Room open day or night.

BUTTERHORN ROLLS

Yield: 3 dozen   Oven: 400-425°

1 cup milk
½ cup shortening
½ cup sugar
1 teaspoon salt

1 package active dry yeast
3 beaten eggs
4½ cups flour

Scald milk; add shortening, sugar, and salt. Cool to lukewarm. Add crumbled yeast to warm milk mixture and stir until softened. Add eggs and flour; mix to a smooth soft dough. Knead lightly on floured board. Place dough in greased bowl; cover and let rise in warm place until double in bulk. Divide dough into thirds; roll each third on a lightly floured board to a 9-inch circle. Cut into 12-16 triangular pieces. Roll each triangle, starting with wide end and rolling to center. Arrange on greased cookie sheet and brush with melted butter. Cover and let rise until very light, about 1 hour. Bake in hot oven for 15 minutes.

ANGEL FLAKE BISCUITS

Yield: 6 dozen   Oven: 450°

5 cups flour
2 teaspoons salt
1 teaspoon baking soda
3 tablespoons baking powder
3 tablespoons sugar

1 cup shortening
2 cups buttermilk
1 package yeast, dissolved in
    2 tablespoons warm water

Sift dry ingredients. Cut in shortening until size of pea. Stir in liquids at once. Store dough in a tightly closed plastic bag in refrigerator. Use as needed. Do not let rise at any time. Roll out amount of dough needed. Cut into shape. Bake for 10 minutes on greased sheet.

NO-BEAT POPOVERS

Yield: 8 popovers   Oven: 450°

2 eggs
1 cup milk

1 cup flour
½ teaspoon salt

Break eggs into bowl. Add milk, flour and salt. Mix well with a spoon, disregarding lumps. Fill greased muffin pans half full. Bake 30 minutes. Don't peek.

El Paso Herald   December 16, 1883
The San Antonio Street mud hangs on like a mother-in-law on a visit.

BUTTER BUNS

Yield: 12 buns   Oven: 375°

⅔ cup warm water
1 package active dry yeast
1⅔ cups sifted flour
2 tablespoons sugar

½ teaspoon salt
¼ cup soft shortening or
    butter
1 egg

Measure water into mixing bowl; stir in yeast to dissolve. To yeast add sugar, salt, shortening, egg, and 1 cup of the flour. Beat with electric mixer (slow speed), guiding batter into beater. Add remaining flour; beat until smooth. Fill buttered muffin cups half full. Allow the batter to rise in a warm place until it reaches the tops of the cups. Bake for 20 minutes.

BAKED SPICY TWISTS

Yield: 4 dozen   Oven: 375°

RICH SWEET DOUGH:

¾ cup milk
½ cup sugar
2 teaspoons salt
½ cup margarine

½ cup warm water (105°-115°)
2 packages active dry yeast
1 egg
4 cups unsifted flour

Scald milk. Stir in sugar, salt and margarine. Cool to lukewarm. Measure warm water into large warm bowl and sprinkle in yeast; stir until dissolved. Add lukewarm milk mixture, egg and 2 cups flour. Beat until smooth. Stir in remaining 2 cups flour to make a stiff batter. Cover tightly with wax paper or foil; refrigerate dough at least 2 hours. Dough may be kept in refrigerator three days. To use, cut off amount needed and shape as desired. *This is a no-knead dough that makes a tender roll.*

TO MAKE SPICY TWISTS:

1 recipe Rich Sweet Dough
½ cup sugar

½ teaspoon cinnamon
½ cup melted butter or margarine

Divide one recipe of Rich Sweet Dough in half. Roll ¼-inch thick into an 8x16-inch rectangle. Brush with melted butter. Sprinkle cinnamon and sugar on dough and fold in thirds. Slice with sharp knife. Twist each slice and place on buttered cookie sheet. Bake 10-12 minutes until golden brown. Repeat for second half of dough.

CRANBERRY NUT BREAD

Yield: 1 loaf   Oven: 350°

2 cups flour
1½ cups sugar
1½ teaspoons baking powder
½ teaspoon baking soda
1 teaspoon salt

Juice and rind of 1 orange
2 tablespoons melted shortening
1 egg, well beaten
½ cup chopped pecans
2 cups cranberries, halved*

Sift together flour, sugar, baking powder, soda and salt. Combine in measuring cup orange juice, rind, melted shortening and enough water to make three-fourths cup; stir in beaten egg with dry ingredients. Mix just enough to moisten. Fold in cranberries and nuts. Spoon into loaf pan with wax paper in bottom. Spread evenly, making corners and sides slightly higher than center. Bake 1 hour and 10 minutes. Remove from pan while still warm. Cool on rack.

*1 package of cranberries makes 2 loaves. Cranberries slice easier if frozen.

CURRANT TEA BREAD

Yield: 1 large or 2 small loaves   Oven: 350°

1 cup butter
1 cup brown sugar
3 large eggs
3 cups flour
1 cup currants
1 cup raisins
1 cup chopped walnuts

1 teaspoon baking powder
½ teaspoon baking soda
½ teaspoon salt
1 teaspoon nutmeg
1 teaspoon cinnamon
1¼ cups buttermilk

Cream butter and sugar. Beat in eggs. Mix ¼ cup flour with fruits and nuts. Sift remaining flour with other dry ingredients and add to the creamed mixture alternately with buttermilk. Fold in floured fruit and nuts. Spread in 9-inch loaf pan (or 2 smaller pans).

TOPPING:

¼ cup flour   ¼ cup soft butter
¼ cup brown sugar

Combine flour, sugar and butter and sprinkle over bread. Bake 1 hour.

El Paso Herald   November 29, 1882
Tomorrow is the time when the festive turkey, but pshaw: We won't say it.

APRICOT NUT BREAD

Yield: 1 loaf   Oven: 350°

1 cup dried apricots, diced
1 egg
1 cup sugar
2 tablespoons melted butter
2 cups sifted flour
3 teaspoons baking powder

¼ rounded teaspoon baking
   soda
½ cup orange juice
¼ cup water (use water in which
   apricots were soaked)
1 cup chopped pecans or walnuts

Soak apricots 30 minutes in water. Beat egg until light. Stir in sugar
and mix well. Stir in butter. Alternately add dry and wet ingredients,
stirring well after each addition. Add nuts and apricots. Mix well and pour
into greased loaf pan. Bake for 1 hour or until golden brown.

MAZARINE COFFEE CAKE

Serves: 10   Oven: 350°

1⅓ cups flour
1 teaspoon baking powder
⅓ cup sugar

½ cup margarine
1 egg
½ cup raspberry jam

Grease a round 9-inch cake pan. (A pan with a removable bottom is even
better). Blend dry ingredients; mix in margarine and egg until flour is
moistened. Press dough evenly on bottom and sides of pan. Spread ¼
cup of jam over dough. Cover with plastic wrap or foil and chill while
preparing filling.

FILLING:

½ cup butter or margarine
⅔ cup sugar
1 cup blanched almonds,
   ground or finely chopped

½ teaspoon almond extract
2 eggs
½ cup confectioners sugar
2 teaspoons lemon juice

Cream butter and sugar; stir in almonds and extract. Add eggs, one at a
time, beating well after each addition. Spoon filling over jam. Bake about
50 minutes. Cool cake in pan; carefully remove. Spread remaining ¼ cup
jam over top. Drizzle with glaze by mixing confectioners sugar with lemon
juice until smooth.

SESAME SEED COFFEE RING

Serves: 16   Oven: 375°

1 package active dry yeast   1 teaspoon salt
¼ cup warm water   1 egg
¾ cup lukewarm milk, scalded   ¼ cup soft shortening
    then cooled   3½-3¾ cups flour
¼ cup sugar

Dissolve yeast in water. Stir in remaining ingredients and half the flour.
Mix with spoon until smooth. Add enough remaining flour to handle
easily. Mix and turn onto lightly floured board. Knead until smooth and
workable (5 minutes). Place in greased bowl and turn greased side up.
Cover and let rise in warm place until double (1½ hours). Punch down;
let rise again until almost double (about 30 minutes).

SHAPING:

½ cup sesame seeds   1 teaspoon cinnamon
2 tablespoons butter   Confectioners sugar
¼ cup sugar   Cream

Brown sesame seeds with butter. Stir constantly. Cool. Roll dough on
lightly floured board into 15x9-inch pan. Cover with sesame seeds;
sprinkle with sugar and cinnamon. Roll tightly, beginning at wide side.
Pinch edges together to seal. With sealed side down form into ring on
greased cookie sheet. Pinch ends together. With scissors, cut two-thirds
through ring every inch apart. Turn each section on its side. Let rise
until double (40 minutes). Bake 25 minutes until golden brown. Frost
with confectioners sugar moistened with cream.

PUMPKIN BREAD

Yield: 10 - 16 servings   Oven: 350°

1 cup white sugar   ½ teaspoon salt
½ cup brown sugar   ¼ teaspoon ginger
1 cup canned pumpkin   ½ teaspoon nutmeg
½ cup oil   ½ teaspoon cinnamon
2 eggs, unbeaten   1 cup raisins
2 cups flour   ½ cup nuts, chopped
1 teaspoon soda   ¼ cup water

Mix sugars, pumpkin, oil and eggs together and beat well. Sift flour,
soda, salt and spices. Add to pumpkin mixture and mix well. Stir in
raisins, nuts and water. In greased loaf pan, bake 65-75 minutes.

APRICOT NIBBLE BREAD

Yield: 1 loaf   Oven: 350°

2 3-ounce packages cream cheese, softened
⅓ cup sugar
1 tablespoon flour
2 eggs (one slightly beaten)

1 teaspoon grated orange peel
½ cup orange juice
½ cup water
17-ounce package apricot-nut quick bread mix

Combine cream cheese, sugar and flour; beat in 1 egg and orange peel. Set aside. Combine slightly beaten egg, orange juice and water. Add quick bread mix, stirring until moistened. Turn two-thirds of the batter into greased and floured 9x5x13-inch loaf pan. Pour cream cheese mixture over top; spoon on remaining batter. Bake 1 hour. Cool 10 minutes; remove from pan. Wrap in foil and refrigerate. This recipe can be prepared ahead but cannot be frozen.

ORANGE OATMEAL COFFEE CAKE

Serves: 8   Oven: 400°

1⅓ cups sifted flour
4 teaspoons baking powder
1 teaspoon salt
1⅓ cups quick-cooking rolled oats
Grated peel of 1 or 2 oranges

⅔ cup brown sugar, firmly packed
2 eggs
1 cup milk
⅓ cup melted butter

Re-sift flour with baking powder and salt. Add rolled oats, orange peel and brown sugar. Beat eggs slightly; add milk and melted butter and pour into well in center of dry ingredients. Stir just enough to moisten. Spread batter in a greased 9-inch baking pan. Bake for 30 minutes.

TOPPING:

½ cup brown sugar, firmly packed
2 tablespoons melted butter
¼ cup drained crushed pineapple

2 tablespoons chopped maraschino cherries
2 tablespoons chopped nuts

Combine all ingredients and spread over baked cake. Place under broiler for 3 minutes until topping is bubbly. Serve hot.

El Paso Daily Times   June 3, 1885
Go to Mrs. Lane's Boarding House for good, clean and cheap meals . . . San Antonio Street . . . Regular board $6.00 per week . . . Meals 35¢ or three for a $1.00.

PINKY'S COFFEE CAKE

Serves: 12   Oven: 350°

1 cup butter, softened	1 cup sour cream
2 cups sugar	2 cups cake flour
3 eggs	½ teaspoon salt
½ teaspoon vanilla	1 teaspoon baking powder

Blend butter and sugar until barely mixed. Do not cream or overbeat. Add eggs, one at a time. Add vanilla. Sift flour, salt and baking powder. Alternately add flour mixture and sour cream. Mix 2 minutes on medium speed of electric mixer. Thoroughly grease and lightly flour angel food cake pan.

TOPPING:

½ cup chopped nuts	1 tablespoon cinnamon
¼ cup brown sugar	Slivered almonds for garnish

Mix nuts, brown sugar and cinnamon. Spoon half the cake batter into pan. Sprinkle half the topping over batter. Spoon on remainder of batter and remainder of topping. To marble, run knife around center cutting to bottom of pan. Bake 55 minutes.

POPPY SEED COFFEE CAKE

Serves: 12   Oven: 350°

1 cup buttermilk	1 teaspoon baking soda
1 2-ounce box poppy seeds	1 teaspoon baking powder
1 teaspoon almond extract	½ teaspoon salt
1 cup butter or margarine	4 egg whites
1½ cups sugar	½ cup sugar
4 egg yolks	1 tablespoon cinnamon
2½ cups flour	

Soak poppy seeds in almond extract and buttermilk; set aside. Cream butter and sugar until light and fluffy. Add egg yolks and beat. Sift flour, soda, baking powder and salt. Alternately add dry ingredients and buttermilk mixture to creamed mixture. Beat egg whites until stiff; fold into batter. Grease angel food cake pan; pour in half the batter. Combine sugar and cinnamon and sprinkle half the mixture over batter. Add remaining batter and sprinkle with remaining sugar and cinnamon. Bake for 1 hour and test with cake tester. Cool in pan. This recipe can be prepared ahead and frozen. Defrost for 1 hour or place in oven 30 minutes. Serve warm if desired.

SUNRISE BLUEBERRY MUFFINS

Yield: 24 large muffins   Oven: 375°

½ cup margarine
1 cup sugar
2 eggs
1¾ cups sifted flour
1 teaspoon baking powder
¼ teaspoon salt
¼ teaspoon nutmeg

⅛ teaspoon cloves
¾ cup buttermilk
¾ cup drained blueberries
3 tablespoons melted butter
⅓ cup sugar
1 tablespoon grated orange
   peel

Grease and flour muffin tins or use paper baking cups. Cream butter and sugar until light. Add eggs one at a time, beating well after each addition. Sift flour, baking powder, nutmeg, cloves and salt. Add to creamed mixture alternately with buttermilk. Fold in blueberries. Fill muffin pans two-thirds full. Bake for 20-25 minutes. Dip tops of the muffins in melted butter and mixture of sugar and grated orange peel. This recipe can be made in advance and frozen. Defrost muffins 1 hour before serving and bake in warm oven for 20 minutes.

BANANA MUFFINS

Yield: 15-18 muffins   Oven: 350°

½ cup margarine
1 cup sugar
2 eggs
¾ cup ripe bananas, mashed

1¼ cups flour
½ teaspoon salt
¾ teaspoon baking soda
1½ cups pecans

Cream margarine. Add sugar and eggs; beat. Stir in mashed bananas. Add sifted dry ingredients. Add nuts. Fill paper cups in muffin pan three-quarters full. Bake 20-25 minutes. The muffins can be frozen after they are baked. To serve, defrost 1 hour and place in warm oven for 20 minutes.

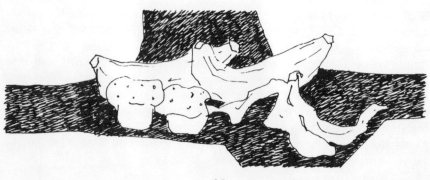

The Sweet Life

CAKES, CANDY, COOKIES

HINTS FOR CAKES, COOKIES & CANDY

Sift cake flour before measuring to assure fine-textured, delicately light results.

Beaten egg whites are best folded in by hand.

Use the displacement method for easy measuring of butter or shortening. Fill a measuring container with 1 cup water and add butter or shortening until water line indicates desired amount of butter or shortening plus 1 cup.

If brown sugar hardens, add a wedge of apple, lemon, or orange and place in a tightly covered jar.

To keep brown sugar from hardening, store in a closed container with a piece of bread.

To prevent cake from sticking to a plate, sift powdered sugar on the plate before placing fresh cake on it.

All ingredients for cakes should be at room temperature.

Loosen a cake that sticks to the bottom of a pan by placing the pan over a cloth wrung out in hot water.

For a fine-textured cake, add a few drops of boiling water to butter and sugar when creaming.

Before frosting a cake, place 2 knives in a glass of very hot water. Keep the glass handy; if the frosting hardens too quickly, use a dipped knife to spread it smoothly.

If a cake browns too quickly before it is done, place a pan of warm water on the oven rack above it.

After putting cake batter in a pan, lift the pan and drop it sharply to the table to release air bubbles. This will prevent the cake from falling.

For a good, quick frosting, boil a small potato until soft. Mash the potato; then beat in confectioners sugar and vanilla.

To keep boiled icing from hardening, add ¾ teaspoon vanilla during cooking.

A little flour or cornstarch sprinkled over the top of a cake will prevent the icing from running off.

To glaze a cake, use 1 tablespoon milk in which a little brown sugar has been dissolved.

The 6 basic types of cookies are drop, bar, molded, pressed, refrigerator, and rolled.

Chill dough for molded, pressed, or rolled cookies.

Drop cookies should be two inches apart on the cookie sheet.

Always place dough on a cool cookie sheet.

Crisp and freshen cookies that have become soft by warming in a very low oven 5 minutes.

To keep candy from boiling over, butter the inside top rim of the pan.

If candy will not harden, add 1 tablespoon corn syrup and cook longer.

CHOCOLATE BUTTERMILK POUND CAKE

Serves: 12-18   Oven: 325°

2 squares unsweetened chocolate
½ cup margarine
2 cups sugar
2 eggs
½ cup buttermilk (no substitute)

2 cups sifted flour
1 cup boiling water
1 teaspoon baking soda
1 tablespoon vanilla

Melt chocolate in deep pan. Cream margarine with 2 cups sugar. Add eggs to margarine and sugar mixture. Add ½ cup buttermilk alternately with 2 cups flour. Boil 1 cup water; pour ½ cup water into chocolate. To the other ½ cup water, add 1 teaspoon baking soda. Blend into chocolate mixture. Stir well with heat under pan allowing mixture to bubble high. Add chocolate mixture to batter little by little, mixing thoroughly. Add 1 tablespoon vanilla and mix well. Pour into well greased and floured bundt or tube pan. Bake for 1 hour and 15 minutes. The cake can also be baked in loaf pans for approximately 1 hour. Dust cake with powdered sugar or top with whipped cream, if desired.

BLACKBERRY JAM CAKE

Serves: 12-16   Oven: 350°

1 cup butter
1½ cups sugar
4 eggs
1 cup buttermilk
3 cups flour
1 teaspoon baking soda
1 teaspoon baking powder
1 teaspoon cinnamon

1 teaspoon ground cloves
1 teaspoon allspice
1 cup raisins (dusted with
    ¼ cup flour)
1½ cups seedless blackberry
    jam
1½ cups pecans

Cream butter and sugar. Stir in eggs, buttermilk and dry ingredients. Mix well. Add raisins, jam and pecans. Bake 45 minutes in a 9x13-inch pan or bundt pan.

ICING:

1 cup sour cream
½ cup butter

2 cups sugar

Melt all ingredients in saucepan and bring to boil. Mixture is very thin, but continue to put a little on cake about every 10 minutes while cake is warm. Use toothpicks to poke holes in cake so icing will soak in.

SAND TORTE POUND CAKE

Serves: 12-16   Oven: 350°

1 cup butter
3 cups sugar
6 eggs
1 cup sour cream

3 cups flour
1/4 teaspoon baking powder
1 1/2 teaspoons vanilla

Cream butter; blend in sugar. Add eggs one at a time, stirring well after each addition. Stir in sour cream. Add flour and baking powder (which have been sifted together). Blend in vanilla. Pour into greased and floured bundt or tube pan. Bake 1 hour and 15 minutes or until tests done. Do not over bake. When fully cooled, sprinkle with powdered sugar. Wrap in plastic and leave 24 hours before serving.

OLD FASHIONED FUDGE CAKE

Yield: 2 9-inch layers   Oven: 350°

2/3 cup soft butter or margarine
1 3/4 cups sugar
2 eggs
1 teaspoon vanilla
2 1/2 squares unsweetened
    chocolate, melted

2 1/2 cups sifted cake flour
1 1/4 teaspoons baking soda
1/2 teaspoon salt
1 1/4 cups ice water

Cream together butter, sugar, eggs and vanilla. Beat mixture 5 minutes at high speed on mixer scraping bowl occasionally. Blend in cooled chocolate. Sift together flour, soda and salt; add to the creamed mixture alternately with ice water, beating well after each addition. Bake in well-greased and floured 9-inch round pans for 30-35 minutes. Frost cake with Chocolate Fortune Frosting.

CHOCOLATE FORTUNE FROSTING:

2 1/2 squares unsweetened
    chocolate
2 cups sifted confectioners sugar
3 tablespoons hot water

1 egg
1/3 cup soft butter
1 teaspoon vanilla

Melt chocolate in mixing bowl over hot water. Remove from heat. With electric mixer blend in sugar and water. Beat in egg; stir in butter and vanilla. Frosting will be thin at this point. Place bowl in ice water and beat until it is of spreading consistency.

GERMAN CHOCOLATE POUND CAKE

Serves: 12-16   Oven: 350°

1 4-ounce bar Baker's German
    Sweet Chocolate
2¾ cups sifted cake flour
1¾ cups sugar
1 teaspoon salt
¼ teaspoon cream of tartar
½ teaspoon baking soda

¼ teaspoon cinnamon
1 cup butter, softened
¾ cup milk
1 teaspoon vanilla
3 whole eggs
1 egg yolk

Melt chocolate over hot water and cool. Stir in softened butter. Sift together dry ingredients. Add to dry ingredients, milk and vanilla, and mix to dampen flour. Beat 2 minutes at medium speed by mixer or 300 vigorous strokes by hand. Add eggs, yolk and chocolate mixture; beat 1 minute longer. Grease and flour a 10-inch tube pan. Line bottom with wax paper. Pour batter into pan. Bake for 1 hour and 5 minutes. Cool in pan for 15 minutes. Remove and cool completely. Glaze.

CHOCOLATE GLAZE:

1 4-ounce bar Baker's German
    Sweet Chocolate
1 tablespoon butter
¼ cup water

1 cup sifted confectioners
    sugar
Dash salt
½ teaspoon vanilla

Melt chocolate and butter in water over low heat. Combine sugar and salt and gradually add to chocolate mixture. Add vanilla and blend well.

SOUR CHERRY CAKE

Serves: 10-12   Oven: 350°

1 cup sugar
½ cup shortening
2 eggs
3 tablespoons sour milk
1 teaspoon baking soda
½ teaspoon lemon extract
¼ teaspoon cinnamon

1½ cups flour
1 cup sour pitted cherries,
    drained
1 cup raisins
1 cup pecans, walnuts or
    almonds, or combination
    of these

Cream sugar and shortening. Add eggs and beat. Mix in sour milk, soda, lemon juice, cinnamon and flour. Add cherries, raisins and nuts. Pour into a greased and floured bundt pan. Sprinkle with 1 teaspoon sugar mixed with ½ teaspoon cinnamon. Bake for 35 minutes.

PLANTATION PRIDE CAKE

Serves: 12-16   Oven: 375°

2 cups sifted flour   1 cup buttermilk or sour milk*
1 tablespoon cocoa   1¾ cups packed brown sugar
½ teaspoon salt   2 eggs
1 teaspoon soda   1 teaspoon vanilla
1½ cups butter

Sift together flour, cocoa, salt and soda. Melt butter and mix with sour milk. Combine milk with brown sugar, eggs and vanilla. In a separate bowl alternately add dry ingredients and milk mixture beginning and ending with dry ingredients. Turn into 13x9-inch greased and floured pan. Bake for 25-30 minutes. Spread with topping. Broil 2-3 minutes, until bubbly and golden, watching carefully.

*To make sour milk mix 2 tablespoons vinegar with one cup milk.

TOPPING:

½ cup butter   ¼ cup evaporated milk
1 cup brown sugar   1 tablespoon vanilla
¾ cup chopped walnuts or pecans

Melt butter and add brown sugar. Heat until sugar dissolves. Add chopped nuts, evaporated milk and vanilla.

CHOCOLATE CHEESECAKE

Serves: 8-12   Oven: 350°

24 chocolate wafers   1 cup sugar
¼ cup butter, melted   2 eggs
¼ teaspoon cinnamon   2 teaspoons cocoa
8 ounces semi-sweet chocolate,   1 teaspoon vanilla
        melted   1½ cups sour cream
3 8-ounce packages cream cheese

Crush wafers and mix with melted butter and cinnamon. Press into 8-inch springform pan and chill. Melt chocolate in top of double boiler over hot water. In a large bowl beat cream cheese until creamy. Add sugar and eggs gradually. Beat in melted chocolate, cocoa, vanilla and sour cream. Pour into crumb-lined pan and bake 45 minutes. Cool for 1 hour. Refrigerate at least 5-6 hours before serving.

ORANGE-GLAZED CAKE

Serves: 12-16   Oven: 325°

1 cup butter
2 cups sugar
4 eggs, beaten
4 cups sifted flour
1 teaspoon baking soda
½ teaspoon salt

1½ cups buttermilk
1 tablespoon grated orange
   rind
1 cup chopped pecans
1 8-ounce package chopped dates

Cream together sugar and butter. Add beaten eggs and continue beating. Sift flour, soda and salt together. Add to creamed mixture, alternating with buttermilk. Mix in orange rind, dates and pecans. Pour into greased and floured tube pan. Bake 1½ hours, or until cake tests done. Before removing from pan, while still hot, punch many holes in cake all the way to the bottom with ice pick or skewer.

GLAZE:

1 cup orange juice
2 cups sugar

2 tablespoons grated orange
   rind

Dissolve sugar in orange juice in small pan over medium heat. Do not boil. Add orange rind and pour hot glaze over cake, letting it drip into holes. Loosen sides of cake from pan so that some of the glaze runs down. Let cake stand in pan for several hours or overnight. It must be entirely cool before removing from pan. Decorate with pecans as desired. This cake may be frozen. Defrost at room temperature.

PINTO BEAN SPICE CAKE

Yield: 20-24 servings   Oven: 375°

1 cup sugar
¼ cup butter
1 egg, beaten
2 cups cooked pinto beans,
   mashed
1 cup flour
1 teaspoon baking soda
½ teaspoon salt

1 teaspoon cinnamon
½ teaspoon cloves
½ teaspoon allspice
2 cups diced raw apples
1 cup raisins
½ cup chopped walnuts
2 teaspoons vanilla

Cream sugar and butter. Add beaten egg and mashed pinto beans. Sift dry ingredients together and add to sugar mixture. Mix well. Add apples, raisins, nuts and vanilla. Pour into a well-greased 10-inch tube pan. Bake for 45 minutes.

SOUR CREAM BANANA PECAN CAKE

Serves: 16   Oven: 350°

¼ cup softened butter
1⅓ cups sugar
2 eggs
1 teaspoon vanilla
2 cups all-purpose flour
1 teaspoon baking powder

1 teaspoon baking soda
1 teaspoon salt
1 cup dairy sour cream
1 cup mashed ripe bananas
   (2 medium)
½ cup chopped pecans

Grease and flour a 13x9x2-inch baking pan. Beat butter until fluffy in large bowl with electric mixer. Gradually add sugar and continue beating until light and fluffy. Beat in eggs, one at a time. Add vanilla. Sift flour, baking powder, baking soda and salt together. Add to sugar mixture alternately with sour cream. Add bananas and pecans; mix just until blended. Turn into prepared pan. Bake for 40 minutes. Cool cake in pan 10 minutes. Turn onto wire rack and cool completely. Frost with caramel frosting.

QUICK CARAMEL FROSTING:

¾ cup butter
¾ cup brown sugar
6 tablespoons evaporated milk

3½ cups powdered sugar
1½ teaspoons vanilla

Heat butter with brown sugar in small pan over low heat, stirring constantly, until sugar melts. Blend in evaporated milk; cool. Gradually beat in sugar until of spreading consistency. Add vanilla.

EASY PEACH CAKE

Serves: 10   Oven: 350°

½ cup butter, softened
1 box yellow cake mix
1 29-ounce can sliced peaches,
   drained

½ cup sugar
1 teaspoon cinnamon
1½ cups sour cream
1 egg

Cut butter into dry cake mix until crumbly. Pat mixture lightly into 13x9x2-inch ungreased pan, building up slight edges. Bake 10 minutes. Arrange peaches on warm crust. Mix sugar and cinnamon and sprinkle on peaches. Blend sour cream and egg; drizzle over peaches. Topping will not completely cover. Bake 25 minutes or until edges are light brown. Do not overbake. Serve warm.

JIM'S CARROT CAKE

Yield: 1 9-inch layer cake   Oven: 325°

2½ cups cake flour, or 2 cups
    plus 1 tablespoon regular
    flour
2 cups sugar
2 teaspoons baking powder
1 teaspoon baking soda
2 teaspoons cinnamon
1 teaspoon salt

1¼ cups salad oil
4 whole eggs
2 teaspoons vanilla
2 cups finely grated carrots
1 cup drained, crushed
    pineapple
1 cup chopped pecans

Mix first six ingredients and sift into mixing bowl. Add salad oil. Beat 2 minutes starting at medium speed, increase to high speed. Add eggs and vanilla and beat for 2 more minutes. By hand, stir in carrots, pineapple and pecans. Pour into two 9-inch greased and floured cake pans. Bake for 45-50 minutes. Cool 15 minutes and turn out on cake rack.

ICING:

1 pound powdered sugar
1 8-ounce package cream
    cheese, softened

⅓ cup margarine
½ cup pecans
2 teaspoons vanilla

Cream all ingredients with an electric mixer. Ice cooled cake.

Variation: The following icing may also be used on this cake.

1 6-ounce package cream cheese
3 tablespoons cream
1½ teaspoons vanilla
½ teaspoon salt

1 pound powdered sugar
¾ cup pecans
½ cup raisins
½ cup coconut

Soften cream cheese; stir in cream and vanilla. Beat 3-7 minutes until light and fluffy. Add salt and powdered sugar, one cup at a time. Stir in pecans, raisins, and coconut.

SARAH'S "SOMETHING" CAKE

Yield: 15 - 18 servings   Oven: 350°

2½ cups all-purpose flour
1 teaspoon cinnamon
1 teaspoon nutmeg
1 teaspoon ground cloves
1 teaspoon baking soda
1 teaspoon baking powder
1 teaspoon salt

1 cup granulated sugar
1 cup dark brown sugar
1 cup oil
3 eggs
1 teaspoon almond extract
1½ cups buttermilk
1 cup shredded coconut

Grease 13x11x3¾-inch pan. Sift together flour, cinnamon, nutmeg, ground cloves, baking soda, baking powder and salt. Set aside. In large mixing bowl mix together sugars, oil, eggs and almond extract. Add buttermilk alternately with dry ingredients. Stir in coconut. Pour into pan and bake 35 minutes.

GLAZE:

1½ cups granulated sugar
¾ cup water
1 cup slivered almonds

½ pint whipping cream
Sugar
Cinnamon

Boil sugar and water together for 3 minutes. Cut warm cake into squares; sprinkle with almonds and boiled sugar water. Return cake to oven for 5 minutes. Allow to cool in pan. Top squares with whipping cream sweetened with sugar and cinnamon before serving.

WAXY PECAN CAKE

Yield: 16 servings   Oven: 300°

6 unbeaten egg whites
1 pound box light brown sugar
2⅔ cups sifted flour

½ teaspoon baking powder
3 cups broken pecans
1 teaspoon vanilla

Cream egg whites and brown sugar. Fold in dry ingredients, pecans and vanilla. Pour into two well-greased and floured 8½x4½x2½-inch loaf pans. Bake for 1 hour and 15-20 minutes, until loaves pull away from sides. The loaves will look cracked on top. This recipe can be prepared ahead and frozen. Defrost in wrapping.

El Paso Daily Times   April 3, 1885
If you want pleasing recollections of Kentucky turf, drink OFC Taylor Whiskey at The Vault.

APPLE CAKE

Serves: 12-16   Oven: 325°

2 large eggs, or 3 medium eggs
2 cups sugar
1½ cups oil
1 teaspoon salt
1 teaspoon baking soda
2 teaspoons baking powder
1 teaspoon cinnamon

1 teaspoon nutmeg
3 cups flour, sifted
½ cup raisins
½ cup broken nuts
1 teaspoon vanilla
1 teaspoon rum or rum flavoring
3 cups raw apples, diced

Beat eggs well. Gradually add sugar and beat again. Pour in oil and beat until smooth. Sift together salt, baking soda, baking powder, cinnamon, nutmeg and flour. Gradually add dry ingredients to egg mixture. Beat in vanilla and rum. Fold in apples, raisins and nuts. Bake in a greased and floured tube pan for 2 hours, but check after the first hour and 30 minutes to see if the cake is done. *This cake keeps well when wrapped in foil and is a good holiday cake.*

ELEGANT CHEESE CAKE

Serves: 12 - 14   Oven: 350°

1 cup zwieback crumbs
2 tablespoons sugar
¼ teaspoon cinnamon
3 tablespoons butter
3 8-ounce packages cream cheese, softened

½ teaspoon salt
3 tablespoons light rum, or 1 tablespoon vanilla
4 egg whites
1 cup sugar

Mix together crumbs, 2 tablespoons sugar, cinnamon and melted butter. Press into bottom of 8 or 9-inch springform pan in an even layer. Cream cheese, salt and rum together until soft and creamy. Beat egg whites until soft peaks are formed; gradually beat in the sugar to make a meringue. Fold egg white mixture into the cheese until well blended. Turn into pan with Zwieback crust. Bake about 25 minutes or until firm in center. Remove from oven. Increase oven temperature to 450° and prepare topping.

SOUR CREAM TOPPING:

2 cups sour cream
2 tablespoons sugar

⅛ teaspoon salt
1 cup strawberries

Combine sour cream with sugar and salt; spread over top of cake. Return to oven for 4-5 minutes. Chill well. Remove sides from pan. Serve strawberries on top.

PRUNE CAKE

Serves: 12   Oven: 375°

1½ cups sugar
1 cup oil
3 eggs
1 cup chopped prunes (cooked
    and unsweetened variety)
2 cups flour
1 teaspoon allspice
1 teaspoon cinnamon

1 teaspoon nutmeg
1 teaspoon cloves
1 teaspoon baking powder
½ teaspoon salt
1 cup buttermilk
1 teaspoon baking soda
1 cup chopped pecans

Mix sugar and oil as thoroughly as possible. Add well beaten eggs and mix until thick. Stir in chopped prunes. Combine all dry ingredients except soda and sift together. Combine buttermilk and soda (mixture will foam). Blend dry ingredients with other mixture alternately with buttermilk and soda. Mix well and add pecans. Bake in three layer pans for about 20 minutes or a tube pan for 60 minutes.

SAUCE:

½ cup sugar
1 tablespoon corn syrup
¼ cup butter

½ cup buttermilk
½ teaspoon baking soda
½ teaspoon vanilla

Combine all ingredients and simmer slowly while the cake bakes. Punch holes in the cake and pour the sauce over.

PUMPKIN CAKE

Serves: 12-16   Oven: 325°

4 eggs
2 cups sugar
2 cups cooked pumpkin
1¼ cups vegetable oil
1½ cups pecans, chopped
3 cups flour
2 teaspoons baking soda

2 teaspoons baking powder
1 teaspoon salt
1 teaspoon cinnamon
½ teaspoon nutmeg
½ teaspoon allspice
Whipping cream

Beat eggs until frothy. Add sugar, pumpkin, vegetable oil and pecans. Mix well. Sift together flour, soda, baking powder, salt, cinnamon, nutmeg and allspice; add to egg mixture. Beat well by hand or on low speed with electric mixer. Grease and flour a tube cake pan or bundt pan and pour batter into pan. Bake for 45-60 minutes. Serve with a dab of whipped cream on each piece. This cake may be stored in foil or frozen. Defrost at room temperature or in a warm oven with the cake wrapped in foil. *Good for Thanksgiving dinner.*

LEMON SUPREME CAKE

Serves: 12   Oven: 325°

4 eggs   1 box Duncan Hines Lemon
¾ cup oil   Supreme cake mix
1 cup apricot nectar

Beat eggs until light and creamy. Add oil and continue beating. Blend in apricot nectar and cake mix. Bake in greased tube pan for 1 hour.

GLAZE:

1 cup confectioners sugar
Enough lemon juice to make sugar
      syrupy

Mix sugar and lemon juice together. When cake is done, pour glaze over the hot cake in the tube pan. Poke holes in cake with a toothpick so glaze will soak in.

DELICIOUS RUM CAKE

Serves: 16   Oven: 350°

1 box yellow cake mix or   ½ cup oil
1 butter pecan cake mix   ½ cup rum
1 3¾-ounce box instant vanilla   ½ cup water
      pudding   ½ cup chopped nuts
4 eggs
Mix together all ingredients except nuts. Beat mixture for 2-3 minutes. Place chopped nuts in bottom of a well-greased tube or bundt pan. Pour batter on top of the nuts. Bake for 50-55 minutes.

SAUCE:

¼ cup water   ½ cup margarine
¼ cup rum   1 cup sugar

Boil above ingredients together for 2-3 minutes. Pour cooked mixture over cake when it is done. Let the cake stand for 30 minutes before turning upside down on a serving plate.

El Paso Daily Herald   March 22, 1893
Home made and reliable for all impurities of the blood . . . Irvin's
Sarsaparilla . . . 75¢ a bottle—6 for $4.00

ALMOND BUTTER CRUNCH

Yield: 1 dozen Oven: 375°

1½ cups blanched almonds, chopped
1 cup butter
1½ cups sugar

3 tablespoons light corn syrup
3 tablespoons water
8 ounces semi-sweet chocolate squares

Place chopped almonds on a cookie sheet; toast in oven for 10 minutes. In medium-sized heavy saucepan combine butter, sugar, corn syrup and water. Cook over medium heat, stirring constantly, until candy thermometer reads 300°. Remove from heat. Stir in 1 cup toasted almonds. Pour into buttered pan, spreading quickly and evenly. Cool and turn onto waxed paper. Melt chocolate squares in top of double boiler over hot water. Spread half the melted chocolate over top of candy and sprinkle with ¼ cup of nuts. Let stand 20 minutes. Turn candy over, spread with remaining chocolate and sprinkle with nuts. Let stand to set. Break into pieces.

APRICOT BALLS

Yield: 4-6 dozen

1 pound dried apricots
1 orange, washed but not peeled
2 cups sugar

2 cups chopped nuts
Powdered sugar

Grind apricots and orange together. Add sugar to apricot-orange mixture. Cook in a heavy pot or skillet slowly for 15 minutes, stirring constantly. Set aside to cool thoroughly. Stir in nuts. Form into small balls and roll in powdered sugar. Store in metal containers.

BEST EVER FUDGE

Yield: 25 squares

2 cups sugar
⅔ cup evaporated milk
12 large marshmallows
½ cup butter
Pinch of salt

6 ounces semi-sweet chocolate chips
1 cup chopped nuts
1 teaspoon vanilla

Mix first five ingredients. Cook over medium heat, stirring until it comes to a boil. Cook 5 minutes longer. Remove from heat and stir in nuts, chocolate chips and vanilla. Place in buttered 9x9-inch pan. When cool cut into squares.

BUTTERMILK PRALINES

Yield: 4 dozen

2 cups sugar
1 teaspoon baking soda
1 cup buttermilk

¾ cup butter
1 teaspoon vanilla
2 cups chopped pecans

In a large pan combine sugar, soda, buttermilk and butter. Cook to soft ball stage. Scrape bottom of pan frequently. Remove from heat. Beat by hand until mixture becomes darker in color. Add vanilla and nuts. Beat until mixture can be dropped onto wax paper. If necessary place candy in pan of warm water to retain softness. The pralines keep indefinitely in a covered container.

CHOCOLATE COCONUT BALLS

Yield: 12 dozen

3 cups chopped nuts
½ cup melted butter
14-ounce can Eagle Brand milk
2 7-ounce cans Angel
 Flake coconut
1½-2 pounds powdered sugar

½ teaspoon almond extract and
 ½ teaspoon vanilla*
3 6-ounce packages chocolate
 chips
¼ pound paraffin

Combine first three ingredients. Add the next three ingredients. Mix and form into small balls. Cool 4 hours or overnight. Melt chocolate chips with paraffin. Dip balls into chocolate with a toothpick.

*1 teaspoon vanilla can be used.

ENGLISH TOFFEE

Yield: 1 pound

1 cup chopped walnuts
¾ cup packed brown sugar
½ cup butter or margarine

½ cup semi-sweet chocolate
 pieces (Hershey's mini-
 morsels are best)

Butter an 8x8x2-inch pan; sprinkle nuts on bottom. In 1½-quart saucepan combine sugar and margarine. Cook over medium heat to soft crack stage (290° on candy thermometer), stirring constantly. Remove from heat and spread over nuts. Sprinkle chocolate pieces on top. When chocolate is soft, spread evenly over toffee. Chill thoroughly. Break into pieces.

CHOCOLATE NUT CLUSTERS

Yield: 3½ dozen large clusters

1 pound sweet chocolate
14-ounce can sweetened
    condensed milk

2 cups unsalted peanuts,
    almonds or pecans

Melt chocolate in top of double boiler. Remove from heat and stir in milk. Blend in nuts until well-coated. Drop by teaspoonfuls onto buttered cookie sheet. Refrigerate several hours.

DATE NUT CANDY ROLL

2 cups sugar
1 cup milk
1 teaspoon vanilla

2 tablespoons butter
1 cup chopped dates
1 cup chopped walnuts

Cook sugar and milk until a drop of the mixture in cold water forms a ball. Stir in vanilla and butter. Beat thoroughly. Add dates. Stir until melted. Add nuts. Remove from heat and stir briskly until thickened. Pour onto wax paper or foil in a long row. Roll. Cool. Slice and serve.

DIVINITY

Yield: 16 squares

3 cups sugar
1 cup water
¾ cup light corn syrup

2 egg whites, beaten
1 cup nuts
1 teaspoon vanilla

Boil sugar, water and syrup until it threads. Pour one-third of mixture over beaten egg whites. Beat well. Cook remainder to a cracking stage. Add slowly to first mixture and beat until creamy. Add nuts and vanilla. Pour into well-buttered pan and cut into squares.

LIQUOR BALLS

1 cup vanilla wafer crumbs
1 cup chopped pecans
1 tablespoon cocoa

¼ cup rum or bourbon
1½ tablespoons light corn syrup
1 cup powdered sugar

Roll wafers into very fine crumbs; add pecans and cocoa. Mix liquor with corn syrup. Combine with wafer mixture. Form into small balls by rolling in palm of hand. Roll balls in powdered sugar. These keep well in a tin can.

LEMON BONBONS

Yield: 4½ . dozen   Oven: 350°

1 cup soft butter
⅓ cup sifted powdered sugar
2 cups sifted flour
⅓ cup finely chopped pecans

1 tablespoon butter
1 cup powdered sugar
2 tablespoons lemon juice
Food coloring

Cream butter and sugar; stir in flour. Chill. Sprinkle nuts on wax paper. Roll dough into balls, Place balls on top of nuts and flatten with bottom of a glass. Bake on cookie sheet 12-14 minutes. Combine remaining butter, sugar, lemon juice and red or green food coloring for frosting. Beat together and dab on the top of each cookie.

MEXICAN SESAME SEED COOKIES

Yield: 4 dozen   Oven: 350°

1 cup lard (not shortening)
1 cup sugar
2 cups flour
¾ teaspoon baking soda

1 teaspoon salt
1 egg
1½ teaspoons almond extract
Sesame seeds

Allow lard to reach room temperature and cream with sugar. Sift flour with baking soda and salt. Beat egg into sugar and lard mixture; add dry ingredients. Stir in almond extract. Form into 1-inch balls. Put on cookie sheets and flatten each ball with the bottom of a glass, dipping glass in flour to prevent sticking. Sprinkle sesame seeds on top. Bake 15-20 minutes.

SOPAIPILLA DULCE
(MEXICAN FRIED COOKIE)

Yield: 2 dozen

4 cups flour
1 teaspoon salt
2 teaspoons baking powder
4 tablespoons lard

4 eggs
1 cup sugar
Water or milk
2 teaspooons cinnamon

Sift flour with salt and baking powder; cut in lard. Beat eggs and add ½ cup sugar to flour mixture. Add enough milk or water to make a medium dough, neither stiff nor soft. Let dough stand for 30 minutes. Roll out ¼-inch thick; cut into 1½-inch squares and fry in deep fat until brown. Drain. To remaining ½ cup sugar, add cinnamon and mix well. While the sopaipillas are still hot, roll in sugar and cinnamon mixture.

BIZCOCHOS
(MEXICAN HOLIDAY COOKIES)

Yield: 8-10 dozen   Oven: 350°

2 cups lard*
1 cup sweet wine or any fruit
    juice
1 cup sugar
1 tablespoon cinnamon

1 tablespoon anise seeds
2 egg yolks
3 cups flour
1 cup sugar
4 teaspoons cinnamon

Whip lard until creamy. Mix wine, 1 cup sugar, 1 tablespoon cinnamon and anise; add this to the lard and mix with wooden spoon. Add egg yolks; mix well. Add sufficient flour to make a soft dough; roll out ½-inch thick. Cut in desired shapes and place on greased cookie sheet. Bake 15 minutes; check often to prevent burning. Mix remaining cinnamon and sugar. Dredge cookies in this mixture while still warm.

*In authentic Mexican cooking, lard (not shortening) is used.

SUGARPLUM COOKIES

Yield: 7 dozen

½ cup butter
2 eggs, slightly beaten
1 cup sugar
1¼ cups dates,
    cut into small pieces
½ cup flour
½ teaspoon salt

1 teaspoon vanilla
1 cup pecans, finely chopped
2½ cups Rice Krispies
2 2-ounce jars red-colored
    sugar
Pillsbury green frosting

Heat butter in medium-sized skillet over medium heat; when practically melted, add eggs and sugar. Mix thoroughly; blend in dates. Cook, stirring constantly, for 5 minutes. Lower heat. Gradually add flour and cook, stirring constantly, until thick (7-10 minutes). Do not overcook. Stir in salt, vanilla, pecans and Rice Krispies and mix thoroughly. Cool to lukewarm. Shape to resemble a strawberry, using about one teaspoon for each. Roll in colored sugar immediately after forming so sugar will stick. Set on wax paper to cool. Using a cake decorator tip, frost large end to resemble green leaves. Let stand at room temperature for 1 hour.

El Paso Daily Herald   February 22, 1893
Telephone 114
On and after this date we will deliver ice for ¾ of a cent per pound wholesale, and 1 cent per pound retail. El Paso Ice and Refrigerator Co.

CHOCOLATE MERINGUE COOKIES

Yield: 3 dozen   Oven: 250°

2 egg whites (room temperature)   ¼ cup shredded coconut
⅛ teaspoon cream of tartar   ½ square semi-sweet
½ cup sugar   chocolate, grated
½ cup chopped pecans   ¼ teaspoon almond extract

In small bowl with mixer at high speed, beat egg whites and cream of tartar until soft peaks form; gradually sprinkle in sugar, 2 tablespoons at a time, beating until each addition is completely dissolved (whites should stand in stiff glossy peaks). Don't scrape sides of bowl during beating. Fold in remaining ingredients until mixed. Drop by rounded teaspoons onto greased cookie sheets about one inch apart. Bake 40 minutes. Cool cookies completely on cookie sheet on wire rack. Store in tightly sealed containers.

NUTTY MERINGUE KISSES

Yield: 8 dozen   Oven: 325°

2 egg whites (room temperature)   1 teaspoon almond or vanilla
1 scant cup sugar   extract
¾ cup chopped pecans

Gradually add sugar while beating egg whites until stiff. Add flavorings and nuts, mixing by hand. On an ungreased cookie sheet lined with aluminum foil, drop ½ teaspoon bits. Cook until edges are slightly tan.

NUT COOKIES

Yield: 12 dozen   Oven: 350°

1 cup butter or margarine   3 cups nuts, chopped
2 cups sugar   2 tablespoons cinnamon
2 eggs   4 cups flour
1 teaspoon baking soda, dis-   Dash salt
    solved in 3 tablespoons
    heavy molasses

Cream butter and sugar; add eggs. Add remaining ingredients. Form into long roll and wrap in wax paper; refrigerate until hardened. Slice and bake until brown and crisp (about 10 minutes).

El Paso Herald   November 9, 1881
Burro load of wood—60¢

CHOCOLATE MINT STICKS

Yield: 2¾ dozen   Oven: 350°

2 eggs
2 squares chocolate
½ cup butter
1 cup sugar

¼ teaspoon peppermint
   extract
½ cup sifted flour
¼ teaspoon salt

Beat eggs until frothy. Melt chocolate and butter over hot water. Combine sugar and eggs and add to chocolate mixture. Add peppermint; beat again, adding flour and salt last. Pour into 9x9-inch greased pan and bake 20-25 minutes. Cool before icing.

ICING:

4 tablespoons butter
1 cup sifted powdered sugar
2 tablespoons cream or evaporated milk

¾ teaspoon peppermint
   extract
¾ teaspoon green food
   coloring

Cream together butter and powdered sugar; add cream, peppermint and coloring. Spread on cake. Cut into 1x3-inch sticks. May be frozen after cutting.

Alternate: Before cutting, dribble 2 squares chocolate melted with 2 tablespoons butter over the top of iced cake.

APRICOT FILLED COOKIES

Yield: 2½ dozen   Oven: 350°

1 cup sifted flour
½ teaspoon baking soda
¼ teaspoon salt

1 cup quick-cooking oatmeal
½ cup melted butter
⅔ cup brown sugar

Sift flour, baking soda and salt together; mix in oatmeal. Mix melted butter and brown sugar together until smooth. Combine with flour mixture and mix well. Spread two-thirds dough mixture in 8-inch greased pan. Press firmly with fork. Top with apricot filling. Top with remaining dough, packing lightly. Bake 30-35 minutes. Cool before cutting.

FILLING:

½ cup dried apricots
½ cup water

½ cup sugar
¼ cup nuts, chopped

Place apricots and water in blender and run until smooth. Add sugar and blend. Pour into small bowl and add chopped nuts.

SAUCEPAN DATE BARS

Yield: 6 dozen   Oven: 350°

1 cup butter	2¾ cups all-purpose flour
1½ cups sugar	½ teaspoon baking soda
2 eggs	½ teaspoon salt
¼ cup buttermilk	½ teaspoon nutmeg
2 cups chopped dates	½ teaspoon cinnamon
1 cup chopped almonds	½ teaspoon ground cloves

Melt butter in saucepan; remove from heat. Add sugar and eggs; beat well. Add buttermilk, dates and nuts; mix well. Mix dry ingredients together and combine with mixture in saucepan. Spread in greased 15x10x2-inch baking dish. Bake 25 minutes. Cool and cut into 2x1-inch bars.

GRINGO BUÑUELOS
(YANKEE COOKIES)

Yield: 6 dozen

1 cup milk	1 teaspoon sugar
1 cup flour	1 teaspoon cinnamon
1 egg	¼ cup sugar
½ teaspoon salt	Liquid shortening

Mix first five ingredients together (it will look like pancake batter). Heat three inches of cooking oil in small pan. Immerse cookie iron until heated through. Dip rosette iron into batter (being careful not to immerse handle of the iron) and then into hot fat to cook. The cookies will slip off the iron after about 15 seconds. Drain on paper towels. Mix cinnamon and remaining sugar; sprinkle on cookies. This recipe can be prepared ahead, put into cookie tins, kept for several days.

El Paso Daily Times   Sunday May 26, 1895
A Song of the Times
Sing a song of six pence
Beef is mighty high
Can't afford to use it
Even in a pie
Hams in great abundance,
Bacon free from fault
Better get the Gold Bond
Never very salt

For sale by Chas. F. Slack & Co. Corner of San Francisco and El Paso Sts.

HONEY DROP COOKIES

Yield: 4 dozen   Oven: 375°

½ cup butter   ½ teaspoon baking soda
2 tablespoons sugar   1½-2 cups sifted flour
½ cup honey   ½ cup chopped raisins
1 egg, well beaten   ½ cup chopped nuts
⅛ teaspoon ground cloves   2 tablespoons water
¼ teaspoon allspice

Cream together butter, sugar and honey. Add egg; mix well. Sift together dry ingredients; add raisins and nuts. Mix well and add to first
mixture along with water to form soft dough. Drop from spoon on greased
cookie sheet. Bake 10-15 minutes.

PRIZE COOKIES

Yield: 5 dozen   Oven: 375°

1 cup brown sugar   ½ teaspoon salt
1 cup granulated sugar   2½ cups oatmeal
1 cup shortening or margarine   2 teaspoons vanilla
2 eggs   ¾ cup flaked coconut
2 cups all-purpose flour   ¾ cup chopped pecans, or
1 teaspoon baking soda   1 cup Post Toasties
1 teaspoon baking powder

Cream shortening with sugars; add eggs and beat until smooth. Sift
together flour, baking soda, baking powder and salt. Add to batter and
blend well. Add oatmeal and vanilla; blend well. Add coconut and pecans.
Drop onto greased cookie sheet by teaspoonfuls. Bake 10-12 minutes
until brown.

VIENNESE BROWNIES

Yield: 1 dozen   Oven: 375°

½ cup butter   2 heaping teaspoons cocoa
1 cup sugar   ½ teaspoon baking powder
3 eggs, separated   1 teaspoon vanilla
½ cup flour   ½ cup chopped nuts

Cream butter and sugar; add egg yolks. Sift flour, cocoa and baking
powder together and add to the creamed mixture. Blend in vanilla and
nuts. Beat egg whites until stiff and fold into mixture. Bake 30 minutes
in greased 8x8-inch pan. Do not overbake. Sprinkle with powdered sugar
when done.

COCA-COLA BROWNIES

Yield: 2 dozen   Oven: 350°

2 cups flour
2 cups sugar
1 cup butter or margarine
3 tablespoons cocoa
1 cup Coca Cola

½ cup buttermilk
2 eggs, beaten
1 teaspoon baking soda
1 teaspoon vanilla
1½ cups miniature marshmallows

Sift together flour and sugar. Heat butter, cocoa and Coca-Cola to boiling point; pour over sugar mixture. Mix buttermilk, eggs, baking soda, marshmallows and vanilla and add to mixture. Mix well. Batter will be thin. Pour into a floured and greased 9x13-inch pan and bake 30 minutes.

FROSTING:

1 pound box powdered sugar,
   sifted
1 cup margarine
3 tablespoons cocoa

6 tablespoons Coca Cola
1 cup nuts, chopped
1 teaspoon vanilla

Combine margarine, cocoa and Coca-Cola and heat to boiling. Pour over sugar. Blend with mixer until smooth; add nuts and vanilla. Pour over cake while frosting is still hot. Cool and cut into squares.

BLONDE TOFFEE BROWNIES

Yield: 3 dozen   Oven: 350°

1½ cups sifted flour
2 teaspoons baking powder
½ teaspoon salt
½ cup butter or margarine
1 cup granulated sugar
½ cup packed brown sugar

2 eggs
1 teaspoon vanilla
1 cup crushed Heath English
   Toffee miniatures
½ cup nuts, chopped fine
   (optional)

Sift flour, baking powder and salt together. Cream butter; add both sugars and cream well. Add eggs and vanilla; beat until fluffy. Blend in dry ingredients. Stir in crushed candy. Spread over bottom of well-greased 13x9x2-inch baking pan. Bake about 30 minutes. When cool, cut into 1x3-inch bars. If desired, bars may be frosted when cool with a white or chocolate butter frosting before cutting.

> El Paso Daily Times   July 25, 1890
> Manitou natural soda water is a most excellent appetizer. Every bottle of Manitou water is put up at the spring.

TOM THUMB COOKIE BARS

Yield: 3 dozen   Oven: 325°

½ cup margarine
½ teaspoon salt
1½ cups brown sugar
1 cup sifted flour
1 teaspoon vanilla

2 eggs, beaten
2 tablespoons flour
½ teaspoon baking powder
2½ cups coconut, flaked
2 cups pecans, chopped

Combine margarine and salt; add ½ cup brown sugar and cream well. Add 1 cup flour and blend. Press mixture into 8x12-inch greased pan. Bake 25 minutes. Add remaining cup of brown sugar and vanilla to eggs, beating until thick and foamy. Add 2 tablespoons flour, baking powder, coconut and nuts and blend. Spread with a fork over baked mixture. Return to oven and bake 35 minutes. Cool and cut into small bars.

SWEDISH GINGER COOKIES

Yield: 8 dozen   Oven: 350°

1 cup butter
1½ cups sugar
1 egg
1½ tablespoons grated orange rind
2 tablespoons dark corn syrup
1 tablespoon water

3¼ cups flour
2 teaspoons baking soda
2 teaspoons cinnamon
1 teaspoon ginger
½ teaspoon ground cloves

Cream butter and sugar; add egg and beat. Add orange rind, corn syrup and water; mix well. Sift dry ingredients together; stir into creamed mixture. Chill well. Roll ⅛-inch thick and cut with cookie cutter. Sprinkle with sugar and bake one inch apart on greased cookie sheet until nicely browned.

SAND TARTS

Yield: 3 dozen   Oven: 300°

1 cup butter
¼ cup confectioners sugar
2 teaspoons vanilla
1 tablespoon water

2 cups sifted enriched
    flour
1 cup finely chopped or
    ground pecans*

Cream butter and sugar; add vanilla and water. Add flour and mix well. Add pecans. Roll dough 1½-inches long and bend into crescent shapes. Bake on ungreased cookie sheet 20 minutes or until delicately browned. While hot, roll in confectioners sugar.

*Almonds or walnuts may be substituted.

Southwestern Souffle

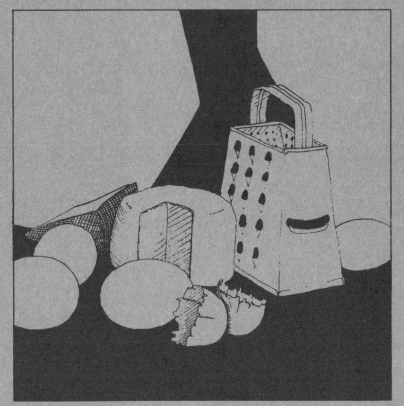

CHEESE AND EGGS

HINTS FOR CHEESE & EGGS

To keep egg yolks from forming a hard crust, place in a bowl and cover with cold water before storing in the refrigerator.

In poaching eggs, a tablespoon of vinegar added to the water will help set the whites. In boiling eggs, vinegar in the water prevents cracking.

Bread crumbs added to scrambled eggs will improve flavor and allow larger servings.

Egg whites beat faster and stiffer if done one at a time in a bowl barely wider than the beater. A teaspoon of cold water added to whites while beating will almost double the volume.

A teaspoon of salt added to the water in which eggs are hardcooked improves flavor and also loosens shells for easy peeling. Eggs should be cooked at a simmer, as fast boiling toughens whites. They should also be turned so the yolk will be in the center.

To keep an omelet from collapsing, add a pinch each of cornstarch and confectioners sugar to the yolks before folding in whites.

Eggs pierced before cooking will not leak even if they crack.

Before frying eggs, sprinkle a little flour onto the oil to prevent spattering.

To determine the age of an egg, place it in a bowl of cold water. If it lies on its side, it is very fresh; if it stands at an angle, it is at least 3 days old; if it stands on end, it is some 10 days old.

Processed cheese, as opposed to natural cheese, has a melting quality often desirable in Mexican dishes and other recipes where melting is important.

To keep cheese fresh, cover with a cloth moistened in vinegar or store, grated, in a covered jar in the refrigerator.

Serve cheese at room temperature. Soft cheese should be taken out of the refrigerator at least an hour before serving.

Cheese can be sliced very thin if the knife is first heated.

One pound cheddar cheese yields 4 cups grated cheese.

When serving strong cheese, also serve strong wine.

Cheese served with pears, apples, grapes, fresh peaches, or figs makes a good dessert. Mild cheeses are preferred for desserts.

Except for very aged or crumbly varieties, cheeses should look fresh and moist.

Runny cheeses such as Brie should be eaten when very soft.

If cheese is "green," leave it out of the refrigerator to ripen.

If cheese comes in a box, check inside for freshness.

Most cheeses will keep for weeks. Exceptions are very runny or rich cheeses, which must be used within a few days.

MOCK CHEESE SOUFFLE WITH MUSHROOM SAUCE

Serves: 4-6   Oven: 350°

8 slices sourdough bread, cut   6 eggs
    in pieces and crust trimmed   2½ cups milk
½ cup butter, softened   Salt and pepper
½ pound Old English cheese,
    grated

Butter bread on both sides and place in buttered 2-quart casserole layered with cheese. Beat eggs and add milk; pour over bread (milk nearly comes to top of casserole). Cover and let stand overnight or at least 5 hours. Bake 1 hour (uncovered last 15 minutes).

MUSHROOM SAUCE:

½ cup onion, chopped   2 cups chicken consommé
¼ cup butter   Salt and pepper to taste
1½ pounds fresh mushrooms   1 cup sour cream
Lemon juice   ½ cup Madeira wine
2 tablespoons cornstarch

Sauté onion in butter and add mushrooms which have been sprinkled with lemon juice. Add cornstarch, consommé and salt and pepper. Cook and stir until slightly thickened; add sour cream and wine just before serving.

HAM AND CHEESE SOUFFLE

Serves: 8-10   Oven: 350°

3 cups cubed cooked ham   1 teaspoon dry mustard
3 cups cubed Swiss cheese   Dash Tabasco sauce
3 cups cubed French bread   3 cups milk
3 tablespoons flour   4 eggs, beaten

Layer ham, cheese and bread in a buttered 3-quart casserole. Sprinkle with flour and dry mustard mixed together. Sprinkle Tabasco sauce as desired. Mix milk with beaten eggs and pour over all. Chill at least 2 hours or overnight. Bake about 1 hour or until puffy and golden on top. Serve immediately. This is very good as a brunch main dish served with fresh fruit salad and sweet rolls.

El Paso Times   July 30, 1890
The melon market was over-crowded yesterday. Ten cents could purchase half a dozen musk melons.

CHILE CHEESE SOUFFLE

Serves: 4-6   Oven: 350°

2 tablespoons butter
2 tablespoons cornstarch
1 cup milk
Dash cayenne
½ teaspoon salt
¼ teaspoon dry mustard

5 tablespoons canned chopped
    green chile, drained
¼ pound Cheddar cheese, grated
6 egg yolks, whipped
6 egg whites, beaten until
    stiff

Melt butter; stir in cornstarch and cook until bubbly. Remove from heat and blend in milk, cayenne, salt and mustard. Cook, stirring until thickened. Stir in chile and cheese. Remove from heat and beat in egg yolks. Fold in 3 egg whites and beat; fold in remaining egg whites and blend. Pour into a greased 2-quart soufflé dish. Place dish in a larger pan filled with boiling water to half-way up side of soufflé dish. Bake about 30 minutes or until a skewer inserted in center comes out almost dry. Serve immediately.

PEÑA BLANCA EGGS

Serves: 6   Oven: 400°

Olive oil
6 cloves garlic
Oregano

Salt
Parsley
6 eggs

Pour into small egg containers (or large muffin tins) enough olive oil to cover bottoms. To each tin add 1 clove garlic, dash of oregano, salt and parsley. Put in oven. When the container is spitting oil, remove from oven and remove garlic. Drop an egg into each container. The eggs cook without returning to the oven. Cover with chile sauce to serve.

CHILE SAUCE:

1 tomato, chopped
1 jalapeño, chopped and
    seeded
1 small onion, chopped

Salt and pepper
Chopped fresh cilantro
    (or 1 teaspoon ground
    coriander)

Mix all ingredients together. Cover eggs with chile sauce to serve. Sauce may be kept covered in refrigerator. *(These are served at Hector Quevedo's Peña Blanca Ranch outside of Casas Grandes, Chihuahua, Mexico).*

El Paso Herald   September 28, 1881

Maximo Aranda is the owner of the largest pear tree in San Elizario. It is 50 feet high and the trunk is 10 feet in circumference.

HUEVOS CON SALSA DE AGUACATES
(EGGS WITH AVOCADO SAUCE)

Serves: 4

2 tablespoons minced onion
2 tablespoons butter or
   margarine
1 4-ounce can green chile
1 tablespoon flour

½ cup milk
8 hot hard cooked eggs
2 avocados, peeled
Salt to taste

Cook onion in butter until soft; add chile, flour and milk. Cook until thick. Peel eggs; keep them warm in hot water. Whirl avocados in blender until smooth. Stir into hot milk sauce, season with salt and pour over the hot sliced eggs.

TEXAS EGGS

Serves: 6

1 bell pepper, diced
1 large tomato, diced
1 large onion, diced
2 tablespoons butter
1 dozen eggs

1 cup grated Cheddar cheese
3-4 jalapeños, or roasted
   and peeled fresh green
   chiles

Seed and chop jalapeños. In skillet, brown onion and bell pepper in butter. Remove from skillet. Beat eggs until frothy. Pour into skillet and cook until soft and very wet. Add all other ingredients and serve.

RANCH EGGS

Serves: 6   Oven: 325°

19-ounce can chile con carne
   (no beans)
6 eggs

½ medium onion, chopped
½ cup Longhorn cheese,
   grated

Mix chile con carne and onion in a saucepan and heat slightly. Pour chile mixture into shallow 1½-quart casserole. Make six holes in the mixture; crack eggs and drop into the holes. Sprinkle cheese over the top of the casserole. Bake 15-20 minutes or until eggs are set.

El Paso Herald   March 9, 1884
The wagging of an idle tongue causes much trouble and heart burning.

EGGS FLORENTINE

Serves: 6   Oven: 350°

3 packages boil-in-the-bag   6 eggs
   frozen spinach   12 tablespoons grated
¼ teaspoon nutmeg   Gruyere cheese

Drop plastic bags of spinach into boiling water; boil 8 minutes. Pour spinach into bowl and season with nutmeg. Divide mixture into six oven-proof egg dishes. Into each break 1 egg; top with salt and pepper and 2 tablespoons cheese. Bake until cheese melts and eggs set. Good with homemade bread and wine for lunch.

EGG AND CHEESE PIE

Serves: 5   Oven: 450°

4 eggs   ¼ pound grated cheese
4 tablespoons flour   (Mozzarella, Swiss or Jack)
1 cup milk   Salt and pepper
2 tablespoons melted butter

Beat eggs well, adding flour gradually. Continue beating and gradually add milk, butter, cheese and salt and pepper to taste. Turn into buttered pie plate or pan and bake 30 minutes. The torte should swell and have a golden, crusty top. Cut like pie and serve with meat, fish or fowl.

ARTICHOKE OMELET

Serves: 4   Oven: 400°

6 canned or 3 fresh artichoke   ½ medium onion, thinly sliced
   hearts, cooked   4 eggs
¼ cup olive oil   Salt and pepper
1 clove garlic, mashed   Tomatoes
2-4 tablespoons minced parsley

Cut artichoke hearts lengthwise into quarters. Heat oil and add garlic, parsley, onion and seasoning. Cook until light brown. Add artichokes. Beat eggs; pour over mixture and cook until bottom is browned. Put in oven for 1 minute. Garnish with thinly sliced fresh tomatoes.

El Paso Herald   December 23, 1883   Christmas Edition
Schuster, B. & Co.
(Ben and Bernard)
Their stock of groceries is very large.

OMELET ABUELITA

Serves: 1-2

3 eggs
1 tablespoon water
½ teaspoon salt
Dash pepper
2-3 drops Tabasco
1 tablespoon chopped parsley

1 tablespoon minced chives
2 tablespoons melted butter
3 tablespoons diced cooked
   bacon
2 tablespoons grated
   Gruyere cheese

Mix eggs and water slightly; add salt, pepper, Tabasco and chives. Pour butter into omelet pan and add bacon. When butter sizzles, add egg mixture and stir rapidly with a fork until mix begins to set. Sprinkle cheese on top and lower heat. When omelet is set, loosen edges and fold over toward middle. Serve on warmed plate.

TORTILLA CHEESE OMELET

Serves: 1

2 teaspoons butter or
   margarine
2 eggs
2 teaspoons water
⅛ teaspoon salt

1 tablespoon chopped
   green chile
½ corn tortilla
¼ cup shredded Jack
   cheese

Heat 1 teaspoon butter in small frying pan or omelet pan over medium heat. When it starts to bubble, put in tortilla and heat until tortilla is limp. Remove to heated platter. Add 1 teaspoon butter to pan. Mix eggs, water, salt and chile. When butter is bubbly pour in egg mixture. Quickly tip pan, lifting edges of omelet to let egg liquid flow underneath. When firm but moist on top, place tortilla on top of eggs; top with cheese. Remove from pan and fold over. Serve with Mexican Sauce (see Index).

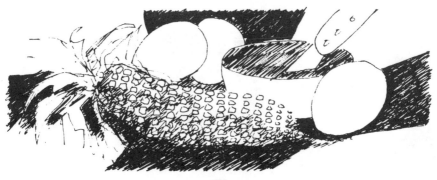

DIABLO OMELET

Serves: 4

8 eggs
1½ teaspoons salt
¼ teaspoon pepper
¼ cup cream or milk
½ cup fresh or canned
 mushrooms, chopped

2 medium tomatoes, peeled
 and chopped
3 tablespoons butter
Pinch garlic powder
1 avocado

Beat eggs slightly, just enough to mix. Add 1 teaspoon salt, ⅛ teaspoon pepper and cream. In small saucepan, sauté mushrooms and tomatoes in 1 tablespoon butter for 4-5 minutes; season with ½ teaspoon salt and ⅛ teaspoon pepper and garlic powder. Peel, pit and dice avocado and add to mushrooms and tomatoes, but do not cook. Heat butter in skillet and make omelet as usual. When almost ready, sprinkle the vegetables over half the omelet and fold. May be served with Mexican Sauce. (see Index).

STRAWBERRY OMELET WITH SOUR CREAM

Serves: 1   Oven: Broil

3 eggs
1 tablespoon light cream
¼ teaspoon salt
2 tablespoons butter

¼ cup sour cream
½ cup frozen or fresh
 strawberries
Powdered sugar

Beat eggs in a bowl; add cream and salt and beat with fork for 30 seconds. Heat butter in skillet until it sizzles. Pour in beaten eggs; stir once or twice with fork. Lift edges as eggs begin to cook and let liquid part run under, shaking pan back and forth to keep omelet free. When cooked but still soft on top, add ⅛ cup sour cream and ¼ cup berries. Slide omelet well to right edge of a platter and fold over. Pour remaining sour cream and berries on top; sprinkle lightly with powdered sugar and place under a hot broiler for 10 seconds.

SAUSAGE AND EGG CASSEROLE

Serves: 6   Oven: 375°

4 hard cooked eggs
4 tablespoons butter or
   margarine
¼ cup sifted all-purpose flour
½ teaspoon salt
Dash pepper
2 cups milk

1 pound bulk pork sausage,
   cooked and drained
16-ounce can whole kernel
   corn, drained
1 cup soft bread crumbs
   (1½ slices)

Slice 2 eggs into 1½-quart casserole. In saucepan blend butter, flour, salt and pepper; add milk all at once. Cook, stirring constantly, until mixture is boiling and thickened. Stir in sausage and corn; pour over sliced eggs. Slice remaining 2 eggs; arrange over top of sausage mixture; sprinkle with bread crumbs. Bake 20-25 minutes or until heated thoroughly.

DEVILED HAM AND EGGS CASSEROLE

Serves: 6   Oven: 350°

10-ounce package frozen
   broccoli, cooked and
   drained
6 hard cooked eggs
3 tablespoons salad dressing
1 tablespoon minced onion
1 teaspoon prepared mustard
½ teaspoon Worcestershire sauce

1 4½-ounce can deviled ham
2 tablespoons butter or
   margarine
2 tablespoons all-purpose flour
1 cup milk
½ teaspoon salt
1 cup sharp processed
   American cheese, diced

Arrange broccoli in 10x6x1½-inch baking dish. Cut eggs in half lengthwise. Remove yolks; mash and mix with the next four ingredients. Add salt and half the ham. Fill egg whites with small dabs of ham and add some yolk mixture, topping with dab of ham. Arrange filled eggs on broccoli. In a saucepan blend flour with melted butter and slowly add milk, stirring until sauce thickens. Add salt and diced cheese continuing to stir until thoroughly blended. Cover eggs and broccoli with sauce. Bake 20-25 minutes.

El Paso Daily Herald   December 15, 1892
Clairette Soap
A Laundry maid pretty and stout,
Was lately in trouble and doubt,
For her best counterpanes
Had some very black stains
But Clairette Soap took them out.

SEAFOOD QUICHE

Serves: 8-12   Oven: 350°

2 9-inch unbaked pie shells
1 6-ounce package frozen crab-
    meat, thawed and drained
    (or canned)
1½ cups cooked, chopped,
    deveined shrimp
1 8-ounce package Swiss cheese,
    chopped

½ cup finely chopped celery
½ cup finely chopped scallions
1 cup mayonnaise
2 tablespoons flour
1 cup dry white wine
4 slightly beaten eggs

Combine crabmeat, shrimp, cheese, celery and scallions. Divide mixture equally between pie shells. Combine mayonnaise, flour, wine and eggs. Pour half mixture over seafood in each pie shell. Bake 35-40 minutes. This recipe may be frozen uncooked. Bake frozen for 50 minutes. Serve with green salad and bread sticks.

HOT CRAB SOUFFLE

Serves: 12-14

8 slices bread
2 cups crabmeat
½ cup mayonnaise
1 small onion, chopped
1 bell pepper, chopped
1 cup celery, chopped

4 eggs
3 cups milk
10¾-ounce can mushroom soup
2 cups grated sharp cheese
Paprika

Cube 4 slices of bread and place in a 3-quart baking dish. Mix crab, mayonnaise, onion, pepper and celery. Spread over bread. Cube the remaining bread and place over mixture. Beat eggs in milk until fluffy. Pour over remaining crab mixture and refrigerate overnight. When ready to bake, spoon undiluted soup over casserole. Top with grated cheese and paprika. Bake 1 hour. This may be frozen before or after baking. If frozen after baking, warm before serving.

SALMON SOUFFLE

Serves: 4-6   Oven: 350°

1 7-ounce can salmon
3 tablespoons butter
3 tablespoons flour
1 cup milk

4 egg yolks
Salt
Worcestershire sauce
6 egg whites

Clean black skin and bones from salmon; mash with juice from the tin. Melt butter in double boiler; stir in flour and blend. Bring milk to a boil and add to butter-flour mixture. Stir until thick and smooth; remove from heat. Beat in egg yolks one at a time; season with salt and Worcestershire to taste. Add salmon to egg mixture. Beat egg whites until stiff and fold into salmon mixture with rubber spatula or wooden spoon. Turn into 8-cup buttered soufflé dish. Bake in preheated oven 30-40 minutes. Serve, if desired, with Hollandaise Sauce (see Index).

Trail's End

DESSERTS AND PASTRIES

HINTS FOR DESSERTS & PASTRIES

When a recipe calls for a whipped topping, follow directions on the label of non-fat dry milk and use instead of whipped cream.

Whip heavy cream and sweeten to taste. Drop on a cookie sheet in serving portions and freeze. When hard, slip off into a plastic bag. Place on desserts before serving.

If whipping cream just won't be whipped, add 4 drops lemon juice or a little plain gelatine powder.

To keep sliced bananas from turning brown, marinate in the juice of any canned fruit for a few minutes.

Egg whites are properly beaten when the peaks flop over slightly. Beating until stiff causes the whites to separate and reduces the quality of the final product.

Grease the container before measuring syrup, molasses, or other sticky substance.

To prevent film from forming on pudding, cover with wax paper while still hot.

Soak walnuts overnight in salt water to get the meats out whole.

Rinse the bowl with boiling water before creaming butter and sugar together.

Crush nuts between sheets of wax paper with a rolling pin.

To keep fruit from baking through the bottom of a pie shell, sprinkle an equal mixture of sugar and flour onto the shell before filling.

Pastry for a 2-crust, 9-inch pie will make 8 to 10 individual tart shells in 3 to 4-inch tart pans.

If pie dough is wrapped tightly, it will keep several days in the refrigerator.

A new pie tin will not usually produce a well-browned under crust until the shininess has worn off the tin through exposure to heat.

In making pie dough, remember that too much flour makes the crust tough, too much shortening makes it dry and crumbly, and too much liquid makes it heavy and soggy.

To shell pecans easily, first pour boiling water over them, let stand a few minutes, and drain.

To keep meringue from shrinking, spread it on the pie so that it touches the crust on all sides and bake in a moderate oven.

If meringue shells get soft, reheat them in a slow oven 15 minutes.

If a custard pie shrinks from the crust, it was baked in too hot an oven.

Use a knife dipped in warm water to cut a cream pie so that the filling won't stick to it.

Shredded coconut added to unbaked pastry for a shell is great for a cream pie filling.

In baking meringue kisses or shells, line the baking sheet with a brown paper bag cut to fit.

When carrying a meringue-topped pie any distance, insert 4 cocktail picks around the center before covering the pie with wax paper. The picks will prevent the paper from touching the meringue.

To prevent soggy crusts, coat pastry shells with egg white before baking.

A few drops of vinegar added to ice water in making pastry will make it fluffier.

CHOCOLATE CREAM ROLL

Serves: 8-12   Oven: 400°

5 eggs, separated   Dash of salt
3 tablespoons cocoa   ¼ teaspoon baking powder
1 cup plus 2 tablespoons   1½ teaspoons vanilla
    sifted confectioners sugar   1 cup whipping cream

Beat egg whites until stiff but not dry; set aside. Beat egg yolks until thick and lemon colored. Sift cocoa, 1 cup sugar, salt and baking powder. Gradually beat into egg yolks. Fold into egg whites. Add 1 teaspoon vanilla. Pour into 13x9x2-inch pan lined on bottom with greased wax paper. Bake in oven 15 minutes. Turn onto wax paper, lightly covered with confectioners sugar. Cool. Carefully peel off paper. Lightly roll and lay flat again. To whipping cream, add 2 tablespoons sugar and ½ teaspoon vanilla and beat. Pour on one end of cake. Lightly roll (cream spreads down as rolled). Cake will stand about three inches high. Frost.

CHOCOLATE FROSTING:

1½ cups confectioners sugar   1 teaspoon vanilla
1 tablespoon softened butter or   Enough cream or milk to
    margarine   moisten for spreading
2 tablespoons cocoa

Combine all ingredients. Spread top, sides and ends with frosting and chill until firm. Cut into slices. Lay flat on dessert plate. This recipe can be prepared two or three days ahead.

CHOCOLATE TORTONI

Serves: 8

2 egg whites   2 teaspoons vanilla
½ cup sugar   ½ cup semi-sweet chocolate
2 cups whipping cream   pieces
2 teaspoons instant coffee   ½ cup toasted almonds, minced
2 egg yolks, slightly beaten

Beat egg whites until stiff. Combine beating and gradually add ¼ cup sugar. Whip cream with ¼ cup sugar and coffee. Add egg yolks and vanilla; fold into egg whites. Melt chocolate over hot (not boiling) water; cool slightly. Quickly fold chocolate and almonds into egg white mixture. Turn into dessert dishes, parfait glasses, paper soufflé cups or custard cups and freeze until firm.

RIO GRANDE MUD

Serves: 15-18   Oven: 325°

2 cups sugar
1 cup shortening
4 eggs
1½ cups flour
⅓ cup cocoa

1 tablespoon vanilla
1 cup chopped nuts
¼ teaspoon salt
16-ounce package miniature
    marshmallows

Cream shortening and sugar. Add eggs and beat. Sift flour, cocoa and salt and add to mixture. Add vanilla and nuts. Pour into 9x13-inch pan. Bake 40-45 minutes. While still warm, cover with marshmallows. When cool, spread icing.

ICING:

½ cup margarine
⅓ cup cocoa
1 pound powdered sugar

½ cup cream, or evaporated
    milk
1 teaspoon vanilla
1 cup nuts

Sift cocoa with powdered sugar. Melt margarine. Add dry ingredients, cream, vanilla and nuts. Blend and spread over cake.

BAKED DEVIL'S FLOAT

Serves: 8   Oven: 350°

1 cup flour
¼ teaspoon salt
¾ cup sugar
2 teaspoons baking powder
1½ tablespoons cocoa

½ cup milk
1 teaspoon vanilla
2 tablespoons melted butter
½ cup nuts (optional)
Whipping cream

Combine dry ingredients. Add milk, vanilla, butter and nuts. Pour into greased square or rectangular pan.

SAUCE:

½ cup sugar
½ cup brown sugar

5 tablespoons cocoa
1 cup hot water

Combine sugars, cocoa and hot water and stir to form a sauce. Pour over ingredients in pan. Bake 40 minutes. Serve with whipped cream.

CHOCOLATE MOUSSE

Serves: 6

4 ounces semi-sweet chocolate squares	4 egg whites
¼ cup water	Dash of salt
4 egg yolks	½ pint whipping cream
½ cup sugar	1 teaspoon orange flavoring

Melt chocolate with water in top of double boiler, stirring occasionally. Set aside. Beat egg yolks; add sugar gradually and beat until mixture is pale yellow (when beaters are lifted out the mixture should fall in a ribbon). Add cooled chocolate and beat until well blended. Place egg whites in a second bowl and beat until foamy. Add salt and beat until stiff. To softened chocolate mixture, stir in about a cup of the beaten egg whites; fold in remaining egg whites. Pour into individual cups or serving dishes and chill several hours. Before serving, top with whipped cream flavored with orange flavoring.

ALMOND ICE BOX DESSERT

Serves: 12

18 lady fingers	7 eggs
3 dozen almond macaroons*	½ pound blanched almonds, ground
1 cup butter	
1½ cups powdered sugar	2-3 tablespoons sherry

Line bottom of spring mold pan with waxed paper. Place split lady fingers around sides of mold, and place macaroons close together on bottom, flat sides down. Fill spaces with broken macaroons and lady fingers. Cream butter and sugar. Add 3 whole eggs, one at a time, beating well after each addition. Separate remaining eggs and add 4 well beaten yolks and beat again. Add almonds (can be ground in blender) and sherry. Fold in stiffly beaten whites of 4 eggs. Pour half of mixture into mold and cover with macaroons. Pour in remaining half and top with macaroon crumbs. Chill at least 30 hours. *This is an elegant party dessert.*

*Order ahead of time from bakery.

El Paso Daily Herald   March 22, 1893
A. Goodman
Wholesale Grocer
Opera House Building
315 El Paso Street
My stock is carefully selected and is the largest in the Southwest.

CHARLOTTE RUSSE WITH STRAWBERRIES

Serves: 10

1½ dozen lady fingers
2 envelopes gelatine
½ cup cold water
2 cups milk
6 egg yolks

1 cup sugar
1 teaspoon vanilla
2 cups heavy cream, whipped
Strawberries, fresh or frozen

Line spring mold pan with split lady fingers. Soften gelatine in cold water. Scald milk. Beat well sugar and egg yolks; stir into milk. Cook until thickened. Just before removing from heat, add gelatine and stir until well dissolved. Add vanilla and set aside. When thoroughly cool, fold in whipped cream and pour into pan lined with lady fingers. Chill. To serve, unmold on cake plate, slice, and spoon on frozen or fresh strawberries. This is a dramatic and delicious dessert and can be made the day ahead.

STRAWBERRY DESSERT

Serves: 10   Oven: 350°

1 cup sifted flour
½ cup brown sugar
½ cup chopped pecans
½ cup melted butter
2 egg whites

1 cup sugar
10-ounce package frozen
    strawberries, thawed
2 teaspoons lemon juice
1 cup whipping cream

Mix flour, brown sugar, pecans and melted butter. Bake for 20 minutes in an ungreased pan, stirring a few times. Cool and spread two-thirds crumbly mixture in a 12x9-inch oblong pan. In a mixing bowl, beat 2 egg whites until stiff; add sugar gradually, lemon juice and strawberries. Fold in whipped cream. Pour over crumb mixture. Sprinkle top with remaining one-third crumbs. Freeze. Remove from freezer 20-30 minutes before serving.

STRAWBERRY TORTE

Serves: 8   Oven: 275°

6 egg whites
2 cups sugar
¼ teaspoon almond extract
1 teaspoon vanilla

1 tablespoon vinegar
2 cups strawberries
2 cups whipping cream

Beat egg whites until stiff but not dry. Gradually add ½ cup sugar, beating constantly. Add almond extract, vanilla and vinegar and fold in 1 cup sugar. Pour into a greased and floured 9-inch springform pan. Bake 1 hour and 15 minutes or until firm and delicately browned. Cool. Remove from springform carefully. Sprinkle remaining sugar on berries. Cover the torte with whipped cream and arrange berries on the top.

PEARS VICTORIA

Serves: 6

12 canned pear halves   2 tablespoons instant coffee
4 tablespoons cocoa

The day before serving, drain pears for 30 minutes. Prepare mixture of cocoa and coffee. Into hollow of each of 6 pear halves, place 1 tablespoon of mixture. Cover treated halves with remaining pear halves. Secure each with toothpick. Refrigerate for 24 hours, turning pears several times. Prior to serving, open pears and cover with sauce.

SAUCE:

1½ cups powdered sugar   2 tablespoons vanilla
2 tablespoons melted butter   2 tablespoons brandy
1 egg   ½ pint whipping cream

Mix at low speed: sugar, butter, egg, vanilla and brandy (may be done 6-8 hours ahead). Just before serving, whip cream and fold into sauce.

ROSY, RUBY PEARS

Serves: 9   Oven: 350°

3 3-ounce packages strawberry   Red food coloring
    Jello   9 pears with stems,
1½ cups boiling apple juice   peeled
2 2-inch cinnamon sticks   ½ pint whipping cream
6 whole cloves   Nutmeg
1 cup Port wine

In a 3-quart casserole dissolve Jello in juice; add cinnamon, cloves, wine and a generous dash of food coloring. Set pared pears in this hot mixture; bake uncovered, basting often for 50 minutes or until tender. Cool pears, turning occasionally to keep color even. Serve topped with whipped cream and a sprinkle of nutmeg. Pears may be frozen after being cooked. To defrost, let stand at room temperature, then heat if desired.

Variation: Refrigerate pears in syrup, turning occasionally. At serving time, lift out of gelatine and serve with whipped cream. (Save gelatine and use for another day's dessert). Makes 9 servings, or halve for 18.

El Paso Herald   December 23, 1883   Christmas Edition
Butcher, Smith and Shipman . . . Mundy Building on El Paso Street
. . . Fine steaks, fresh meats, and game.

BAKED FRUIT CURRY

Serves: 12   Oven: 325°

⅓ cup margarine
¾ cup packed brown sugar
16-ounce can pear halves
16-ounce can peach halves
20-ounce can pineapple slices

¾ teaspoon curry
¼ teaspoon ground cloves
1 teaspoon cinnamon
12 maraschino cherries

Melt margarine; add sugar and spices. Drain and dry fruit and place in 1½-quart casserole. Add butter mixture and garnish with cherries. Bake 1 hour uncovered. Serve with pound cake. Good reheated.

Alternate: Good without cake served with ham or Canadian bacon.

EGG NOG RING

Serves: 12

8 eggs
1 cup granulated sugar
1½ envelopes gelatine
¼ cup water
½ cup boiling water

¾ cup whiskey
Lady fingers
½ pint whipping cream
Chopped, blanched almonds
1 dozen macaroons, crumbled

Separate eggs and beat whites until stiff. Add sugar and continue beating until peaks are formed. Beat yolks well. Dissolve gelatine in ¼ cup cold water; pour boiling water over it. Pour gelatine mixture over egg whites. Add whiskey to well beaten egg yolks. Line a ring mold with lady fingers. Combine the egg mixtures and pour into mold. Chill overnight. When ready to serve, turn ring onto platter. Whip cream until stiff and add almonds and macaroons. Fill center of ring with whipped cream mixture.

ICE CREAM BOMBE

Serves: 12

4 cups chocolate wafers, finely
     crushed (2 8-ounce boxes)
1 cup melted butter
1 quart pistachio ice cream

1 quart chocolate ice cream
1 quart vanilla ice cream
Flaked coconut

Crush wafers and combine with butter. Set aside ⅔ cup of crumb mixture. Press remaining mixture over bottom and sides of 9-inch springform pan. Freeze for 15 minutes or until firm. Remove from freezer and quickly spread softened vanilla ice cream over bottom in an even layer. Sprinkle with ⅓ cup crumbs. Repeat, spreading pistachio ice cream and sprinkling with ⅓ cup of crumbs. Spread chocolate ice cream evenly over crumbs. Cover with foil and return to freezer until ready to serve. To serve, chill plates. Invert pan over serving plate and release. Garnish with coconut. Cut with knife dipped in water.

MANGO ICE CREAM

Yield: 1 gallon

5 eggs
2½ cups sugar
3 tablespoons vanilla
Pinch of salt
2 13-ounce cans evaporated
milk

1 quart half-and-half
1 2-pound can mangos
Juice of 1 lime

Beat eggs and sugar at high speed on electric mixer for 10 minutes. Add vanilla and salt and mix for 1 minute. Add evaporated milk and half-and-half and beat on low speed. In blender mix mangos (juice and fruit). Pour egg mixture into electric ice cream freezer; add mangos and lime juice. Fill freezer to within four inches of the top. Freeze with six parts cracked ice to one part ice cream salt. It will take about 50-60 minutes to freeze. May be stored in deep freezer. (In order to pack the ice cream freezer, drain off water and pack with one part salt to four parts ice.)

ICE CREAM CHARLOTTE

Serves: 8

3 dozen lady fingers
2 quarts coffee ice cream
6 tablespoons rum
1 cup heavy cream

Chocolate curls
Glacé cherries (or drained
maraschino cherries)
Chocolate or caramel sauce

Line bottom and sides of 8-inch springform pan, or mold, with split lady fingers. Quickly whip ice cream in electric mixer, gradually adding the rum. Return to freezer. Whip cream until stiff. Fold into ice cream and spoon half into pan over lady fingers. Cover with layer of lady fingers and remaining cream. Cover with foil; freeze until firm (4 or 5 hours). Remove from mold; place on cake stand and decorate with cherries and chocolate curls. Serve in wedges with sauce.

GRINGO FLAN

Serves: 6

½ cup sugar
1 can Eagle Brand milk
13-ounce can evaporated milk

6 eggs, well beaten
¼ teaspoon salt
1 teaspoon vanilla

Caramelize sugar in top of double boiler. Mix all other ingredients well with wire whisk. Pour over caramelized sugar in double boiler. Cook on top of stove for 1-3 hours, covered. Test with toothpick by inserting into flan until toothpick comes out clean. Turn into a 9-inch pie pan or dish with high sides. Chill. Cut in wedges to serve.

FLAN DE NARANJA CON ALMENDRAS*
(ORANGE CUSTARD WITH ALMONDS)

Serves: 6   Oven: 325°

1 quart half-and-half, or   1 teaspoon grated orange rind
   light cream   1 teaspoon vanilla
4 whole eggs and 2 egg yolks   1 cup sugar
¼ cup orange juice (fresh or   ½ cup water
   frozen, not concentrate)   2 cups toasted almonds
2 tablespoons sugar

Scald cream; cook until it reduces to about 3 cups. Add vanilla and set
aside. Beat together eggs and egg yolks, orange juice, 2 tablespoons
sugar and orange rind. Gradually pour hot cream mixture into egg mixture, stirring vigorously. Set aside. Dissolve 1 cup sugar in water and
heat this syrup in heavy skillet until golden brown. Mix in toasted almonds. Pour this mixture into six custard cups and tip and turn the cups
until the inside of each is evenly coated. Let caramel set. Pour custard
into cups; set cups in pan of hot water. Bake for about 25 minutes or
until knife inserted near center comes out clean. Cool and unmold cus-
tards on small individual dessert plates or cups with bottom sides up.
*Spanish recipe from Valencia.

KATHRYN'S ALMENDRADO

Serves: 8-10

1½ envelopes gelatine   ½ teaspoon vanilla
½ cup cold water   ½ teaspoon almond extract
¼ cup boiling water   Pinch of salt
6 egg whites   Red and green food coloring
½ cup sugar

Soak gelatine in cold water. Add boiling water and stir to dissolve; cool.
Beat egg whites until stiff; add the sugar alternately with the gelatine
mixture using electric mixer at high speed. Add vanilla, almond extract
and salt. Be sure to whip thoroughly so the gelatine will completely blend
with the egg whites. Makes about two quarts of foam. Divide mixture into
three equal parts, leaving one part white and tinting one part red and the
other green (to resemble the Mexican flag). Pour the three layers into an
oblong loaf pan and chill. Serve covering each slice with sauce.

SAUCE:
5 egg yolks   ½ teaspoon vanilla
2 cups milk   ½ teaspoon almond extract
¼ cup sugar   Sliced toasted almonds
⅛ teaspoon salt

Scald milk. Beat eggs; add sugar and salt and slowly add to milk. Add
flavoring stirring constantly until sauce thickens slightly. Chill and serve
over slice of almendrado. Garnish with sliced toasted almonds.

SPANISH CREAM WITH CARAMEL SAUCE

Serves: 6

1 tablespoon gelatine	3 eggs, separated
2½ cups milk	¼ teaspoon salt
½ cup sugar	1 teaspoon vanilla

Soak gelatine in milk for 10 minutes. Place over hot water in double boiler. When gelatine is dissolved, add sugar. Pour slowly over slightly beaten egg yolks, stirring while pouring. Return to double boiler. Cook and stir until mixture begins to thicken. Remove from heat and add salt and vanilla. When cool, fold in stiffly beaten egg whites and pour into wet mold. Chill in refrigerator. Serve with Caramel Sauce.

CARAMEL SAUCE:

1½ cups brown sugar	4 tablespoons butter
⅔ cup corn syrup	⅜ cup heavy cream

Cook sugar, syrup and butter until a small amount forms a soft ball when placed in a cup of cold water. Remove from heat and stir in cream. Chill.

CAPIROTADA
(MEXICAN BREAD PUDDING)

Serves: 12   Oven: 350°

2 cups brown sugar	6-8 teaspoons butter
2 cups water	¼ pound Velveeta cheese
1 teaspoon cinnamon	¼ pound Longhorn cheese
½ teaspoon ground cloves	1 cup raisins
6-8 slices dried bread	

Mix brown sugar, water, cinnamon and cloves. Bring to a boil and cook until sugar is dissolved. Simmer 10 minutes. Lightly butter bread and place in oven until butter is melted. Cut bread into 2-inch squares. In baking dish, arrange a layer of bread. Place a small cube of Velveeta cheese, a cube of Longhorn cheese and a few raisins on each piece of bread. Repeat until all bread is used. Pour the brown sugar mixture over this. Liquid should fill half the dish; if not, add more water. Cover and bake until all the juice is absorbed. Good with lemon custard, ice cream or lemon sherbet.

El Paso Daily Times   July 20, 1890
City Meat Market
San Antonio Street
"Largest refrigerator in town"

RUM CHIFFON PIE

Serves: 6-8

1 envelope unflavored gelatine	½ cup water
¼ cup water	1 cup whipping cream
3 eggs, separated	Chocolate curls or toasted
1 cup sugar	almonds
¼ cup rum	9-inch baked pie shell or
Dash salt	vanilla wafer crust

Soften gelatine in ¼ cup water. Beat egg yolks slightly in top of double boiler. Stir in ½ cup sugar, rum, salt and ½ cup water. Cook over hot water stirring until mixture coats spoon. Stir in softened gelatine until dissolved. Cool mixture in refrigerator. Beat egg whites until fluffy; add remaining sugar gradually and continue beating until stiff. Fold cooled custard mixture into egg whites. Whip cream stiff; fold half into filling mixture and pour into pie shell. Spread remaining cream over top and sprinkle with chocolate curls or toasted almonds. Chill until firm.

LEMON CLOUD PIE

Serves: 6-8   Oven: 400°

CRUST:

1 cup sifted flour	1 teaspoon grated lemon
¼ cup shortening	rind
1 slightly beaten egg	1 teaspoon lemon juice

Cut shortening into flour until particles are fine. Combine egg, lemon rind and juice. Sprinkle over flour mixture while stirring with fork until moist enough to hold dough together. If necessary, add 1-2 tablespoons water. Form into a ball. Flatten to ½-inch thickness. Roll out between wax paper. Put in pie pan. Bake shell for 12-15 minutes.

LEMON CHEESE FILLING:

1 cup sugar	⅓ cup lemon juice
¼ cup cornstarch	2 slightly beaten egg yolks
1 cup water	4 ounces cream cheese
1 teaspoon grated lemon rind	2 egg whites

Combine ¾ cup sugar, cornstarch, water, rind, juice and egg yolks in saucepan. Cook over medium heat; stir constantly until thick. Remove from heat and add cream cheese. Cool. Meanwhile, beat egg whites until soft mounds form. Gradually add remaining sugar. Fold into mixture. Spoon into baked pie shell. Sprinkle with any leftover crumbled baked pastry pieces. Chill 2 hours.

LEMON ANGEL FLUFF PIE

Serves: 6   Oven: 250°

CRUST:

4 egg whites   1 cup sugar
¼ teaspoon cream of tartar

Beat egg whites until frothy. Add ¼ teaspoon cream of tartar. Beat until peaks are formed and gradually add sugar. Beat until stiff and glossy. Fill a greased 10-inch pie plate with mixture. Place in cold oven (turn on oven as soon as door is closed). Bake 1 hour.

FILLING:

6 egg yolks   3 teaspoons grated lemon
¾ cup sugar   rind
4½ tablespoons fresh lemon   ½ pint whipping cream
    juice

Beat egg yolks, sugar, lemon juice and lemon rind until lemon-colored. In top of double boiler cook (beating with hand mixer) over hot water until thickened. Let cool in refrigerator. Whip cream. When lemon mixture is as thick as Jello, place half the whipping cream on top of pie shell; carefully slice the lemon mixture (meringue can be easily crushed) and lightly cover whipping cream layer. Spread remaining whipping cream. Refrigerate several hours before serving. It is best to make pie in the morning to be served that evening.

ANGEL MANGO PIE

Serves: 6   Oven: 275°

4 egg whites   Juice of 2 large or 4
1 cup sugar (superfine)   small limes
1 teaspoon vinegar   1 can sweetened condensed
1 teaspoon vanilla   milk
30-ounce can mangos,   2 drops almond extract
    drained well   ½ cup whipping cream

Beat egg whites until thick but not stiff. Gradually add sugar. Beat vinegar into mixture; add vanilla. Pour into well-greased 9-inch pie plate. Bake 1 hour. Purée drained mangos in blender. Mix together lime juice, condensed milk, almond extract and mangos. In small bowl, whip cream and blend into mango mixture. Chill well. At serving time, spoon into meringue shell and cut into wedges.

STRAWBERRY BAVARIAN PIE

Serves: 6 - 7   Oven: 300°

⅓ cup butter or margarine,   1 envelope unflavored gelatine
   melted   2 teaspoons lemon juice
2½ cups flaked coconut   ½ cup water
2 pints fresh strawberries   1 cup whipping cream
¾ cup sugar

Combine margarine and coconut and press into 9-inch pie pan. Bake for
30-35 minutes or until browned. Cool. Thinly slice 1½ pints of strawberries; reserve remainder for garnish. In large bowl combine sliced
strawberries and sugar; mix well and set aside until sugar dissolves.
Soften gelatine in water; place in saucepan over low heat until dissolved. Add gelatine and lemon juice to sweetened strawberries. Whip
cream until stiff; fold into strawberry mixture. Chill until mixture mounds
when dropped from a spoon. Pour into crust. Chill until set (about 6
hours). Garnish with remaining berries.

GRASSHOPPER CHIFFON PIE

Serves: 8   Oven: 375°

1⅓ cup crushed chocolate   2 cups boiling water
   wafers   ¾ cup cold water
¼ cup sugar   ⅓ cup creme de menthe
¼ cup softened butter or   (green)
   margarine   ⅓ cup creme de cacao
1 6-ounce package lime Jello   1 teaspoon vanilla
4 tablespoons sugar   1 egg white
⅛ teaspoon salt   1 cup whipping cream

Combine first three ingredients and mix well. Press firmly over bottom
and sides of a 9-inch pan. Chill at least 1 hour or bake 8 minutes and
chill before filling. Dissolve Jello, 2 tablespoons sugar and salt in boiling
water; add cold water, liqueurs and vanilla. Chill until slightly thick. Beat
egg white until foamy; add remaining sugar gradually, continuing to beat
until egg is stiff and glossy and meringue stands in shiny soft peaks.
Whip cream until stiff. Measure ½ cup Jello mixture and set aside. Fold
meringue and whipped cream into remaining Jello mixture and chill until
thick. Spoon into crust. Drizzle reserved clear Jello over top of pie. Pull
spoon through filling in zig-zag to marble. Chill until firm. Garnish with
chocolate curls.

El Paso Herald   September 7, 1881
Editor's note:
It will be a great day when the railroads arrive in El Paso.

PUMPKIN PIE WITH WINE

Serves: 6-8   Oven: 400°

2 eggs
1½ cups cooked pumpkin
1 cup brown sugar
½ teaspoon salt
½ teaspoon cinnamon

½ teaspoon nutmeg
½ cup half-and-half
3 tablespoons sherry wine
1 unbaked pie shell

Beat eggs slightly and combine with all other ingredients. Pour mixture into unbaked pie shell and bake for 10 minutes. Reduce temperature to 350° and continue baking 30-40 minutes until filling is well set.

RASPBERRY PARFAIT PIE

Serves: 6-8

1 9-inch pie shell, baked
1½ cups fresh or frozen
    raspberries*
1¼ cups water

1 3-ounce package raspberry
    flavored gelatine
1 pint vanilla ice cream
Whipping cream

Wash berries and drain. Pour water into 2-quart saucepan and bring to a boil. Remove from heat. Add gelatine and stir until dissolved. Cut ice cream into six or eight pieces; add to hot gelatine mixture and stir until ice cream is completely melted. Chill in refrigerator until mixture is thick but not set (about 25 minutes). Fold in berries and pour into pie shell. Chill until firm. Serve with whipped cream.

*With quick-frozen raspberries, thaw and drain and measure liquid. Add water to make 1¼ cups; heat and use to dissolve gelatine.

PEACHY PRALINE PIE

Serves: 8   Oven: 400°

1 9-inch unbaked pie shell
¾ cup sugar
3 tablespoons flour
4 cups sliced peeled peaches
1½ tablespoons lemon juice

⅓ cup brown sugar
¼ cup flour
½ cup chopped pecans
3 tablespoons margarine

Combine sugar and flour in large bowl. Add peaches and lemon juice. Combine brown sugar, flour and pecans in small bowl. Cut in butter until crumbly. Sprinkle one-third pecan mixture over bottom of pie shell, cover with peach mixture and sprinkle remaining pecan mixture over peaches. Bake until peaches are tender (about 40 minutes).

PECAN TARTS

Serves: 24   Oven: 375°

1 3-ounce package cream cheese,   ¾ cup firmly packed brown
    softened   sugar
½ cup butter, softened   1 teaspoon vanilla
1 cup sifted all-purpose flour   1 tablespoon butter, softened
1 egg, slightly beaten   Dash of salt
                                 ⅔ cup chopped pecans

In a large mixing bowl blend cream cheese and ½ cup butter until smooth. Add flour; blend well. Chill dough in refrigerator about 2 hours or overnight. Shape dough into about 24 1-inch balls. Press into tiny muffin or tart pans (1¾-inch in diameter). Blend egg, brown sugar, vanilla, tablespoon butter, salt and pecans in a small bowl. Fill pastry cups with mixture. Bake for 20 minutes. Cool on wire racks before removing from pans.

PECAN CHESS PIE

Serves: 6-8   Oven: 325°

1 9-inch unbaked pie shell   2 eggs
1 cup brown sugar   2 tablespoons milk
½ cup sugar   1 teaspoon vanilla
1 rounded teaspoon flour   1 cup chopped pecans
½ cup butter, melted   Whipping cream (optional)

Mix together dry ingredients and add to melted butter. Mix with a fork. Add eggs, milk and vanilla and whip with fork. Pour into pie shell. Sprinkle pecans over top. Bake about 45 minutes. Allow to cool. Top with whipped cream.

PECAN PIE

Serves: 6-8   Oven: 400°

1 cup sugar   1½ cups pecans, chopped
3 eggs, slightly beaten   2 tablespoons butter
1 cup corn syrup   ¼ teaspoon salt
1 teaspoon vanilla   1 9-inch unbaked pie shell

Add sugar to eggs, blend all other ingredients. Pour into shell. Bake for 15 minutes. Reduce heat to 350° and bake for 35-40 minutes.

PECAN APPLE PIE

Serves: 8   Oven: 425°

5-7 green apples   ½ teaspoon cinnamon
¾ cup sugar   Dash of salt
¼ teaspoon nutmeg   2 tablespoons chopped pecans
2 tablespoons flour   1 9-inch unbaked pie shell

Peel, core and thinly slice apples to make 6 cups. Combine with sugar, flour, cinnamon, nutmeg and salt. Let set 20 minutes. Sprinkle pecans over bottom of pastry shell. Turn apple mixture into shell on top of pecans. Prepare topping.

TOPPING:

¼ cup melted butter   ½ teaspoon cinnamon
⅓ cup flour   ¼ cup pecans
½ cup brown sugar

Combine topping ingredients. Sprinkle over apples. Bake 40-45 minutes.

APPLE MINCEMEAT CRISP

Serves: 6-8   Oven: 400°

1 9-inch unbaked pie shell   ½ cup cognac
6 cooking apples   1 tablespoon sugar
6 tablespoons butter   2-3 cups mincemeat
Pinch of salt   Butter

Peel and cut apples into sixths. Melt butter in heavy skillet; add apples and salt. Cover and steam over medium heat until apples are soft but not mushy. Break apples up; add ¼ cup cognac and sugar and spread in pie shell. Add as much mincemeat as possible; add another ¼ cup cognac and dot with butter. Bake 35-40 minutes or until crust is crisp. Cool slightly.

TOPPING:

1 pound jar apricot preserves   1 cup whipping cream
1 package slivered almonds,   2 tablespoons sugar
        toasted   2 tablespoons cognac

Melt preserves and brush top of pie with glaze; sprinkle with toasted almonds. Whip cream and add sugar and cognac. Top each slice with a generous portion of cream mixture.

HONEY APPLE CRISP

Serves: 6   Oven: 350°

4 cups sliced cooking apples   1 cup sifted all-purpose flour
¼ cup granulated sugar   ½ cup packed brown sugar
1 tablespoon lemon juice   1 teaspoon salt
¼ cup Sauterne wine   ½ cup butter
½ cup honey

Spread apples in a 2-quart baking dish. Sprinkle with granulated sugar, lemon juice and wine. Pour honey over top. Mix flour, brown sugar and salt. Work in butter until crumbly. Spread over apples. Bake for about 40 minutes or until apples are tender and crust is crispy brown. This is best served warm, and it is good after ham or pork chops.

PINK ADOBE APPLE PIE

Serves: 8   Oven: 400°

5-7 apples   ¼ teaspoon cinnamon
2 cups flour   ½ cup sugar
¾ cup lard or shortening   ¼ cup raisins
1 teaspoon salt   1 cup brown sugar
6-7 tablespoons water   2 tablespoons flour
2 tablespoons lemon juice   ½ cup pecans or walnuts
¼ teaspoon nutmeg   ¼ cup water

With fingers, work together flour, lard and salt until mixture resembles coarse meal (this is the secret of pie dough). Add water a little at a time, mixing with a fork until dough can be gathered together. Divide into two parts. Roll half the dough to line a 9-inch pie plate. Fill with peeled, thinly sliced apples; sprinkle with lemon juice, nutmeg and cinnamon. Spread sugar and raisins over apples. Combine brown sugar with flour and spread over all. Sprinkle nuts on top and dot with butter. Sprinkle water over all. Roll out remaining dough to make top crust. Seal edges and flute. Brush crust lightly with a little milk. Bake at 400° for 10 minutes; reduce heat to 350° and bake 30 minutes. Serve with sauce.

SAUCE:

½ cup butter   1½ cups confectioners sugar
1 tablespoon water   1 teaspoon brandy or rum

Over low heat melt butter with water. Remove from heat and beat in sugar and brandy. If too thick add a little hot water.

MARBLE-TOP CHOCOLATE RUM PIE

Serves: 6 - 8

1 9-inch pie shell, baked
¾ cup sugar
1 envelope unflavored gelatine
Dash of salt
1 cup milk
2 egg yolks, beaten

6 ounces semi-sweet chocolate
⅓ cup rum
2 egg whites
1 cup whipping cream
1 teaspoon vanilla

In heavy saucepan combine ½ cup sugar, gelatine and salt. Stir in milk and egg yolks. Cook and stir over low heat until slightly thickened. Remove from heat; melt chocolate in warm mixture. Add rum. Chill until partially set. Beat egg whites until soft peaks are formed. Gradually add ¼ cup sugar and continue beating until stiff peaks are formed. Fold into chocolate mixture. Whip cream with vanilla. Layer whipped cream and chocolate mixture in pastry shell, ending with cream. Swirl the top to marble chocolate and cream. Chill until firm.

CHOCOLATE TOFFEE BAR PIE

Serves: 8   Oven: 400°

12 slices zwieback
¼ cup butter
¼ cup sugar
¼ teaspoon cinnamon
10 Heath bars (small)
16 large marshmallows

¼ cup blanched, toasted
   almonds
½ cup milk
Dash of salt
1 cup whipping cream

Make a 9-inch crust of zwieback crumbs combined with butter, sugar and cinnamon and bake 10-15 minutes. In top of double boiler melt candy bars, marshmallows, milk, almonds and salt. Cool thoroughly. Fold in stiffly whipped cream. Pour into baked shell and chill until firm.

FRENCH CHOCOLATE PIE

Serves: 6 - 8   Oven: 300°

2 egg whites
⅛ teaspoon salt
⅛ teaspoon cream of tartar
½ cup sugar
½ cup pecans, chopped

½ teaspoon vanilla
¼ pound sweet chocolate
3 tablespoons water
1 cup whipping cream

Combine egg whites, salt, cream of tartar in bowl. Beat until foamy. Add sugar gradually until blended. Continue beating until mixture holds a stiff peak. Fold in nuts and vanilla. Spoon into a greased 8-inch pie pan. Bake 50-55 minutes. Cool. Place chocolate and water in pan over low heat. Stir until chocolate is melted. Cool. Whip cream to soft consistency. Fold chocolate mixture into cream. Spoon into meringue shell. Garnish with chocolate shavings and chill 2 hours or longer before serving.

VALENTINE EMPANADAS

Yield: 24   Oven: 400°

1 cup sifted all-purpose flour
⅛ teaspoon salt
½ cup butter or margarine
4 ounces cream cheese

10-ounce jar apricot pre-
    serves
2 beaten eggs
Sugar

Sift flour and salt into bowl; add butter and cream cheese (in small pieces). With pastry blender, cut butter and cheese into flour mixture until well blended. Lightly shape into ball; wrap in wax paper or foil. Refrigerate until well-chilled. On floured surface roll out dough ⅛-inch thick. Use 3¼x2½-inch heart-shaped cookie cutter; cut out hearts. Place 1 teaspoon apricot preserves in center of half the hearts. Brush edges with beaten egg and cover with another heart; with fork, lightly press edges together. Arrange on lightly greased cookie sheets. Brush top with beaten egg; sprinkle with sugar. Bake 10-12 minutes or until golden; cool on rack.

ALMOND EMPANADITAS

Yield: 3 dozen

2 cups flour
2 teaspoons baking powder
1 teaspoon salt
½ cup shortening
½-⅔ cup ice water
¾ cup chopped almonds

½ cup sugar
1 teaspoon cinnamon
1 egg white
¼ teaspoon almond extract
1 cup confectioners sugar

Sift flour, baking powder and salt. Cut in shortening until mixture resembles crumbs. Add ice water, 1 tablespoon at a time, tossing with fork until all flour is moistened. Shape into ball and roll onto lightly floured surface to ⅛-inch thickness. Cut into 2½-inch circles. Mix almonds, sugar and cinnamon. Beat egg white with almond extract until frothy. Stir in almond mixture. Place one teaspoon filling on each circle. Wet edges and seal with a fork. Fry in deep fat fryer at 400° until light brown, turning once. (A deep fat fryer is essential for preparing these.) Drain and dredge while hot in confectioners sugar.

El Paso Herald   December 16, 1883

Yesterday in our rambles around town we noticed about a dozen different kinds of game suspended from the front of the Diamond G Restaurant. Black tailed deer, elk, bear, grouse, Missouri Prairie chickens, quail, turkey and chickens abounded in profusion. It is a cold day when the Diamond G. gets left in such matters.

From the Roost

FOWL

HINTS FOR FOWL

Fried or baked chicken is delicious "all the way to the bone" when it has been marinated in the refrigerator overnight in buttermilk, sour milk, or sour cream.

Salt cut chicken 3 hours before frying to draw out the blood.

Birds called broiler-fryers in the supermarket are suitable for broiling, frying, roasting, braising, or poaching.

To thaw a frozen turkey in the refrigerator, allow 1 to 2 days for a 4 to 12-pound bird, 2 to 3 days for a 12 to 20-pound bird, and 3 to 4 days for a 20 to 24-pound bird. Thawing at room temperature takes about half the given time.

Cook a turkey 20 minutes per pound at 325° if it weighs 16 pounds or less, 15 minutes per pound if it is larger.

After taking a turkey from the oven, wait 20 minutes before carving to allow the juices to settle.

Remove the pan lid or foil from a turkey during the last 30 minutes in the oven so it will brown.

Poultry should not be kept frozen over 6 months.

One 5 pound chicken is a better buy than two 2½ pound chickens because of the more favorable meat to bone ratio.

A few slices of lemon added to stewing chicken will make it more tender and delicious.

To stuff poultry quickly, use salad tongs.

CHICKEN AND AVOCADO CASSEROLE

Serves: 8   Oven: 350°

2 medium fryers
1 large chopped onion
2-3 stalks chopped celery
    and leaves
Salt to taste
Pepper to taste
Seasoned salt to taste
2 tablespoons butter
3 tablespoons flour
1 cup chicken stock

1 cup light cream
½ cup grated sharp cheese
½ teaspoon salt
Dash hot pepper sauce
1 7-ounce can mushrooms,
    drained
½ cup toasted slivered
    almonds
2 sliced avocados

Boil fryers with onion, celery, salt, pepper and seasoned salt with enough water to cover. Cook until meat almost falls off the bones. Strain broth and cool; skim off excess fat. Leave chicken in rather large pieces when boning. In a saucepan melt butter (may use a little chicken fat also in making up the 2 tablespoons butter). Blend in flour. Stir in 1 cup chicken stock and light cream, stirring until thickened. Add cheese, salt and pepper sauce. In bottom of buttered casserole place the meat and mushrooms. Cover with sauce; bake covered with foil 25 minutes. Add sliced avocados; sprinkle top with ½ cup toasted almonds. Return to oven until avocados are warmed through. Serve with wild rice, green beans and green salad. For a buffet supper serve chicken and avocado casserole over layer of spaghetti.

CHICKEN BROCCOLI CASSEROLE

Serves: 4   Oven: 350°

10-ounce package frozen broccoli
    spears
1 2½ pound chicken
10¾-ounce can cream of
    chicken soup
½ cup sour cream

½ cup mayonnaise
Curry powder to taste
½ cup Parmesan cheese
1 tablespoon lemon juice
Sherry to taste (up to 2
    tablespoons)

Cook broccoli as directed until barely tender. Cook and bone chicken; cut into medium-sized pieces. Place chicken in greased 1½-quart oblong baking dish. Cover with broccoli. Mix soup, sour cream, mayonnaise, Parmesan cheese, curry powder, lemon juice and sherry. Pour over broccoli and chicken. Bake 30-40 minutes.

El Paso Herald   November 23, 1881
Butter is frequently scarce on our market. A butter and cheese factory would pay well in our valley.

CHICKEN AND RICE MILANESE

Serves: 8-10   Oven: 400°

5 pound roasting chicken
2 teaspoons salt
⅛ teaspoon pepper
2 tablespoons parsley
1 onion, sliced
1 cup raw rice
2 tablespoons butter
2 cloves garlic
2 teaspoons salt
3½ cups canned tomatoes

2½ cups canned spaghetti
   sauce with mushrooms
1 cup onion, chopped
1 bell pepper, chopped
½ pound boiled ham, diced
1 4-ounce can mushrooms
   with juice
⅛ teaspoon oregano
⅛ teaspoon basil
⅛ teaspoon pepper

Cook chicken in water with 2 teaspoons salt, pepper, parsley and sliced onion until tender enough to fall off the bone. Drain and save broth. Remove chicken from bones leaving good-sized pieces (be certain there are no skins or stringy tendons left in the meat). Cook rice in butter until just golden brown, stirring constantly. Add 2 cups chicken broth and simmer over low heat while preparing rest of recipe. Mash garlic to a pulp and mix 2 teaspoons salt with garlic. Add to the rice. Add remaining ingredients to cooked rice and pour into a large casserole. Bake 1 hour. Casserole should be moist and juicy. If it should dry out in baking, add a little more chicken broth or spaghettl sauce the last 15 minutes of baking. This casserole can be frozen.

CHICKEN BREASTS SUPREME

Serves: 8   Oven: 350°

8 chicken breasts
8 slices boiled ham
8 slices Swiss cheese
1 cup chopped pimentos
1 cup sliced mushrooms
3 tablespoons flour

1½ teaspoons paprika
⅛ teaspoon pepper
¼ cup butter
3 chicken bouillon cubes
1 cup dry white wine
Slivered almonds

Skin and bone chicken. Flatten boney tip of breast. On one side, place a slice of ham, cheese, some pimento and mushrooms. Fold and tie. Dust with seasoned flour and brown in butter. Pour mixture of wine and bouillon over chicken. Cover and bake for 1 hour. Make gravy from drippings. Pour over breasts. Garnish with almonds.

The El Paso Herald   December 16, 1883

The good people of El Paso will eat their Christmas turkey at the rate of 10¢ a pound. The bad people will steal theirs

---

CHICKEN VALENCIA

Serves: 4   Oven: 350°

2½ pound fryer
1 cup flour
2 tablespoons butter
3 tablespoons vegetable oil
3 medium tomatoes, peeled and
   quartered
¼ cup pimento-stuffed olives,
   sliced
1 cup chopped onion
1 large bell pepper,
   seeded and chopped

1 teaspoon leaf basil,
   crumbled
1 teaspoon seasoned salt
1 teaspoon paprika
1 cup water
⅓ cup Parmesan cheese
1 envelope (1 teaspoon)
   instant chicken broth
2 large oranges, pared and
   sectioned

Cut fryer into serving pieces. Coat chicken in flour; tap off excess. Reserve 1 tablespoon flour. In large skillet, sauté chicken in butter and oil about 15 minutes or until golden brown. Place chicken in 2½-quart baking dish and add tomatoes and olives. Add onion and bell pepper to drippings in skillet; sauté until tender. Stir in basil and the 1 tablespoon reserved flour seasoned with salt and paprika. Cook 1 minute stirring constantly. Stir in water and chicken broth; cook and stir until sauce thickens and bubbles. Stir in cheese and orange sections. Pour over chicken and vegetables; cover. Bake 50 minutes or until chicken is tender.

GRINGO CHICKEN CASSEROLE

Serves: 6-8   Oven: 350°

2 chickens, boned and diced
1 medium onion, chopped fine
1 clove garlic, minced
1 bell pepper, chopped fine
4 tablespoons margarine
10-ounce can green chile and
   tomatoes

10¾-ounce can mushroom soup,
   undiluted
10¾-ounce can cream of
   chicken soup, undiluted
1 package corn tortillas
1½ pounds sharp Cheddar
   cheese, grated

Boil chicken until tender. Reserve broth. Sauté onions, garlic and pepper in margarine. Mix with canned ingredients. Tear tortillas into pieces; dip into chicken broth. In buttered casserole place a layer of tortillas, onion, bell pepper, soup mixture, chicken and cheese. Repeat and top with cheese; bake 20-30 minutes.

El Paso Herald   December 23, 1883   Christmas Edition
Stuart & Sutherland grocery house has recently moved to Mundy
Blvd.

CHICKEN JERUSALEM

Serves: 6

12 chicken thighs, or 6 boned
   breasts
½ cup butter
2 green onions, chopped
½ cup white wine
½ cup water

2 teaspoons salt
1 cup sliced mushrooms
2 14-ounce cans artichoke
   hearts
Parmesan cheese

Brown chicken in butter. Add chopped onions, wine and water. Simmer 45 minutes. Add mushrooms, salt and artichoke hearts. Cook slowly 15 minutes. Serve with noodles sprinkled with parsley. Top with Parmesan cheese.

CHICKEN IN ORANGE SAUCE

Serves: 8-10   Oven: 350°

3 medium or 2 large chickens,
   cut up
12-ounce can frozen orange
   juice
12 ounces water

2 cups brown sugar
1 cup sherry
½ cup Heinz Barbeque Sauce
   with Onions

Simmer juice, water, sugar, sherry and barbeque sauce for 5 minutes. Pour over raw chicken. Bake uncovered 2½ hours, turning chicken often.

CHICKEN PARMESAN

Serves: 6   Oven: 375°

½ cup pancake mix
¼ teaspoon salt
⅛ teaspoon pepper
4 whole chicken breasts, split
10¾-ounce can cream of
   mushroom soup

⅓ cup dry onion soup mix
   (about ½ of one package)
⅓ cup milk
½ cup grated Parmesan cheese
Parsley

In a bowl combine pancake mix, salt and pepper. Roll breasts in mixture to coat well. Place chicken in a 3-quart baking dish. Combine mushroom soup, onion soup mix and milk in a bowl and blend until smooth. Pour over chicken. Cover dish tightly with foil. Bake 1 hour. Remove foil and sprinkle cheese on top. Bake uncovered 20 minutes. Garnish with parsley.

CRISPY CHICKEN ROLLS

Serves: 6

3 whole chicken breasts, halved
  and boned
1¼ cups cooked shrimp,
  chopped
¾ cup butter or margarine
¼ cup chopped green onions

2½ teaspoons salt
¼ cup salad oil
1 cup all-purpose flour
1¼ teaspoons double acting
  baking powder
¾ cup water

Remove skin from chicken breasts; pound to ¼-inch thickness. Combine shrimp, butter, green onions and 1½ teaspoons salt. Spoon mixture onto each breast. Wrap and secure with toothpicks; cover and refrigerate until ready to cook. Heat oil to 370° in Dutch oven or electric skillet. In medium bowl mix flour, baking powder, 1 teaspoon salt and ¾ cup water. Whip until well blended. Dip 3 chicken rolls, one at a time, into flour mixture and then into hot oil. Fry until golden (10-15 minutes). Drain on paper towels. Repeat with remaining 3 rolls. Remove toothpicks and serve immediately to retain crispness. (May be browned and cooked in 350° oven for 20 minutes.)

CHICKEN MADEIRA

Serves: 6

3 chicken breasts, halved
6 chicken thighs
½ cup butter
½ teaspoon grated lemon peel
1 teaspoon grated orange peel
¼ cup lemon juice
½ cup orange juice

½ teaspoon tarragon
Salt and pepper to taste
1 cup Madeira wine (or 1 cup
  sherry*)
Grated Parmesan cheese
1 cup heavy cream
1 8-ounce package egg noodles

Fry chicken in butter until white. Remove from skillet and put in a shallow baking dish, skin side down. To the butter in skillet, add all other ingredients except cheese, cream and noodles. Pour over chicken. Sprinkle each piece of chicken with grated cheese. Broil, basting with sauce. Turn chicken and sprinkle with more cheese. Broil and baste until done, about 20 minutes on each side. Allow chicken to cool somewhat and add cream to sauce (cream will curdle if added to hot chicken). Serve over cooked egg noodles.

*More wine may be added as desired.

El Paso Herald   December 23, 1883   Christmas Edition
The El Paso Valley produces 100,000 bales of wheat.

CHICKEN BREASTS PIQUANT

Serves: 6   Oven: 375°

3 chicken breasts, split
¾ cup Rosé wine
½ cup soy sauce
¼ cup salad oil
2 tablespoons mushroom liquid
1 clove garlic, minced

1 teaspoon ginger
½ teaspoon oregano
1 tablespoon brown sugar
1 4-ounce can mushrooms,
    drained (liquid reserved)

Arrange chicken breasts in baking dish. Combine all other ingredients except mushrooms and pour over chicken. Cover and bake 1½ hours. Add mushrooms the last 15 minutes of baking time. If not browned, place under broiler for a few minutes.

CHICKEN BREASTS IN WINE

Serves: 6   Oven: 350°

3 chicken breasts, split
16-ounce can small whole
    baby onions, drained
1 4-ounce can sliced mushrooms,
    drained

10¾-ounce can cream
    of mushroom soup
¼ cup white wine
1 8-ounce package sharp
    Cheddar cheese, grated

Arrange chicken breasts in 2-quart casserole. Top with onions and mushrooms. Mix together cream of mushroom soup and wine; pour over chicken. Sprinkle with half the grated cheese. Cover and bake 1 hour. Uncover, and add remaining cheese. Bake uncovered an additional 30 minutes.

BARBECUED STUFFED CHICKEN BREASTS

Serves: 6

1 2¼-ounce can deviled ham
½ cup crushed saltine crackers
½ teaspoon grated onion
¼ teaspoon poultry seasoning

6 whole chicken breasts, boned
Salt
Margarine (melted)

Combine deviled ham, cracker crumbs, onion, and poultry seasoning; mix well. Wash and dry chicken. Place a spoonful of stuffing in center of each chicken breast. Roll up and tie with string or secure with skewers. Place on greased barbecue grill or oven broiler; broil slowly, basting with margarine and turning every 5-7 minutes. Cook 30-45 minutes.

CHICKEN CREPES

Serves: 8 (2 per person)   Oven: 350°

CREPES:

1¼ cups flour	½ teaspoon salt
3 eggs	3 tablespoons butter, melted
1 cup milk	3 tablespoons vegetable oil
¼ cup water	

Combine all ingredients except butter and oil. Whip in blender until smooth. Chill batter (covered) for at least 1 hour. Heat a 6-inch crepe pan until a drop of water evaporates instantly. Brush with butter combined with oil. Pour in 2 tablespoons of batter, quickly rolling to spread over pan. Cook until edges brown; turn, brown other side. Repeat with more batter. Refrigerate or freeze, tightly covered, for at least one day before using.

FILLING:

1 large frying chicken (3-4 pounds)	10¾-ounce can cream of chicken soup
Celery, chopped	1 teaspoon sugar
Onion, chopped	½ teaspoon nutmeg
Bay leaf	1½ teaspoons salt
Water	1 teaspoon pepper
3 bunches green onions, chopped	1 teaspoon dry mustard
½ pound fresh mushrooms, chopped	2 tablespoons sherry
¼ cup butter	1 tablespoon monosodium glutamate
10-ounce package frozen spinach, cooked and drained	

Simmer chicken with celery, onion, bay leaf and enough water to cover. Bone and chop chicken. Sauté green onions and mushrooms in butter until just tender. Add spinach, soup (undiluted), chicken and all remaining ingredients. Mix well. Place a heaping spoonful of filling in center of each crepe; roll one turn. Fold edges in and roll until tight; place in a flat ovenproof dish, seam side down. Cover with Mornay sauce and bake until hot (20-30 minutes). Serve with extra sauce. Crepes can be made, filled and frozen. Keep crepes separated. When frozen, remove and store in plastic bags. Sauce cannot be frozen.

MORNAY SAUCE:

½ cup butter	2 pounds Velveeta cheese
1 cup flour	12 ounces beer
4 cups milk	2 tablespoons sherry

Melt butter; add flour and cook until bubbly. Add milk slowly and cook until smooth. Boil 1 minute. Cut cheese into small chunks and beat into hot sauce. Using electric mixer, beat 15 minutes. Add beer a little at a time, until sauce reaches desired consistency. Do not overbeat after adding beer. Add sherry. If stored for a few days, beat again to restore lightness.

CHICKEN CURRY

Serves: 10

2 3½ pound chickens
2 teaspoons salt
2 tablespoons lemon juice

4 ounces salt butter
Pepper to taste
Water

Cook chickens in water with salt, lemon juice, salt butter and pepper; bone and set aside.

CURRY SAUCE:

¼ cup olive oil
¼ cup vegetable oil
2 yellow onions
1 large carrot
2 stalks celery
1 green apple
4 tablespoons Indian curry
    powder
4 tablespoons flour
1 teaspoon tomato paste
1 teaspoon B-V meat paste
2½ cups chicken stock

2 tablespoons lemon juice
1 tablespoon shredded coconut
1 tablespoon honey
2 tablespoons guava jelly
1 small stick cinnamon
1 small piece ginger root or
    crystallized ginger
3 crushed cardamom seeds
1 large clove garlic, bruised
1 clove
½ teaspoon dry mustard
Salt and cayenne to taste

Slice onions, carrot, celery and apple; cook in skillet in oils for 5 minutes. Add curry powder and cook 5 minutes; add flour and cook another 5 minutes. Prepare sauce by combining all other ingredients. Add chicken and simmer for at least 1 hour. Sauce may be prepared and frozen. Chicken is best prepared 1-2 days before serving. Serve with wild rice and any combination of condiments.

CONDIMENTS:

Raisins
Coconut, grated
Nuts, chopped finely

Hard cooked eggs, chopped
Chutney

Serve in separate bowls with curry.

El Paso Herald   September 28, 1881
Inflation at railroad entry:
Corn is selling at 2½ cents a pound. Eggs have gone up to 40 cents a dozen and butter is 40 cents a pound.
Trains are coming in on a regular basis.

CHICKEN TARRAGON
Serves: 6

3 whole chicken breasts
1 onion, thinly sliced
1 carrot, thinly sliced
¼ teaspoon dried tarragon
½ cup white wine
Boiling water
3 tablespoons butter

3 tablespoons flour
½ teaspoon salt
Dash of pepper
2 tablespoons butter
1 egg yolk, slightly beaten
3 tablespoons heavy cream

Split and skin breasts. Place chicken, onion, carrot, tarragon and wine in a large saucepan. Add boiling water to cover chicken. Cover; simmer 25 minutes or until tender. Remove chicken and keep warm. Strain liquid. Boil gently until liquid is reduced to 2 cups. Melt 3 tablespoons butter. Stir in flour, salt and pepper. Gradually add the 2 cups chicken broth. Cook, stirring constantly, until mixture is smooth and thickened. Add the 2 tablespoons butter and simmer gently 5 minutes, stirring occasionally. Combine the egg yolk and cream; stir into hot sauce. Pour over chicken breasts to serve.

CHICKEN-ZUCCHINI FLIPS
Serves: 4-6

¼ cup chopped onion
¼ cup sliced celery
2 tablespoons butter
10¾-ounce can cream of
    chicken soup
¼ cup milk
2 cups diced, cooked chicken
2 eggs, beaten

¼ cup flour
2 tablespoons Parmesan
    cheese
1 teaspoon snipped parsley
1 teaspoon chives
Salt and pepper
3 medium zucchini squash,
    shredded and drained

Sauté onion and celery in butter; add soup and milk. Stir in chicken and heat thoroughly. Keep warm. In bowl combine eggs, flour, cheese, parsley, chives, salt and pepper and zucchini. Mix well. Drop one-fourth cup batter on hot greased griddle and flatten slightly. Cook until browned. Turn and brown the other side. Remove and keep warm. The batter makes eight crepes. Spoon chicken filling on crepe. Fold over. Top with remaining sauce.

BARBECUE SAUCE FOR CHICKENS
Yield: 4 cups (enough for 2-3 chickens)

2 cups vinegar
1⅓ cups salad oil
4 teaspoons Worcestershire
    sauce
2 teaspoons grated onion

2 cloves garlic, minced
3 teaspoons salt
1 teaspoon paprika
1 6-ounce can tomato paste
1 teaspoon Tabasco

Mix all ingredients together and simmer 15 minutes. Chicken pieces or quarters may be marinated in sauce overnight or longer. Drain and cook over charcoal fire outside. If marinated, chicken doesn't need to be basted.

TURKEY DEL REY

Serves: 6   Oven: 350°

8 ounces thin spaghetti   ¼ cup grated Parmesan cheese
¼ cup butter   1 egg yolk, slightly beaten
¼ cup flour   2 cups cooked cubed turkey
1 teaspoon salt   ¼ cup chopped bell pepper
¼ teaspoon nutmeg   ½ pound sliced mushrooms
2 cups turkey broth   1 teaspoon minced scallions
1 cup light cream   ½ cup slivered almonds
1 cup dry sherry

Cook spaghetti in boiling salted water and drain. Melt butter over low heat and blend in flour, salt and nutmeg. Stir until mixture is smooth. Remove from heat, stir in broth and cream and simmer, stirring for 1 minute. Stir in wine and cheese. Add a little of the warm sauce to the egg yolk and return all to the rest of the sauce. Pour over spaghetti. Add turkey, bell pepper, mushrooms and scallions to spaghetti and mix together. Pour into a 2-quart buttered baking dish; sprinkle with almonds. Bake uncovered for 30 minutes. Let stand 10 minutes before serving.

TURKEY MONET

Serves: 4

2 tablespoons butter   1 package frozen cooked
2 tablespoons flour   asparagus, or broccoli
Pinch of salt   4 large slices turkey
Pinch of pepper   Pimento
Pinch of cayenne   Olives
1 cup milk   Parsley
4-6 ounces Velveeta or American
    cheese

Make a white sauce using first six ingredients. Add cheese and stir until smooth. Warm the turkey in water. Place turkey on top of asparagus and ladle cheese sauce over all. Garnish with pimento, olives and parsley. Good with broiled tomatoes.

El Paso Herald   December 13, 1882

Our clever friend Mr. T. M. Collins of San Elizario sent to the Herald office a *beet* raised in his garden that weighs thirty eight pounds. It is the biggest we ever saw except a *beat* we have on our books who is six feet long and weighs 175 pounds.

Wild Wild West

GAME

HINTS FOR GAME

Use glass, ceramic, or enamelware containers for marinating game. Wine marinades are preferred, because they enhance the flavor without changing it.

Game birds weighing $3\frac{1}{2}$ to 4 pounds, ready to cook, should serve 4.

Salt game birds and refrigerate 2 days before freezing. To thaw birds without drying, soak them overnight in milk or salt water.

To reduce the gamey taste of venison, soak it overnight in milk.

A few grapes in the cooking pan give a special flavor to most game, including venison and birds.

Wipe game birds with a damp cloth; do not scald or wash them.

Game birds with dark meat usually cook in less time than birds with white meat.

As wild birds have very little fat, this must be supplemented in cooking.

"QUACK-IN-A-SACK"

Serves: 3-4   Oven: 475°

1 medium-sized goose	4 slices dry toasted bread,
2 cloves garlic	cut in ½-inch squares
1 small onion	1 apple, peeled and chopped
¼ cup salad oil	1 cup ground meat, cooked
White and black pepper	2 tablespoons raisins
Salt	

When using a wild goose, soak for at least 12 hours in heavily salted water. Purée in blender: garlic, onion, salad oil, salt and pepper to taste. Mix well and rub inside and outside of goose. Prepare stuffing by combining toasted bread squares, apple, ground meat and raisins. Flour goose by placing the goose in a large bag with flour and shaking. Stuff the goose and place it in a heavy paper bag which has been greased inside. Seal the bag and place in a large pan. Bake for 30 minutes. Reduce heat to 325° and bake for 2 hours.

GLAZED DUCK WITH PLUM SAUCE

Serves: 4   Oven: 325°

1 5-pound duck	17-ounce jar purple plums
1 teaspoon salt	½ bay leaf
½ teaspoon pepper	6 whole cloves
1 onion, sliced	2 tablespoons red wine vinegar
1 celery stalk, sliced	4 teaspoons cornstarch
¾ cup Port wine	1 tablespoon water

Rub body of duck with salt and pepper. Cut off one slice of onion and reserve for sauce. Place remaining onion, celery and ¼ cup Port inside duck. Truss and place on rack in oven. Roast for 3 hours, pouring off fat periodically. To prepare sauce, drain syrup from plums and add water to make 1 cup. Combine remaining ½ cup Port, onion slice, bay leaf, cloves and vinegar; simmer 5 minutes. Blend cornstarch with 1 tablespoon water and stir into sauce. Cook until clear and thick, stirring constantly; strain. Add dash of salt and set aside ½ cup sauce for glaze. Combine remaining sauce with plums. Brush duck with reserved glaze after 3 hours of cooking. Continue roasting 20 minutes brushing two or three more times with glaze. Reheat sauce and serve with duck.

El Paso Herald   December 23, 1883   Christmas Edition
Vault Saloon (M. J. McKelligon)
Sometimes known as "the little church around the corner". Good food and drink . . . convenient garden in the rear.

DOVE EN CASSEROLE

Serves: 4   Oven: 350°

12 dove
½ cup butter
Salt and pepper
2 ounces dried Italian
    mushrooms, broken in
    small pieces
1 cup onion, minced

Parsley, chopped
Thyme, chopped
2 tablespoons flour
4 cups game bird stock*
1 cup dry sherry
1 cup sliced stuffed olives

Brown birds in hot butter; season lightly with salt and pepper. Remove to casserole. Brown mushrooms, onions and herbs in the same butter for 5 minutes. Add flour and stir until lightly browned and bubbly. Add stock and stir until smooth. Add sherry and olives; simmer an additional minute and check seasoning. Cover and bake until tender (about 1½-2 hours).

*Chicken or beef bouillon can be used.

ROAST DOVE WITH WILD RICE DRESSING

Serves: 2   Oven: 350°

6 dove
¼ cup diced bell pepper
¼ cup chopped onion
6 tablespoons butter or
    margarine
2 cups cooked wild or
    brown rice

½ cup chopped olives
½ cup canned mushrooms
¼ teaspoon paprika
½ cup hot water

Cook bell pepper and onion in 4 tablespoons butter until tender. Combine with rice, olives, mushrooms and paprika. Add additional butter if necessary to make mixture moist. Stuff dove with this mixture. Place in an uncovered roasting pan and roast 1 hour basting frequently with a mixture of 2 tablespoons butter and hot water. Serve while hot.

DOVE CASSEROLE

Serves: 4   Oven: 350°

12 dove   ½ cup finely chopped onion
½ cup butter or margarine   1 cup white wine
1 cup fresh mushrooms   1 cup heavy cream
2 tablespoons parsley   Salt and pepper

Wash and dry dove; rub with salt and pepper and sauté lightly in butter. Remove and place dove breast down in a casserole or heavy skillet. Sauté mushrooms, parsley and onion in the remaining butter. Add wine; pour over birds. Bake 2 hours basting frequently. Add more wine if necessary. Add cream, heat and serve immediately. Garnish with white grapes (split and seeded) or artichoke hearts.

BARBECUED DOVE

Serves: 4

12 dove   6 slices bacon
Milk   Wishbone Italian dressing
6 canned jalapeños   Salt and pepper

Marinate dove in milk overnight. Remove and dry. Place ½ jalapeño inside cavity of each dove. Wrap ½ slice of bacon around each dove; secure with toothpick. Sprinkle with salt and pepper. Barbecue over slow fire with generous applications of Italian dressing (about 30 minutes).

GOURMET OLE

Serves: 6   Oven: 250°

18 dove or 12 quail   1 bottle Cabernet Sauvignon,
3 teaspoons seasoned salt   or any favorite good wine
3 teaspoons lemon pepper   16-ounce can S & W spiced
1 cup flour   grapes
2 cups butter or margarine   1 8-ounce jar kumquats

Lightly roll birds in flour, salt and pepper. In a skillet, melt butter and swiftly brown birds. Drain on paper towel. Place birds in large covered casserole or roasting pan. Pour wine over birds and bake 2 hours. Baste several times. Add drained grapes and kumquats the last 5 minutes and broil for 5-8 minutes. Serve with wild rice and fresh mushrooms, spoonbread and chilled watercress salad with gourmet cheese and fruit for dessert.

QUAIL

Serves: 2   Oven: 300°-325°

4 quail   ¼ cup onion, finely chopped
Salt   1 tablespoon parsley,
¼ cup flour   finely chopped
⅓ cup butter   ½ cup Sauterne wine
½ cup mushrooms, finely   ½ cup heavy cream
    chopped

Salt and flour birds; brown in butter. Place in casserole. Sauté mushrooms, onions and parsley in same butter. Pour over birds. Add Sauterne. Bake 1 hour, basting occasionally. Add heavy cream and heat
thoroughly. Serve with wild rice.

FRIED QUAIL—CREAM GRAVY

Serves: 4

8 quail (breast split   1 teaspoon salt
    to lie flat)   1 teaspoon pepper
1 cup milk   ½ cup flour
2 eggs   2 cups shortening

Place milk, eggs, salt and pepper in blender and blend well. Dredge quail
in flour; dip in milk batter. Coat with flour. Heat shortening in large skillet until hot. Place quail in hot oil and reduce heat immediately to medium. Cover and fry 5 minutes on each side. Raise heat again and brown.
Remove quail; drain on paper towel.

CREAM GRAVY:

4 tablespoons shortening   1-1½ cups milk
    (from frying quail)   Salt and pepper to taste
4 tablespoons flour

Drain all but 4 tablespoons of oil from skillet. Add flour and blend over
medium heat until bubbly. Add milk, salt and pepper. Cook until thickened. Serve over quail and mashed potatoes.

El Paso Herald   December 20, 1882
Products of our El Paso valley . . . Grains and all kinds of fruits and
vegetables. Grape is the staple fruit. The El Paso onion is already
famous. Alfalfa and tobacco are also grown. The editor comments
that undoubtedly cotton and rice could be grown successfully.

QUAIL WITH WINE SAUCE

Serves: 4   Oven: 350°

8 quail*	1½ teaspoons salt
⅓ cup oil	Cooked rice or toast points
1 small onion, chopped	2 tablespoons flour
½ pound sliced mushrooms	3 tablespoons Sauterne wine
1 cup chicken broth	

In dutch oven over medium heat, brown birds in oil on all sides. Remove birds. Brown onions until golden; add mushrooms. Stir in broth and salt. Add birds; cover and bake for 1 hour. When tender (test birds with fork) remove birds to warm place. Reserve liquid and prepare sauce. Blend flour and wine until smooth. Gradually stir into hot liquid and cook until slightly thickened. Pour over birds. Serve preferably on rice or toast points.

*Allow at least 2 quail per person (men may prefer more).

QUAIL WRAPPED IN BACON

Serves: 4   Oven: 325°

8 quail	8 slices uncooked bacon
1 teaspoon salt	¼ cup melted margarine
1 teaspoon pepper	½ cup flour
1 box Uncle Ben's Long Grain Wild Rice	½ cup dry sherry

Cook the rice according to the directions on the box while preparing the quail for stuffing. Clean quail; sprinkle body cavities with ½ teaspoon salt and pepper. Stuff each cavity with 2 tablespoons of cooked rice. Place the remaining rice in a colander on top of a pan of hot water; cover the colander, allowing the rice to steam and remain hot while the quail are cooking. Wrap each quail with one slice of bacon; secure with a toothpick. Sprinkle remaining salt and pepper on quail. Melt the margarine in a skillet. Roll quail in flour and lightly brown in margarine. Place quail in a roasting pan without a cover. Pour sherry over quail. Bake for 45 minutes. Serve with remaining rice.

QUAIL IN HEAVY CREAM

Serves: 4   Oven: 350°

8 quail   Pepper
4 bacon slices   2 cups chicken broth
4 tablespoons butter   1 cup heavy cream
8 shallots or green onions   ¼ cup cream-style prepared
Cognac or brandy   horseradish
Salt   Parsley

Cut quail down the back so breasts are split and lie flat. Clean quail; cover each breast with ½ slice of bacon and secure with toothpick. Brown in an iron skillet with butter and shallots. Pour a little cognac or brandy over quail and ignite. Salt and pepper to taste. Add broth; bake uncovered for 30 minutes, basting frequently. Add cream and horse-radish; cook 20 minutes more. Place quail on a platter and cover with sauce. Garnish with parsley.

QUAIL TARRAGON

Serves: 4   Oven: 400°

8 quail   1 cup butter
½ cup flour   ¾ cup Sauterne wine
Salt and pepper   1 teaspoon tarragon

Wash birds well; salt and pepper to taste and dredge with flour. In a skillet sauté birds in ½ cup butter, turning often until brown. Transfer quail to a rack in a shallow baking pan. Place a small piece of butter in the chest cavity of each bird. De-glaze skillet with ¼ cup Sauterne and pour over birds. Bake quail for 40 minutes, basting every 10 minutes with a mixture of ½ cup Sauterne, ¼ cup melted butter and 1 teaspoon tarragon. Roasting pan can be de-glazed with remaining basting sauce. Pour over the birds when serving.

CHARCOAL QUAIL

Serves: 4

8 quail   4 slices of bacon

Allow 2 quail per person. Soak overnight in salt water in refrigerator. Wrap each quail with ½ slice bacon, anchoring with a toothpick. Cook outside over charcoals.

PHEASANT

Serves: 4   Oven: 350°

2 slices bacon
2 disjointed pheasant
1 teaspoon monosodium
   glutamate
2 tablespoons "seasoning"*
1 teaspoon salt
½ teaspoon pepper
1 cup water

½ cup Claret or Burgundy wine
1 bay leaf
1 carrot, sliced
1 stalk celery
2 tablespoons flour
⅛ teaspoon oregano
⅛ teaspoon marjoram
½ cup orange juice

In heavy skillet cook bacon and set aside. Thoroughly brown pheasant which have been sprinkled with monosodium glutamate. Sprinkle with "seasoning", salt and pepper. Add water, wine, bay leaf, carrot and celery. Cover skillet and bake for 1 hour. Mix together remaining ingredients and stir until smooth. Add to sauce around birds and return to oven an additional 20 minutes. Before serving, discard celery and adjust flavor and body of gravy. Bacon may be crumbled over birds or discarded.

*To make seasoning, mix together 1 package spaghetti sauce mix, 1 package dried onion soup mix and 1 package dried chicken soup with rice.

PHEASANT WITH BRANDY

Serves: 6   Oven: 375°

3 pheasant*
8 green onions, peeled and
   thinly sliced
¼ cup butter
½ cup brandy
2 cups chicken broth

1 teaspoon salt
Pepper
6 slices lean bacon
2 cups heavy cream
¼ cup prepared horseradish

Sauté onions in roasting pan in butter. Add pheasant and sauté until birds are browned on all sides. Pour brandy over birds; ignite. When flame dies, add chicken stock, salt and pepper. Put bacon strips over pheasant breasts and roast uncovered 45 minutes basting frequently with pan juices. Stir in cream and horseradish and continue roasting 15 minutes, basting often. Serve at once.

*Cornish game hens can be substituted when pheasant isn't available.

> El Paso Herald   November 29, 1882
> Quails are a dollar a dozen. Wild ducks are 50¢ a piece. Venison is worth 15¢ per pound.

PHEASANT IN SOUR CREAM

Serves: 2

1½-pound pheasant
3 tablespoons flour
1½ teaspoons salt
Pepper
3 tablespoons butter

1½ cups water
¼ teaspoon sugar
½ teaspoon paprika
1 cup sour cream

Cut pheasant into serving pieces. Wash and drain well. Dredge with flour, salt and pepper. Brown slowly in butter on all sides over medium heat 10-15 minutes. Blend any remaining flour into pan. Add ½ cup water and blend until smooth. Lower heat, cover and simmer for 1¾ hours, adding water as needed. When done, add remaining ingredients and blend well. Heat just to boiling. Serve with white rice and tossed green salad.

PHEASANT BAVARIAN

Serves: 4   Oven: 375°

2 pheasant*
¼ cup butter
2 cups coarsely chopped tart
    apples
½ cup Calvados brandy
2 cups heavy cream

¼ cup fresh lemon juice
2 teaspoons salt
½ teaspoon pepper
1 tablespoon cornstarch
1 tablespoon cold water

Cut pheasant into quarters. In a skillet sauté birds in butter until brown. Remove. Sauté apples in same skillet. Place apples in 2-quart casserole, then birds. Pour brandy in same skillet with drippings; pour over birds. Cover tightly and bake 45 minutes. Add cream, lemon juice, salt and pepper; bake uncovered for 30 more minutes. Remove birds. Mix water and cornstarch and add to pan drippings to make gravy.

*Chicken may be used.

LEMON PHEASANT

Serves: 4

2 pheasant
½ cup flour
2 teaspoons salt
¼ teaspoon pepper
½ cup vegetable oil

¼ cup lemon juice
10½-ounce can consommé
1 clove garlic, minced
1¼ cups water

Salt pheasant and refrigerate overnight. Cut pheasant into individual servings. Roll in flour, salt and pepper. Brown birds well in hot oil in heavy skillet. Add lemon juice, consommé, garlic and water. Cover; simmer about 1 hour or until tender. Thicken liquid for gravy.

PHEASANT CAROL ANN

Serves: 4   Oven: 350°

2 pheasant, split in half
Salt and pepper
6 bacon slices
1 cup butter

2 tablespoons lemon juice
½ cup blanched, slivered
    almonds

Salt and pepper each pheasant half. Place bone side down in roasting pan. Cover with bacon slices. Roast in oven, basting frequently with ½ cup butter and pan juices, until tender (about 1 hour). (When the age of the bird is in doubt, cover with foil at mid-point in roasting.) When the bird is tender, add ½ cup melted butter; blend in lemon juice and almonds. Return to oven for 10 minutes basting once more. Serve with rice and spiced cranberry sauce.

VENISON CUTLETS WITH MANDARIN ORANGES

Serves: 6

12 venison cutlets
Salt and pepper
¼ cup butter
1 tablespoon cognac

¼ cup mandarin orange juice
1-2 tablespoons currant jelly
½ cup mandarin orange
    sections

Sprinkle cutlets with salt and pepper; sauté in butter over medium high heat, browning both sides. Remove to heated platter and keep hot. Add cognac, mandarin orange juice and jelly to pan drippings. Mix well, bring to a boil and cook for 1 minute. In a small saucepan heat mandarin orange sections in orange juice mixture. Place in small bowl in center of platter. Spoon sauce over meat. Serve immediately.

VENISON STROGANOFF

Serves: 4   Oven: 300°

2 pounds lean, boned, trimmed
    venison (steaks, chops or
    roast)
½ cup flour
¼ cup oil
1 large onion, sliced
Water

8 ounces sour cream
1 4-ounce can mushrooms
1 tablespoon Worcestershire
    sauce
Salt
Pepper
Paprika

Brown floured venison in oil over medium high heat. Add sliced onion and cook until soft. Add water to cover. Cover and bake just until tender (2 hours) to retain wild taste. (To reduce wild taste, cook all day in slow oven.) Shortly before serving, add sour cream, mushrooms, Worcestershire sauce, salt and pepper. Top with paprika.

VENISON CHILE

Serves: 8-10

½ pound pinto beans
2 tablespoons salt
5 cups canned tomatoes
3 bell peppers, chopped
1½ pounds onions, chopped
1½ teaspoons salad oil
½ cup chopped parsley
2 cloves garlic, crushed

½ cup butter
1 pound ground pork
2½ pounds ground venison
1½ teaspoons monosodium
    glutamate
½ cup chile powder
1½ teaspoons pepper
1½ teaspoons cumin seed

Wash beans thoroughly; soak overnight in water two inches above beans. Wash again and simmer with salt until tender (about 4 hours). Simmer tomatoes in separate pan 5 minutes. Sauté onions and bell pepper in salad oil; add to tomatoes and cook until tender. Add garlic and parsley. Melt butter in large skillet and sauté venison and pork which has been sprinkled with monosodium glutamate for 15 minutes. Drain off grease; add meat to tomato and onion mixture. Stir in chile powder and cook 10 minutes; add beans, pepper and cumin seed. Simmer covered for 1 hour, uncovered for 30 minutes.

El Paso Herald   December 20, 1882
Salt! Salt! Salt!
The cheapest and best salt that can be brought to El Paso or Chihuahua. Sierra Blanca, Texas. John E. Barlow agent. Zimpleman's Salt Springs.

The Chuckwagon

MEAT

HINTS FOR MEATS

Meat from lambs 3 to 5 months old is known as spring lamb and is so stamped on every cut. The younger the animal, the more delicate the flavor.

Raw meat is tender if it has a little connective tissue, but tough if it has a large amount.

Tender cuts of meat are best cooked by dry heat, tough cuts by moist, slow heat.

A pound of boneless meat yields 4 servings; a pound of meat with a small amount of bone yields 3 servings; a pound of meat with a large amount of bone yields 2 servings.

To retain juices and flavor, salt meat only after it is three-fourths cooked. Allow ¾ teaspoon salt to a pound of ground meat, 1 teaspoon salt to a pound of solid meat.

Meat loaf mixture may be baked in greased muffin tins for faster cooking and attractive serving.

To prevent meat from sticking, sprinkle salt or garlic salt in the pan, heat, and then add the meat.

To separate ground meat, use a potato masher in the frying pan.

For delicious, juicy hamburger steak, mix ¼ cup milk into each pound of meat.

When boiling tough meat, add a little vinegar to tenderize.

Sprinkle bacon with a little flour before frying to keep it from curling.

Rolling sausage in flour before frying prevents shrinking.

Carve meats, except steak, across the grain.

Before placing ham in a pan for baking, slit the rind lengthwise on the underside. The rind will pull away and can be removed easily without lifting the ham from the pan.

CHIPPED BEEF IN SOUR CREAM

Serves: 4-6

½ pound chipped beef
2 tablespoons butter
1 pint sour cream
1 6-ounce jar artichoke
   hearts

Dash cayenne or
   paprika
½ cup dry white wine
1 heaping tablespoon
   Parmesan cheese

Shred chipped beef; cover with water and parboil for 1-2 minutes. Melt butter in skillet over low heat. Add sour cream and stir until all lumps have disappeared. Thinly slice artichoke hearts; stir into cream along with cayenne, wine, cheese and beef. Stir to make a smooth sauce. If sauce seems thin, add a "sift" of flour; if too thick, add a little water. Keep the sauce over medium heat until fully-blended and piping hot. Serve over hot buttered toast with an extra sprinkle of Parmesan cheese. *Perfect dish for late Sunday breakfast—very rich.*

GRILLED STEAK WITH RED WINE AND SHALLOT SAUCE

Serves: 4

Sirloin steak
Soy Sauce
Salt

Black pepper, freshly ground
1 teaspoon dried thyme,
   crumbled

Brush sirloin steak with soy sauce and sprinkle well with salt, pepper and thyme. Let stand for 1 hour. Brush again with soy sauce and grill closely over brisk fire 3-4 minutes on each side for rare steak. Carve in thin slices on the diagonal; serve with sauce.

SAUCE:

1¼ cups chopped shallots or
   green onions
1¼ cups red wine

½ cup butter
Salt
2 tablespoons chopped parsley

Combine shallots and wine; bring just to a boil. Add butter and salt to taste. Stir until butter is melted. Add parsley. Steak must be rare or medium rare for maximum flavor.

El Paso Herald   December 23, 1883   Christmas Edition
Look and Swain—First class restaurant—Our food "would put the surliest old bachelor in Texas in a humor to kiss a molasses bedaubed baby".

GRILLED STEAK SOUTHWESTERN

Serves: 6-8

½ cup wine vinegar
½ cup firmly packed light
   brown sugar
¼ cup catsup
¼ cup soy sauce
2 tablespoons Worcestershire
   sauce

1 teaspoon prepared mustard
½ teaspoon garlic salt
3 pounds top round, cut
   1½-2 inches thick
1 teaspoon coarsely ground
   pepper

Combine first seven ingredients for marinade. Sprinkle both sides of steak with pepper and rub in with palm of hand. Place steak in marinade; cover and refrigerate 24 hours, turning several times. Place steak on grill five inches from hot coals. Grill to desired doneness (about 15 minutes per side), brushing occasionally with marinade.

GLAZE:

¾ cup sour cream
2 teaspoons prepared horseradish

1 teaspoon chopped green
   onion

In a bowl combine horseradish and onion with sour cream. Spread top of steak with mixture and continue cooking until glazed (3-5 minutes). To serve, slice thinly across grain. This is good with stuffed potatoes with cheese topping, fruit salad, fresh green beans and rolls.

BEEF KABOBS

Serves: 4

½ cup oil
3 tablespoons lemon juice
1 tablespoon wine vinegar
1 large onion, minced
½ teaspoon garlic salt
½ teaspoon thyme
½ teaspoon chile powder
1 teaspoon oregano

Salt and pepper to taste
2 pounds tenderloin or
   sirloin steak
Small onions
Cherry tomatoes
Mushrooms, stemmed
Bell pepper chunks

Combine all ingredients except meat and vegetables. Pour mixture over meat and marinate overnight. Place meat on skewers alternating with vegetables which have been dipped in marinade. Barbecue for 15 minutes. Baste often.

STEAK DIANE

Serves: 2

4 beef tenderloins, very thinly sliced	**Pepper**
	Butter
Salt	

Beat tenderloins with meat mallet to flatten. Sprinkle with salt and pepper. In hot skillet, brown meat in enough butter to keep from sticking to pan.

SAUCE:

4 tablespoons butter	**1½ tablespoons Worcestershire**
½ cup chopped green onions	**sauce**
(including tops)	**2 tablespoons Port wine**
½ cup sliced fresh mushrooms	

Brown onions and mushrooms in butter until soft. Add Worcestershire sauce and wine. Pour over meat and serve.

Variation: A simple sauce of 4 tablespoons butter and 3 teaspoons Worcestershire sauce can be used instead of the above sauce.

PEPPER STEAK

Serves: 4

1 flank steak	**2 medium bell peppers,**
1 tablespoon dry wine	**seeded, deribbed and**
3 tablespoons soy sauce	**cut into ½-inch squares**
½-1 teaspoon sugar	**¼ cup vegetable oil**
2 teaspoons cornstarch	

Cut flank steak lengthwise into 1½-inch strips, then crosswise into ¼-inch slices. Mix wine, soy sauce, sugar and cornstarch. Marinate steak in this mixture 1-6 hours. Set large skillet over high heat for about 30 seconds. Pour in 1 tablespoon oil and heat another 30 seconds. Stir and fry bell pepper squares for 3 minutes or until tender-crisp. Remove to drain. Add 3 tablespoons oil to skillet and heat almost to smoking point. Fry steak for about 2 minutes or to desired doneness. Add bell pepper and cook 1 minute.

El Paso Herald   December 16, 1883
The Diamond G is a model of neatness, cleanliness and convenient arrangement. Our table will "tickle the palate of the bon vivant".

SOUTHWESTERN PEPPER STEAK

Serves: 6

1 pound flank steak	2 celery stalks
4 teaspoons cornstarch	1 onion
5 tablespoons soy sauce	2 bell peppers
¾ cup beef broth or bouillon	16-ounce can bean sprouts,
⅓ cup chopped chile	drained
4 tablespoons salad oil	Salt and pepper

Prepare broth mixture of cornstarch and soy sauce; stir in beef broth and add chopped chile. Cut steak in half lengthwise; slice the halves diagonally across the grain into ⅛-inch thick slices. Heat 1 tablespoon of oil in frying pan until very hot. Cook half the meat at a time until lightly browned, adding more oil if necessary. Remove meat to dish. Add 1 tablespoon oil to pan. Cut celery stalks, onion and bell pepper into 1-inch pieces. Cook celery and onion about 2 minutes or until onion is tender-crisp. Add bell pepper and cook and stir 1 minute longer, adding more oil if necessary. Place on dish with meat. Add broth mixture to pan. Stir until thickened and boiling. Return meat and vegetables to pan; add bean sprouts and cook until hot. Season with salt and pepper. Serve with rice.

ROULADIN

Serves: 8

16 slices top round, sliced very thin on slicing machine	8 medium onions, sliced (separated into rings)
1 6-ounce bottle prepared mustard	1 24-ounce bottle sliced kosher dill pickles
8 medium fresh tomatoes, sliced	1 pound bacon
	Water
	Red wine

Spread each slice of meat generously with mustard. Top with 1 slice bacon, 3 slices tomato, several onion rings and several slices pickle. Start at one end of the prepared meat and roll to the other end keeping in all the ingredients. Secure open ends with toothpicks. Put about ½-inch water and wine in the bottom of an electric skillet or other large skillet with lid. Cook over medium heat for about 1¼ hours. Check often to make sure liquid does not cook completely down. Add more liquid if necessary. Turn once while cooking. This tastes better if cooked a day or two ahead of time. Serve with a little of the natural juice over the top. Can be frozen. To serve, remove from freezer for 1 hour and heat slowly until hot. Good served with tossed vebetable salad, green bean casserole and lemon pie.

ROLLED BEEF

Serves: 4-6

¼ cup melted butter or margarine	2 parsley sprigs, snipped
1 medium onion, chopped	2 pounds sirloin tip
4 cups fresh bread cubes	3 tablespoons flour
½ teaspoon salt	Salt
¼ teaspoon pepper	3 tablespoons shortening
½ teaspoon poultry seasoning	1½ cups hot water
4-5 celery leaves, chopped	Bottled meat sauce

In large bowl combine melted butter, onion, bread cubes, salt, pepper, poultry seasonings, celery leaves and parsley. Cut sirloin tips into eight slices ⅛-inch thick. Arrange bread mixture in center of each beef slice; roll up and tie securely both ways with string or secure with toothpicks. Roll beef in combination of flour and salt. Melt shortening and brown beef rolls well on all sides for about 15 minutes. Add hot water, cover and simmer until tender (about 35 minutes). Remove strings and lift gently to a heated platter. Keep warm. To pan drippings add bottled meat sauce to taste. Pour this sauce over the meat. Garnish with tomato wedges.

STANDING RIB ROAST

Yield: Roast with 4 ribs serves 6   Oven: 375°

Standing rib roast   **Salt and pepper**

Salt and pepper beef. Insert meat thermometer into center of roast. Let stand at room temperature 20-30 minutes. Place roast in shallow pan, fat side up. Roast in oven 1 hour. Turn off heat. During resting period, beef continues to cook slowly and evenly throughout. Turn oven temperature to 300°. Allow roast to reheat until desired internal temperature is reached. Beef will be pink and juicy when temperature reaches 130°. Serve with wine sauce.

WINE SAUCE:

2 tablespoons cornstarch	1 cup water
10½-ounce can beef bouillon	Salt and pepper
½ cup red table wine	

Measure ¼ cup drippings from roasting pan; blend in cornstarch. Add bouillon, water and wine. Cook, stirring constantly, until sauce thickens. Season with salt and pepper.

SWISS STEAK PARMESAN

Serves: 4-6

2½ pounds round steak
2 tablespoons flour
1 teaspoon salt
½ teaspoon paprika
½ teaspoon instant coffee
⅛ teaspoon garlic powder

2 tablespoons vegetable oil
¼ cup thinly sliced onion
½ cup beef bouillon
½ cup white wine
½ cup Parmesan cheese

Score steak. Mix flour, salt, paprika, coffee and garlic powder. Rub into steak. Brown meat in hot oil; add onions, bouillon and wine. Cover and simmer until tender (approximately 1½ hours). Before serving sprinkle with cheese.

SAVORY-SWEET ROAST WITH NOODLES

Serves: 6-8

3 pounds chuck roast
¼ cup cooking oil
2 cups onions, sliced
2 8-ounce cans seasoned
    tomato sauce
2 tablespoons brown sugar
1 teaspoon dry mustard
½ teaspoon salt

1 cup water
¼ cup lemon juice
¼ cup red wine vinegar
1 tablespoon Worcestershire
    sauce
1 6-ounce package curly
    noodles (Rotini,
    Skroodles)

Brown roast in oil; put onions on top. Mix remaining ingredients except noodles and pour over meat and onions. Cover and simmer for 2 hours. Add noodles and more water if needed and cook 30 minutes longer.

BEEF SUPREME

Serves: 6   Oven: 425°

½ pound bacon
3 pounds lean stew meat
1 tablespoon olive oil
2 carrots, sliced thinly
1 onion, sliced thinly
4 tablespoons flour
Salt
Pepper

3 cups red wine
3 cups bouillon
2 tablespoons tomato paste
2 cloves garlic
½ teaspoon thyme
1 small bay leaf
3 stalks parsley

Blanch bacon 10 minutes in water; drain. Sauté and remove. Pat dry lean stew meat. Sauté over high heat in 1 tablespoon (more if necessary) olive oil; remove. Sauté carrots and onion; add to casserole with beef and bacon. Sprinkle 2 tablespoons flour with salt and pepper over beef; toss. Place in oven 5 minutes. Toss again and sprinkle another 2 tablespoons flour, salt and pepper over meat. Return to oven for additional 5 minutes. Lower oven to 325°. Remove casserole. Mix red wine, bouillon, tomato paste, mashed garlic, thyme, bay leaf and parsley; simmer on top of stove. Pour over meat in casserole; return to oven for 3-4 hours. While meat is braising, prepare onions and mushrooms.

ONIONS:

18-24 small white onions
1½ tablespoons butter
1½ tablespoons oil
½ cup bouillon, wine or water

Parsley
½ bay leaf
¼ teaspoon thyme

Brown onions in butter and oil. Add bouillon, parsley, bay leaf and thyme. Cover and simmer slowly until almost all the liquid has evaporated. Set aside.

MUSHROOMS:

4 tablespoons butter
4 tablespoons oil

½ pound mushrooms

Heat butter and oil over high heat. When foam has subsided, add mushrooms. Toss and shake pan 4-5 minutes. When liquid reappears and mushrooms are browned, they are done. Add mushrooms and onions to casserole last 20 minutes. *Takes time, but it is the best ever—fantastic flavor!*

El Paso Herald   November 23, 1881

Turkeys are roosting high. In fact too high to be visible to the naked eye.

BEEF CARBONADES

Serves: 8-10　　　　　　　　　　　　　　　　　　　Oven: 325°

4 pounds lean beef, cubed
2 pounds large onions, thickly
　　sliced
6 cloves garlic, crushed
3 tablespoons brown sugar
¼ cup red wine vinegar

½ cup chopped parsley
2 small bay leaves
2 teaspoons thyme
Salt and pepper to taste
2 10-ounce cans beef broth
24 ounces beer

In large skillet brown floured meat in hot oil; remove to 6-quart casserole.
Brown onions and garlic in same pan, adding oil as needed. Remove to
casserole. Combine sugar, vinegar, parsley, bay leaves, thyme, salt and
pepper and broth with drippings and pour over meat mixture; add beer.
Cover and cook for 2 hours. Serve with dumplings or noodles.

BEEF AND CHEESE PIE

Serves: 6　　　　　　　　　　　　　　　　　　　　　Oven: 375°

1 cup biscuit mix
1 egg yolk
2½-3 tablespoons milk
1½ pounds lean ground beef
1 teaspoon salt
1 medium onion, chopped

¼ teaspoon pepper
1 egg
1 egg white
1 pint cottage cheese
½ cup Parmesan cheese

Stir biscuit mix, egg yolk and milk with a fork until blended; form into a
ball. Roll on lightly floured board and place in a 9-inch pie pan; flute
edges. Brown meat with salt until juices begin to form; add onion and
pepper. Cook, stirring frequently, until meat loses all pinkness; drain.
Turn into prepared crust. Mix together egg, egg white and cottage cheese.
Spoon over meat. Sprinkle Parmesan cheese on top. Bake 25 minutes or
until top is set.

Variation: 1 teaspoon Beau Monde, 1 teaspoon chile powder, ¾ teaspoon Italian
seasoning may be added to meat while cooking.

El Paso Daily Herald　　　　　　　December 26, 1892
The new Hotel Vendome open for business
John Friedenbloom, proprietor
Rates—$10 per week—$2.50 to $4.50 per day
Only first class hotel in the city. Passenger elevator always in running
order. Electric lights. Large airy rooms fitted with hot and cold water.
Porcelain lined bath tubs. We have our own dairy and our table will
be constantly supplied with pure milk and cream. The drinking water
is from La Noria Mesa and is absolutely pure. Only hotel employing
French cooks.

TOPSY TURVY TACO CORNBREAD DINNER

Serves: 6   Oven: 350°

1½ pounds ground beef
1 egg
1 tablespoon instant onion
1 8-ounce can tomato sauce
1 package taco seasoning mix
1 8¼-ounce package cornbread
    muffin mix

Sliced olives
1 tomato, wedged
1 avocado, peeled and wedged
Shredded lettuce

Combine beef, egg, onion, tomato sauce and taco seasoning. Spread in even layer in bottom of 10-inch baking dish. Bake 20 minutes. Prepare cornbread mix as directed on package. Drain excess juices and spread over top of meat. Turn oven up to 400° and continue baking until bread is browned. Pour off any juices and turn upside down onto serving dish. Garnish with tomato, avocado, olives and shredded lettuce.

HAMBURGER-CHEESE CASSEROLE

Serves: 8   Oven. 350°

1 pound lean ground beef
Salt to taste
2 8-ounce cans tomato sauce
1 8-ounce package noodles, cooked
1 cup small curd cottage cheese
1 8-ounce package cream cheese,
    softened

¼ cup sour cream
⅓ cup chopped green onions
1 tablespoon chopped bell
    pepper or chopped
    green chile
2 tablespoons softened
    butter

Brown ground beef with salt. Add tomato sauce. Combine cheeses, sour cream, onions and pepper in bowl. Butter a 2-quart casserole. Make a layer of half the noodles; cover with cheese mixture. Add remaining noodles. Spread with butter. Top with hamburger mixture. Bake 20-30 minutes.

SAUSAGE DINNER

Serves: 6-8   Oven: 375°

2 pounds pork sausage
1 2-ounce jar chopped pimento
1 small onion, chopped
½ bell pepper, chopped
6 stalks thinly sliced celery

5½ cups boiling water
2 packages chicken noodle soup
1 cup rice
½ cup slivered almonds
1 4-ounce can sliced mushrooms

Fry sausage; pour off fat. Add pimento, onion, bell pepper, celery, water, soup mix and rice; boil for 7 minutes. Mixture will be thin. Add almonds and mushrooms. Bake covered 30 minutes; uncovered 10 minutes.

EGGPLANT-MEAT CASSEROLE

Serves: 8   Oven: 350°

1 pound ground round
3 tablespoons butter
3 onions, chopped
2 cups tomato purée
⅛ teaspoon basil
⅛ teaspoon oregano
½ cup chopped bell pepper
1 teaspoon salt
⅛ teaspoon pepper

Dash garlic powder
6 pork sausages
2 large eggplants
3 eggs, beaten
1 cup salad oil
½ pound Mozzarella cheese, grated
1 Italian pepperoni sausage,
    sliced thin

In skillet, sauté ground round in butter. Add onions and cook until golden. Add tomato purée, basil, oregano, bell pepper, salt, pepper and garlic. In another skillet, sauté pork sausages until brown. Peel and thinly slice eggplants. Dip into beaten eggs and sauté in hot salad oil until both sides are brown. Drain on paper towels. In a 2½-quart casserole arrange one third of each: meat mixture, eggplant, Mozzarella, pork and sausage and pepperoni. Repeat until all is used, ending with cheese on top. Bake for 1 hour.

BARBECUED FRANKS

Serves: 20

1 4-ounce bottle catsup
4 tablespoons vinegar
½ cup chile catsup
Few drops Tabasco
3 tablespoons Worcestershire
    sauce
4 tablespoons hot water
2 tablespoons melted butter
2 medium onions, chopped

2 tablespoons flour
½ teaspoon salt
¼ teaspoon paprika
2 teaspoons dry mustard,
    or 4 tablespoons
    prepared mustard
4 teaspoons brown sugar
20 frankfurters

Mix all ingredients except franks; heat. Prick skins of franks several times and marinate in sauce 3-4 hours or overnight in refrigerator. Simmer 1 hour and serve on hot dog buns.

El Paso Herald   June 21, 1882
                M. Schoenfeld
                Dealer in stoves and ranges
                Tin and Hardware
                Double action force and lift pumps

BARBECUED SPARERIBS

Serves: 4   Oven: 400°

4 pounds country-style   ¼ cup lemon juice
    spareribs   ⅓ cup brown sugar
Salt   ¼ cup Worcestershire sauce
Pepper   ½ teaspoon allspice
1 6-ounce can tomato paste   2 cloves garlic, crushed
¼ cup catsup   1 small onion, minced
2 cups water   1½ teaspoons salt
2 tablespoons vinegar

Separate ribs; salt and pepper and place in a large flat dish. Mix other
ingredients and pour over ribs; cover and refrigerate 24 hours. Drain
marinade. Roast in oven for 30 minutes; grill over charcoal, turning and
basting until tender and glazed.

BARBECUED CHUCK ROAST

Serves: 4-6

3-4 pound chuck roast   1½ teaspoons A-1 sauce
¼ cup olive oil   ½ teaspoon dry mustard
1 teaspoon crushed rosemary   2 teaspoons soy sauce
¼ cup wine vinegar   ¼ cup sherry
2 tablespoons catsup   ½ teaspoon Worcestershire sauce

Combine all ingredients except roast. Marinate roast in mixture 8 hours;
cook 20 minutes on each side over slow coals for medium rare.

BARBECUED BRISKET

Serves: ½ pound per person   Oven: 450°

5-7 pound brisket   ½ cup lemon juice
2 cups catsup   2 teaspoons celery seed
2 teaspoons chile powder   2 cups water
2-3 tablespoons liquid smoke   2 teaspoons salt
½ cup Worcestershire sauce

Brown brisket in oven for 30 minutes. Combine ingredients; bring to a
boil and pour over meat. Lower oven to 300° and bake 2-3 hours or
until tender. Baste frequently.

Note: It is much neater to omit browning brisket and combine meat and other ingredients in a cooking bag. The meat browns naturally and the basting is done.

BARBECUED FLANK STEAK

Serves: 4

2 pounds flank steak
1 clove garlic
2-3 tablespoons soy sauce
1 tablespoon tomato paste

1 tablespoon oil
¼ teaspoon pepper
½ teaspoon oregano

Score flank steak diagonally on both sides. Combine all ingredients in blender until smooth. Pour sauce over steak and marinate overnight. Broil 4-7 minutes per side over hot coals.

Variation: Combine the following and mix well. Use as a marinade over flank steak and cook as above.

¾ cup oil
½ cup soy sauce
2 tablespoons vinegar
2 tablespoons honey

1½ teaspoons ginger
1 teaspoon garlic powder
1 scallion with tops,
 finely chopped

BEEF BRISKET IN BEER

Serves: 8-10   Oven: 350°

4 pound beef brisket
Salt and pepper
2 sliced onions
2 teaspoons Tabasco sauce
2 tablespoons brown sugar

1 clove garlic, minced
12-ounce can beer
 (cold or warm)
2 tablespoons flour
½ cup water

Trim fat from brisket. Season with salt and pepper. Place in a 13x9x2-inch baking dish. Cover meat with onions. Combine other ingredients except flour and pour over the meat. Cover with foil; bake 3½ hours. Uncover and bake 30 minutes more, basting occasionally. Remove meat to platter. Skim excess fat from drippings. Measure liquid and add water to make 1 cup. Blend flour and ½ cup water. Combine with drippings in saucepan. Serve gravy with roast.

FARM DINNER

Serves: 6-7

3½ pound corned beef brisket
2 medium cloves garlic
2 teaspoons whole peppercorns
6 small white onions, peeled

6 carrots, peeled
1 medium head cabbage, halved
6-8 medium potatoes

Cover brisket in water. Add garlic and peppercorns and simmer over low heat for 4½ hours. Add onions and continue simmering. In 20-25 minutes, add carrots. Cook 30 minutes; add cabbage. In 15 minutes, add potatoes. Simmer until potatoes are tender. Remove brisket and cool. Slice thin. Serve on large platter surrounded by vegetables. Good with mustard and horseradish.

VEAL SABROSA

Serves: 6

¼ cup flour
½ cup Parmesan cheese
1 teaspoon salt
⅛ teaspoon pepper
1½ pounds veal cutlets, sliced
    ¼-inch thick in 2-inch
    strips

2 tablespoons olive oil
1 clove garlic
½ cup dry white wine
½ cup consommé
1 tablespoon lemon juice
Chopped parsley

Mix flour, cheese, salt and pepper together. Wipe meat dry; sprinkle with flour mixture and pound it into meat. Heat olive oil with garlic and brown meat lightly on both sides. Remove garlic; add wine, consommé and lemon juice. Cover and simmer slowly for about 30 minutes. Sprinkle with chopped parsley and serve from hot platter.

BAKED VEAL CUTLETS

Serves: 8   Oven: 350°

8 thin veal cutlets (not breaded)
8 thin slices boiled ham
8 thin slices Swiss cheese
3 tablespoons butter, melted
½ cup corn flakes, finely
    crushed

½ cup heavy cream
10¾-ounce can cream of
    mushroom soup
2 tablespoons Sauterne wine

Place ham and cheese inside veal; roll and secure with toothpicks. Brush with butter and roll in corn flakes. Place in ungreased pan and bake for 40 minutes (can be frozen now or set aside to finish later). Combine remaining ingredients; pour over cutlets. Cover and bake 30 minutes. Serve with hot rice.

VEAL IN WINE WITH MUSHROOMS

Serves: 24

6 4½-ounce cans mushroom
    caps
¾ cup oil
9 pounds veal
    (cut in 1-inch cubes)
6 10¾-ounces cans condensed
    cream of mushroom soup

3 cups white wine
1½ cups chopped onion
3 teaspoons oregano
3 cups sour cream

Drain mushrooms; measure liquid adding enough water to make 3 cups. Sauté veal in heated oil until browned. Stir in mushroom liquid, soup, 1½ cups wine, onion and oregano. Bring to a boil; cover and reduce heat. Simmer, stirring occasionally, until veal is tender (about 1½ hours). Just before serving, add remaining 1½ cups wine, mushrooms and sour cream. Serve over hot rice. This can be prepared one day ahead and everything but sour cream can be frozen.

HAM JAMBALAYA

Serves: 6

5 slices bacon
1½ cups regular, long-grained
   rice
1 medium onion, minced
1 medium bell pepper, minced
1 clove garlic, crushed
16-ounce can tomatoes
13¾-ounce can chicken broth

1 bay leaf
½ teaspoon salt
½ teaspoon thyme leaves
1 pound cooked ham, cubed
   (2½ cups)
½ pound shelled, deveined
   shrimp
4 drops Tabasco sauce

In medium skillet fry bacon until crisp. Drain well and crumble; set aside. In same skillet over medium heat, cook rice, onion, bell pepper and garlic in bacon grease until rice is slightly browned. Stir in tomatoes and liquid, broth and spices. Cover and simmer 15 minutes. Stir in ham, shrimp and Tabasco. Cook, covered, 15-20 minutes until rice is tender, stirring occasionally. Spoon onto platter and sprinkle with bacon.

HOT HAM SAUCE

Yield: 1 quart

1 20-ounce can crushed
   pineapple
12-ounce can apricot nectar
1½ cups catsup

1½ tablespoons Worcestershire
   sauce
1 tablespoon lemon juice

Blend all ingredients in large saucepan and simmer 15 minutes. Serve hot on ham slices.

HAM SAUCE

3 eggs
4 tablespoons mustard
2 tablespoons vinegar

½ cup sugar
¼ teaspoon salt
1 4½-ounce can condensed milk

Beat eggs in saucepan; add mustard, vinegar, sugar and salt. Cook over medium heat until thick. Remove from heat; add milk and beat with spoon. Keep refrigerated.

HOT MUSTARD SAUCE

½ cup vinegar
1 2-ounce can Coleman
   mustard

1 egg, well beaten
Pinch of salt
⅓ cup sugar

Mix vinegar and mustard and soak overnight. Add egg, salt and sugar. Cook and stir constantly in top of double boiler until thickened. Excellent for fondue sauce or with egg rolls at a pick-up buffet.

HAM IN PATTY SHELLS

Serves: 18

6 tablespoons butter or margarine	½ cup all-purpose flour
½ cup finely chopped onion	4 cups milk
½ cup finely chopped bell pepper	3 tablespoons dry sherry
1 pound button mushrooms, sliced	1 teaspoon salt
1 tablespoon lemon juice	½ teaspoon dry mustard
	⅛ teaspoon white pepper
	8 cups diced ham
	18 fresh or frozen patty shells

Melt butter in large saucepan over medium heat. Sauté onion and bell pepper 1 minute. Add mushrooms and lemon juice. Continue cooking until vegetables are tender. Stir in flour. Cook 1 minute, stirring constantly. Remove from heat. Gradually stir in milk and sherry. Add salt, mustard and pepper. Return pan to heat. Cook, stirring constantly, until mixture thickens and comes to a boil. Add ham. Bring to boil; cook 1 minute. Serve in chafing dish and spoon into patty shells. This cannot be frozen.

PORK CHOPS CREME

Serves: 6   Oven: 350°

6 1-inch pork chops	½ teaspoon salt
1 clove garlic	¼ teaspoon pepper
4 tablespoons shortening	½ teaspoon paprika
½ pint sour cream	3 bay leaves
1 tablespoon vinegar	Minced parsley
1 tablespoon Worcestershire sauce	

Rub pork chops with garlic and brown in shortening. Mix sour cream with next five ingredients. Pour over meat and place ½ bay leaf on each chop. Sprinkle with parsley. Bake for 40 minutes. Flavor is enhanced when prepared in the morning for dinner.

PORK CHOPS MI CASA

Serves: 4

4 large pork loin chops	1 teaspoon salt
1 teaspoon Beau Monde seasoning	16-ounce can stewed tomatoes
1½ teaspoons chile powder	1 cup dry white wine

Cut a small piece of fat from edge of pork chops and render in a large skillet. Sauté chops until golden. Sprinkle with Beau Monde seasoning, chile powder and salt. Stir in tomatoes and wine. Cover and simmer for 45 minutes. Remove lid and simmer 5-10 minutes to reduce liquid.

PORK CHOPS AND SAUERKRAUT

Serves: 4-6   Oven: 350°

½ pound sliced bacon, diced
19-ounce can sauerkraut,
    drained and rinsed
15-ounce jar applesauce
1 tablespoon brown sugar

½ teaspoon dry mustard
¼ cup dry white wine (optional)
Dash of pepper
¼ teaspoon paprika
6 medium shoulder pork chops

Sauté bacon until crisp; drain. To sauerkraut add bacon, applesauce, brown sugar, mustard, white wine and pepper. Turn into a shallow casserole. Sprinkle with paprika. Sauté chops in bacon drippings until golden on both sides. Place on top of sauerkraut. Cover and bake for about 1 hour or until chops are tender.

LEG OF LAMB AMERICAN

Serves: 6-8   Oven: 325°

1 leg of lamb
⅔ cup grape jelly
¼ cup vinegar
½ teaspoon thyme

1 clove garlic, crushed
2 tablespoons salt
½ teaspoon pepper

Place leg of lamb on rack in roasting pan. Roast uncovered for 2 hours. Drain drippings. Combine all ingredients to make marinade. Pour marinade over lamb and roast 30 minutes or more until done.

BARBECUED LEG OF LAMB

Serves: 6

4 pound leg of lamb, butterflied
½ teaspoon garlic powder
1 teaspoon Bouquet Garni

⅓ cup olive oil
3 tablespoons red wine
    vinegar

Combine Bouquet Garni and garlic powder; rub well into meat. Place in glass baking dish or bowl. Combine oil and vinegar and pour over lamb. Marinate several hours at room temperature or overnight in refrigerator. Barbecue for approximately 1-1½ hours, turning every 10-15 minutes and brushing with marinade. Cut into ¼-inch slices.

El Paso Herald   December 23, 1883   Christmas Edition
P. C. Dunne is the proprietor of a fish and oyster and fresh meat depot on Santa Fe Street opposite to the State National Bank Building. His meats are first class. He has fresh fish daily.

LAMB CURRY

Serves: 24

4 medium onions
4 cloves garlic
4 tablespoons ground coriander
4 teaspoons salt
4 teaspoons cumin seed
1½ teaspoons each: black
    pepper, ground cloves,
    and ground cardamom

1 teaspoon ground ginger
1 teaspoon cinnamon
1 teaspoon poppy seed
½ cup lemon juice
4 cups yogurt
10 pound boneless lamb
Curry powder to taste
½ cup butter

Put 2 onions and 2 cloves of garlic into an electric blender. Add all spices and lemon juice. Whirl until smooth and thoroughly blended. Blend in yogurt. Pour this sauce over lamb which has been cut into 1½-inch cubes. Be sure each piece is coated. Cover and let stand 1-2 hours or overnight. Melt butter in a large frying pan; thinly slice the remaining onion and garlic and sauté in butter until golden. Add meat and the marinade. Cover and simmer slowly until lamb is tender (about 2 hours).

MARINATED LAMB

Serves: 8-10   Oven: 300°

1 boned leg of lamb
1 teaspoon marjoram
1 teaspoon thyme
1 teaspoon rosemary
¼ cup chopped parsley

½ cup chopped onion
1 clove garlic, minced
½ cup olive oil
½ cup lemon juice

Combine herbs, onion, garlic, oil and lemon juice. Place leg of lamb in flat dish and cover with marinade. Cover with foil and refrigerate for 24 hours, turning occasionally. Place lamb in roasting pan with marinade. Cook for 3 hours.

DELICIOUS LIVER

Serves: 6

6 thin slices calf's liver
6 slices bacon
¾ cup yellow corn meal

10-ounce can onion soup,
    undiluted
1 6-ounce can taco sauce or
    picante sauce

Fry bacon until crisp. Drain on paper towels. Dip liver in corn meal and brown in bacon fat. Add onion soup and taco sauce. Cover and simmer 45 minutes. Serve with crumbled bacon on top.

SWEETBREAD

Serves: 4-6   Oven: 350°

1 pair sweetbread
Salt
Whole spice (if desired)
Butter
3 ounces white wine
1 8-ounce can mushrooms
    (stems and pieces)

1 onion, chopped
1 cup celery, chopped
Parsley (optional)
Pepper
2 cups thick white sauce

Soak sweetbread 12 hours in cold water with 2 tablespoons salt. Remove; wash well. Barely cover with boiling water, small amount of salt and whole spice; boil 5 minutes. Dry well; remove skin and break up. In a pan for the oven, sauté sweetbread in butter until brown; add 1 jigger wine. Bake about 30 minutes. While sweetbread is baking, sauté mushrooms, onion, parsley and celery until browned. Add the other jigger of wine and season with pepper. Make white sauce from flour, mushroom liquid and/or milk and add to mushroom mixture. Combine with sweetbread; heat and serve in chafing dish.

STEAK MARINADE SAUCE

2 cloves garlic, crushed
½ cup soy sauce
¼ cup brown sugar
2 tablespoons olive oil

¼ teaspoon cracked pepper
2 small pieces ginger
    root, crushed

Mix all ingredients in a jar; shake well. Marinate steaks at least 1 hour before broiling. Baste steaks frequently while broiling. This is also good on 1½-inch pork chops.

STANLEY'S BARBECUE SAUCE

Yield: 1 quart

1 quart water
¾ jar B.V. beef bouillion
¼ cup butter
¾ bottle A-1 sauce

1 tablespoon Worcestershire
    sauce
Juice of 1 lemon
½-1 cup chopped onions

Boil water and add remaining ingredients. Simmer 30 minutes. Delicious on steak.

El Paso Herald   November 9, 1881
We don't hear of any turkeys in town for Thanksgiving and Christmas.

JALAPEÑO PEPPER JELLY

Yield: 4 pints or 8-½ pints

1 cup bell pepper, chopped
8-9 fresh jalapeños, chopped fine
6⅓ cups sugar
1⅓ cups white vinegar
Red or green food coloring
     (if desired)

1 bottle Certo
2-3 tablespoons fresh lime juice
Melted paraffin

Combine bell pepper, jalapeños, sugar and vinegar in a saucepan. Add food coloring. Bring to a boil; remove from heat and add Certo. Return to heat until boiling point is reached; remove. Add lime juice. Pour into sterilized jars, stirring often to distribute peppers. Pour melted paraffin on top of jars to seal.

CHILE EN ESCABECHE
(CURED CHILE)

Yield: 2 pints

12 green chiles
1 large onion, thinly sliced
5 large garlic buds, pressed
½ cup oil
1 cup white vinegar

½ cup water
2 teaspoons salt
1 teaspoon oregano
3-4 bay leaves

Sauté onion and garlic in oil until clear. Add vinegar, water, salt, oregano and bay leaves. Bring to a boil. Add chiles which have been roasted, peeled and seeded. Simmer about 10 minutes. Store in jars and refrigerate. Good with meat.

CULI SAUCE

Yield: 10 pints

10-ounce can green chiles,
     or 6 fresh green chiles,
     roasted and peeled
8 medium onions
8 cups vinegar
2 cups sugar

24 ripe peeled tomatoes
2 tablespoons salt
1 tablespoon cinnamon
1 tablespoon cloves
1 tablespoon allspice
1 tablespoon nutmeg

Chop chiles and onions; add all other ingredients. Cook together in large pot until thickened. Pour into jars and seal while hot. Delicious as a condiment with meats.

ALBEMARLE PEACH CHUTNEY

Yield: 5 quarts

7 pounds firm, fresh peaches	¼ cup scraped ginger root*
1 pint cider vinegar	1½ tablespoons salt
2 pounds dark brown sugar	2 tablespoons paprika
½ cup grated onion	2 tablespoons cumin powder
2 pounds seedless raisins	Grated rind and juice of 2 lemons
5 apples, pared and diced	
2 tablespoons white mustard seed	

Peel and cut peaches in slices about ¾-inch thick (enough to make about 4 quarts). Cover with vinegar and brown sugar. Set aside. Combine all remaining ingredients and cook over a low heat, stirring constantly, until the mixture is thoroughly blended. In a separate saucepan, cook the peach mixture for several minutes or until the peaches are tender but still hold their shape. Combine both mixtures and cook together for a few minutes. Pour into sterilized jars and seal securely.

*3 tablespoons ground ginger, or 2⅞-ounce bottle of Spice Island crystallized ginger can be used.

MIKE'S BARBECUE SAUCE

Yield: 1 quart

2 large onions, chopped	2½ teaspoons prepared mustard
4 tablespoons sugar	
7 tablespoons vinegar	¼ teaspoon garlic powder
¼ teaspoon black pepper	½ cup margarine
1 cup catsup	½ teaspoon chile powder
1 cup water	2 chopped jalapeños
2 teaspoons paprika	Dash Louisiana hot sauce
2 teaspoons salt	

Combine all ingredients in blender at high speed until blended thoroughly. Cook slowly 30 minutes. Add water, a little at a time, if sauce gets too thick. Will keep in refrigerator for two months and can be frozen.

El Paso Herald   November 29, 1882

A resident claimed that a flight of ducks landed on El Paso Street. El Paso and San Antonio Streets make first class mud puddles when it rains . . . Repairing streets in El Paso is one of the lost arts, if it ever was one of the discovered arts.

Desert Greens

SALADS AND DRESSINGS

HINTS FOR SALADS & DRESSINGS

Greens cannot be properly coated with salad oil unless they are absolutely dry.

Greens that are torn rather than cut make a more appealing salad and are less likely to wilt or discolor.

Salad ingredients prepared long in advance lose nutritive value and become limp.

About 1 teaspoon of salad oil will cover a medium head of lettuce. A preliminary coating of oil before dressing is added will hold the nutrients.

Tomatoes cut vertically bleed less.

Fresh tomatoes keep longer if stored with stems down.

To crisp salad greens, add 1 tablespoon vinegar to a pan of water and soak vegetables 15 minutes

Rap a head of lettuce on a counter top; the core then can be pulled out easily.

To crisp celery, wash an Irish potato, cut it into about 6 pieces, and place in a container with the celery. Cover with water and refrigerate. Or, soak celery in cold water containing 1 teaspoon sugar for about an hour.

To ripen an avocado, place in a flour canister for 24 hours.

Sweet pickle juice may be used instead of vinegar in making coleslaw dressing.

When making potato salad, slice the boiled potatoes and immediately coat gently with vinegar. No more "mashed" potato salad!

Always lightly grease the mold for congealed salad.

To unmold a salad easily, set it in a larger pan of tepid water for a moment and shake gently. Hold a serving plate over the mold and turn mold upside down. If it doesn't slip easily onto the serving dish, dip the mold a few moments more in tepid water and repeat.

Never boil gelatine and never add fresh pineapple to it.

The following fruits will sink in a molded salad: canned apricots, peaches, and pears; Royal Ann cherries; whole strawberries; prunes; plums; and fresh orange sections.

The following will float in a molded salad: fresh apple cubes, banana slices, grapefruit sections, fresh peaches and pear slices; strawberry halves, marshmallows, and broken nut meats.

One envelope unflavored gelatine is equal to 1 tablespoon and is enough to set 2 cups of liquid.

To cut marshmallows or dates, wet kitchen shears in hot water.

To prevent bananas from turning brown, marinate a few minutes in the juice of any canned fruit used in the salad.

STUFFED AVOCADOS

Serves: 6

3 avocados
1 head romaine lettuce
½ cup finely minced celery
½ cup cubed apple
½ cup chopped, blanched
  almonds

¼ cup bottled creamy
  French dressing
¼ cup mayonnaise
Paprika to taste

Cut avocados in half lengthwise and peel. Place on individual plates lined with lettuce. Combine celery, apple and almonds; add French dressing and mix well. Fill avocado halves with the mixture, top with a little mayonnaise, and sprinkle with paprika.

COLD BEAN SALAD

Serves: 24

2 cans garbanzo beans
2 cans green beans
2 cans wax beans
2 cans kidney beans
2 cans water chestnuts, thinly
  sliced

1 fresh green onion, chopped
2 cups Green Goddess dressing
  (see Index)
3 avocados

Drain beans well and rinse; combine with water chestnuts, onion and dressing in large bowl. Refrigerate several hours or overnight. Garnish with sliced avocados before serving.

CAULIFLOWER SALAD

Serves: 6

1 medium head cauliflower
½ cup oil and vinegar dressing
½ cup stuffed green olives,
  chopped

1 avocado, diced
½ cup Bleu cheese, crumbled
3 tomatoes, cut in wedges

Break up cauliflower and soak in cold water for 1 hour. Break into smaller pieces and marinate for 2 hours in oil and vinegar dressing. Add remaining ingredients just before serving.

El Paso Herald   November 29, 1882
We have been having fowl weather, and Thanksgiving day will still be fowler.

COUNTRY COLE SLAW

Serves: 8

2 cups finely shredded cabbage
1 medium onion, minced
¼ cup bell pepper, minced
¼ cup chopped parsley (optional)

¼ cup minced pimento (optional)
6 sliced stuffed olives
    (optional)
1 teaspoon celery seed (optional)

Combine all ingredients. Cover with dressing and marinate for 24 hours. Serve garnished with tomatoes. This salad keeps several days in the refrigerator.

DRESSING:

3 tablespoons sugar
1 teaspoon salt
1 teaspoon pepper

1 tablespoon vinegar
3 tablespoons salad oil

Dissolve sugar, salt and pepper in vinegar; add oil very slowly. Beat until there is no separation of oil and vinegar.

TACO SALAD

Serves: 10

1½ pounds ground beef
1½ cups onion
1 cup celery
1 cup bell pepper
3 cloves garlic
1 teaspoon salt
1 teaspoon chile powder

½ teaspoon cumin
10-ounce can tomatoes and
    green chiles
1 pound Velveeta cheese
1 large head lettuce
2 large fresh tomatoes
⅓ package Fritos (11 ounce)

Brown ground beef and set aside. Chop onion, celery and bell pepper; sauté with minced garlic in remaining juices. Combine meat with mixture and spices; simmer for 20 minutes. Cut lettuce coarsely and dice tomatoes; toss together in a large bowl and add slightly crushed Fritos. In top of double boiler put canned tomatoes and chiles with Velveeta cheese which has been cubed. Stir frequently until melted. When ready to serve, add hot meat to lettuce and toss to mix. Pour cheese sauce in bowl to use as dressing for salad.

El Paso Daily Times   Sunday May 26, 1895
                    Ranch Saloon
                    Always Fresh Beer on Tap
                    Best 15¢ Hot Lunch in the City
                    From 11 to 2 o'clock

POTATO SALAD CAESAR

Serves: 8

4 cups cooked potatoes, diced
1½-2 quarts romaine, broken
2 cups croutons
2 tablespoons melted butter
Pinch of garlic powder

¼ cup grated Parmesan cheese
¼ cup crumbled Roquefort
   cheese
6-8 anchovies
½ cup sliced, pitted ripe olives

Prepare dressing and toss with potatoes. Chill (can be done the day before). In a large salad bowl combine chilled potato mixture with romaine. Toss croutons with butter and garlic powder and add to mixture. Add cheeses, anchovies and olives; toss together. *This is great with fried or barbecued chicken.*

DRESSING:

½ cup salad oil
1 teaspoon Worcestershire
1 teaspoon salt
⅛ teaspoon pepper

⅛ teaspoon garlic powder
¼ cup lemon juice
1 egg
¼ cup minced onion

Beat together all ingredients and toss with potatoes.

MUSHROOM SALAD

Serves: 4-6

1 pound fresh mushrooms
1 cup chopped celery (inner
   stalks and tiny leaves)
2 pimentos, cut in strips
1 hard cooked egg, sliced

2 tablespoons minced chives,
   green onions or scallions
Salt and pepper
Oil and vinegar dressing

Rinse mushrooms lightly and dry well. Cut caps and stems into bite-sized pieces. Mix all ingredients in bowl and toss with dressing. Marinating salad in refrigerator 30 minutes adds to flavor. Sprinkle lightly with salt and freshly ground black pepper. Remove salad from dressing and arrange with lettuce or romaine leaves on salad plates.

Variation: Delicious tossed with a variety of greens and artichoke hearts. Bottled Italian dressing can be used. The marinated ingredients could be done an hour or so ahead, but greens should be tossed at the last minute.

El Paso Herald   November 9, 1881
The editor states that there were 44,000 grape vines in one growers
land in Mexico opposite El Paso.

SWEET 'N SOUR ASPARAGUS SALAD

Serves: 6

1 pound fresh asparagus spears
6 slices bacon
¼ cup wine vinegar
2 teaspoons sugar
Dash of salt

Dash of pepper
2 finely chopped green
  onions (2 teaspoons)
Shredded lettuce
2 hard cooked eggs, sliced

Cook asparagus in boiling, salted water 8-10 minutes, just until tender. Drain. Meanwhile, cook bacon until crisp. Drain, crumble and set aside. Add vinegar, sugar, salt, pepper and onion to drippings in skillet. Add asparagus and heat through. Arrange a bed of lettuce on six salad bowls. Remove asparagus from skillet and arrange on lettuce. Top with egg slices. Pour hot bacon dressing over each salad. Sprinkle with bacon.

WINE-MARINATED ARTICHOKE HEARTS

Serves: 4-6

2 9-ounce packages frozen
  artichoke hearts
1 cup salad oil
½ cup white wine vinegar
¼ cup white wine

¼ cup chopped red onion
1 tablespoon chopped parsley
1 teaspoon finely chopped garlic
½ teaspoon salt
½ teaspoon seasoned pepper

Cook artichoke hearts according to package directions. Drain and cool. Combine all other ingredients and mix well. Pour over artichoke hearts and let stand at least 3 hours before serving. This is especially good with prime rib and Yorkshire pudding.

Alternate: The marinade is also good on green beans.

CUCUMBER AND RED ONION SALAD

Serves: 6-8

1½ cups sour cream
½ clove garlic
¾ teaspoon salt
Dash Tabasco sauce
2 tablespoons vinegar

1 teaspoon mustard
Sugar to taste
1 tablespoon chopped parsley
2 cucumbers, sliced (unpared)
1 red onion, sliced

Mix first eight ingredients. Add cucumbers and onions. Chill.

MOLDED CUCUMBER SALAD

Serves: 11-12 individual molds

1 6-ounce package lime Jello
1 8¼-ounce can crushed
   pineapple
1 teaspoon lemon juice
½ cup mayonnaise

1 cup sour cream or sour
   half-and-half
1 pound cottage cheese
1 diced cucumber

Drain pineapple and reserve juice. Add water to pineapple juice to make 1 cup. Heat to boiling and use to melt Jello. Add all other ingredients except pineapple in order given. Add pineapple last. Mix thoroughly and refrigerate in lightly greased mold. Turn out just before serving.

DUTCH BOY LETTUCE SALAD

Serves: 8-10

4 slices bacon
1 egg
⅓ cup sour cream
¼ cup vinegar
2 tablespoons sugar

Dash of salt
½ head lettuce, torn
½ pound fresh spinach, torn
3-4 green onions, sliced

In large skillet, cook bacon until crisp. Drain, reserving 1 tablespoon drippings in skillet. Crumble bacon and set aside. Combine slightly beaten egg, sour cream, vinegar, sugar and salt; stir into reserved drippings. Cook and stir until thickened. Add lettuce, spinach and onion, tossing until coated. Serve immediately.

SPINACH AND BACON SALAD BOWL

Serves: 6

¾ cup oil and vinegar dressing
6 cloves garlic
8 slices bacon

1 pound crisp, young spinach
3 hard cooked eggs, finely
   chopped

Two hours before serving, add quartered and peeled garlic to the oil and vinegar dressing. Sauté bacon until crisp; drain on paper towels and crumble. Tear the spinach and place in salad bowl. Add bacon and eggs. Remove garlic from the dressing and toss with spinach.

CANLIS' SALAD

Serves: 4-6

2 tablespoons olive oil	2 heads romaine
Salt	¼ cup chopped green onions
1 clove garlic	½ cup grated Romano cheese
2 peeled tomatoes	1 pound finely chopped bacon

Pour approximately 2 tablespoons good imported olive oil in a large wooden bowl. Sprinkle with salt, and rub firmly with a large clove of garlic (the oil will act as a lubricant and the salt as an abrasive). Remove garlic. Place tomatoes, cut in eighths, into bowl; add romaine, torn into 1-inch strips. Other salad vegetables may be added, but place heavy vegetables in first. Top with romaine and add remaining ingredients. Prepare dressing.

DRESSING:

3 ounces olive oil	¼ teaspoon oregano
Juice of 2 lemons	1 coddled egg
½ teaspoon chopped fresh mint	1 cup croutons

Pour olive oil, lemon juice and seasonings into a bowl. Add egg and whip vigorously. When ready to serve, pour dressing over salad. Add croutons last. Toss thoroughly.

CORNED BEEF SALAD MOLD

Serves: 8

1 envelope unflavored gelatine	3 hard cooked eggs
¼ cup cold water	2 cups chopped celery
1½ cups tomato juice, heated	½ cup chopped cucumber
1 teaspoon lemon juice	1 tablespoon chopped onion
½ teaspoon salt	1 cup mayonnaise or salad
12-ounce can corned beef, shredded	dressing
	1 4-ounce can taco sauce

Soften gelatine in cold water. Dissolve in tomato juice. Add lemon juice and salt. Chill until partially set; fold in corned beef and remaining ingredients. Chill in 1½-quart mold until firm. Garnish with greens and chopped eggs. Good served with hot rolls or biscuits.

HEARTY TUNA SALAD

Serves: 4 - 6

10-ounce package frozen Italian green beans

2 7-ounce cans white tuna, drained and flaked

1 cup sliced celery

1 8-ounce can water chestnuts

1 cup chow mein noodles

Cook beans according to package. Drain and cool. Combine beans, tuna, celery and water chestnuts. Add dressing and chill for several hours. Just before serving, toss with chow mein noodles. Serve in lettuce cups.

DRESSING:

½ cup mayonnaise

1½ tablespoons soy sauce

1 tablespoon lemon juice

Dash of garlic powder

Combine all ingredients. Serve on tuna salad.

MEXICAN TUNA SALAD

Serves: 4-6

½ head lettuce, torn

2 tomatoes, chopped

½ cup chopped green onions

½ cup chopped olives

1 cup grated Cheddar cheese

1 cup tuna

1 cup small Fritos

Prepare salad dressing. Combine above ingredients in bowl and pour dressing over when ready to serve.

DRESSING:

½ cup mashed avocado

½ cup sour cream

⅓ cup mayonnaise

1 teaspoon lemon juice

1 clove garlic

1 teaspoon sugar

½ teaspoon chile powder

¼ teaspoon Tabasco

¼ teaspoon salt

Combine all ingredients.

El Paso Daily Herald   February 8, 1898
"The Oyster Fiesta"
At least 250 members of the McGinty Club and invited non-resident guests filled Choin Hall last night on the occasion of the long expected oyster blow out of the McGinty Club.

MOLDED GAZPACHO SALAD

Serves: 6-8

2 envelopes unflavored gelatine
10-ounce can tomato juice
⅓ cup red wine vinegar
1 teaspoon salt
Dash of Tabasco
2 small tomatoes, peeled and
    diced

1 medium cucumber, pared
    and diced
½ medium bell pepper,
    diced
¼ cup chopped onion
1 tablespoon chopped chives

In a medium saucepan sprinkle gelatine over ¾ cup tomato juice to soften. Stir constantly over low heat until gelatine is dissolved. Remove from heat. Stir in remaining tomato juice, vinegar, salt and Tabasco. Set in a bowl of ice, stirring occasionally, until mixture is consistency of unbeaten egg whites (about 15 minutes). Fold in tomato, cucumber, bell pepper, onion and chives. Pour in a 1½-quart mold that has been rinsed in cold water. Refrigerate until firm (at least 6 hours). Serve with Avocado Dressing.

AVOCADO DRESSING:

Yield: 2 cups

1 large ripe avocado (about 1
    pound)
½ cup sour cream
½ cup light cream
1 tablespoon grated onion

Dash of cayenne
1½ teaspoon salt
⅛ teaspoon sugar
1 clove garlic, crushed
1 tablespoon lemon juice

Peel avocado. Cut into chunks. Blend in blender with sour cream, light cream and rest of ingredients until smooth. Place plastic wrap directly on surface of dressing. Refrigerate covered for several hours.

MEXICAN ABALONE (OR CLAM) SALAD

2 8-ounce cans chopped abalone
    (or clams)
1 large onion, chopped
2 4-ounce cans chopped green
    chile
2 tomatoes, chopped

3 tablespoons olive oil
1 teaspoon vinegar
Juice of 2 limes (fresh)
Garlic salt to taste
Salt and pepper

Mix all ingredients together several hours before serving. Serve with crackers as a dip or as a first course at dinner.

CARNE A LA VINAGRETA
(MARINATED BEEF SALAD)

Serves: 6

4 cups cooked lean beef, cut in strips
1 large onion, thinly sliced
2 tablespoons capers
2 tablespoons minced parsley
½ cup olive oil

¼ cup red wine vinegar
1 teaspoon crumbled oregano
1 teaspoon prepared mustard
½ teaspoon salt
1 avocado, sliced

Put meat strips on rimmed platter and cover with onions. Sprinkle with capers and parsley. Mix together oil, vinegar, oregano, mustard and salt. Pour over meat. Cover and chill at least 3 hours to mingle flavors. Garnish with slices of avocado.

CHILE AND TOMATO ASPIC

Serves: 8-10

2 3-ounce packages lemon Jello
2 cups boiling water
2 10-ounce cans tomatoes and green chiles

1 teaspoon salt
Juice of ½ lemon
½ cup diced celery

Dissolve Jello in boiling water. Add tomatoes and green chiles, salt and lemon juice. Place in refrigerator until thickened (about 30 minutes). Add celery. Pour into ring mold or small individual molds to set. Serve on lettuce with mayonnaise dressing.

Variation: Chunks of avocado may be added with the celery.

MEXICAN SALAD

Serves: 4

8 fresh green chiles
2 medium tomatoes, peeled and sliced
3 small green onions, chopped

3 tablespoons vegetable oil
1 tablespoon vinegar
1½ teaspoons sugar
Salt to taste

Roast and peel chiles; cut into strips. Place chiles and tomatoes on bed of lettuce leaves. Top with green onions. Mix remaining ingredients and pour over chiles. Chill. Serve with a Mexican dinner.

MANGO SALAD

Serves: 12

3 3-ounce packages lemon Jello
1 29-ounce can mangos,
    drained
3 cups boiling liquid (mango
    juice plus water)
1 8-ounce package cream cheese

Juice of 1 lime
Sour cream
Brown sugar
Grated coconut

Dissolve Jello in boiling liquid of mango juice and water; set aside. Put drained mangos and cream cheese into blender and blend until creamy. Add to Jello mixture and stir in lime juice. Pour into ring mold, individual molds or oblong pan and chill 4-6 hours or overnight. Serve on bed of lettuce and top with any or all: sour cream, brown sugar and coconut.

BLUEBERRY SALAD

Serves: 15

1 3-ounce package lemon Jello
1 cup boiling water
½ pint sour cream
3 3-ounce packages rasp-
    berry Jello

3 cups boiling water
2 15-ounce cans blueberries

Dissolve lemon Jello in 1 cup boiling water. Cool and blend with sour cream in blender. Pour in 3-quart mold or casserole. Refrigerate until congealed. Dissolve raspberry Jello in 3 cups boiling water. Drain blueberries and reserve liquid. Add 2 cups blueberry syrup to Jello (add water to syrup to make 2 cups). Cool. Add blueberries to mixture and pour over sour cream mixture. Refrigerate until congealed. Slice and serve on lettuce leaves.

MANDARIN LUNCHEON SALAD

Serves: 4-5

2 11-ounce cans mandarin oranges
½ cup blanched almonds, sliced
2 cups diced, cooked turkey
16-ounce can bean sprouts

2 hard cooked eggs, chopped
1 teaspoon chopped chives
½ teaspoon curry powder
¾ cup mayonnaise

Drain orange segments. Toast almonds until golden. Combine with turkey, drained bean sprouts, eggs, chives, curry powder and mayonnaise. Lightly mix in 1 cup orange segments. Mound on individual lettuce leaves. Garnish with remaining orange segments. Good with chicken, crabmeat or tuna.

ARTICHOKE HEARTS VINAIGRETTE

Serves: 8

2 9-ounce packages frozen arti-
    choke hearts
½ cup olive oil
½ teaspoon salt
¼ teaspoon leaf oregano,
    crumbled

¼ teaspoon leaf thyme,
    crumbled
½ teaspoon paprika
¼ cup wine vinegar
Crisp salad greens

Cook and drain artichoke hearts. Combine with remaining ingredients, except salad greens. Refrigerate 12-24 hours. Drain and discard marinade. Serve artichokes with salad greens. This dressing can be used on any vegetable. Do not freeze.

ZUCCHINI SALAD

Serves: 4-6

1 head romaine
½ cup radishes, sliced

1 large zucchini squash, un-
    cooked and sliced thin

Tear romaine into pieces and add radishes and zucchini. Prepare dressing.

DRESSING:

½ cup mayonnaise
½ cup Italian dressing
2 tablespoons Cheddar cheese,
    grated

2 tablespoons grated onion
½ teaspoon anchovy paste
6 slices toast

Combine all ingredients except toast. Mix thoroughly. Cut toast into cubes to make croutons. Pour dressing and croutons on salad and toss just before serving.

SPINACH SALAD

Serves: 4

2 bunches spinach
4 green onions, chopped
Pepper
Salt
4 slices bacon, fried and
broken into pieces

Bacon drippings
2 tablespoons wine vinegar
Juice of ½ lemon
Pinch of sugar
1 hard cooked egg

Wash fresh spinach thoroughly and chill with chopped green onions. Season with coarse black pepper and salt. Warm bacon drippings, vinegar, lemon juice and sugar over low heat. Remove from heat and pour over chilled spinach. Sprinkle chopped eggs and bacon pieces over the salad. Serve immediately.

PIMENTO SALAD DRESSING

Yield: 1 cup

1 4-ounce can pimentos, plus juice
2 tablespoons Bleu cheese
⅓ cup salad oil
¼ cup vinegar

1½ teaspoons sugar
½ teaspoon salt
1 thin slice of small onion
¼ teaspoon pepper

Blend in blender just a few seconds until smooth. *This is an unusual, bright-colored dressing, good on vegetable or citrus salads.*

BACON DRESSING

Serves: 6-8

12 slices bacon
6 tablespoons bacon grease
9 tablespoons vinegar
3 teaspoons flour
1 tablespoon water

2 egg yolks
½ teaspoon salt
6 tablespoons sour cream
3 tablespoons sugar

Cut bacon into ½-inch squares and fry. Remove all grease except 6 tablespoons. Add vinegar to cooled grease. Add water to egg yolks while other mixture cools. Blend eggs with flour. Add this mixture to pan. Stir constantly until mixture thickens; add cream, salt and sugar. If a thinner consistency is desired, add 2 tablespoons water. Bring mixture to boil and pour over romaine lettuce broken into pieces.

OIL AND VINEGAR DRESSING

Yield: 1 cup

6 ounces olive oil
2 ounces vinegar
1 teaspoon salt
½ teaspoon freshly ground pepper

¼ cup chopped marjoram, rosemary or tarragon
Dash Worcestershire sauce
(optional)

Blend all ingredients together. Chill well before serving. Worcestershire sauce may be used for a slight garlic flavor.

RED WINE DRESSING

Yield: 3 cups

1 teaspoon salt
½ teaspoon freshly ground
pepper
¼ teaspoon sugar
½ teaspoon dry mustard
¼ teaspoon mustard
Dash Tabasco sauce
1 teaspoon lemon juice

¼ teaspoon chopped garlic
½ teaspoon chopped tarragon
leaves
4 tablespoons tarragon vinegar
2 tablespoons red wine
1¾ cups salad oil
¼ cup olive oil

Combine all ingredients in order and shake thoroughly in a jar before using.

"CUM-BACK" DRESSING

Yield: 3 cups

1 cup mayonnaise
1 clove garlic, quartered
1 medium onion, chopped
Dash of Tabasco
1 teaspoon pepper
1 tablespoon Worcestershire
sauce
½ cup salad oil

½ cup chile catsup
½ cup catsup
Juice of 1 lemon
1 teaspoon paprika
1 tablespoon creamy horseradish
Salt to taste

Put mayonnaise in blender. Add garlic and onion; beat until vegetables are liquified. Add remaining ingredients and mix well. Chill 24 hours before using. Serve over head lettuce or tossed salad. This will keep for weeks.

BLEU CHEESE DRESSING

Yield: 2½ cups

¾ cup salad oil
¼ cup vinegar
1 cup sour cream
1 teaspoon salt

1 medium clove garlic, minced
Sprinkle of seasoned pepper
¼ pound Bleu cheese

Place in blender ¼ cup of salad oil and ¼ cup of vinegar; blend. Mix in sour cream; add remaining oil and seasonings and blend. Crumble Bleu cheese into mixture and blend only a second so that Bleu cheese remains in chunks. Refrigerate until serving. This dressing is wonderful as a dip for fresh vegetables such as cauliflower buds, carrot sticks, celery sticks, radishes. Also delicious served on a tossed green salad with tomatoes.

GREEN GODDESS DRESSING

Yield: salad dressing for 12

1 clove garlic, crushed
3 tablespoons chopped green
    onions
1 cup chopped parsley

1 tablespoon wine vinegar
½ cup sour cream
1 cup mayonnaise
2 teaspoons anchovy paste

Combine all ingredients in order. Serve on salad greens.

SESAME SEED DRESSING

Yield: 3 cups

1 cup sugar
1 teaspoon paprika
½ teaspoon dry mustard
1 teaspoon salt
1 teaspoon Worcestershire sauce

1 tablespoon onion juice
    (grate a fresh onion)
2 cups salad oil
1 cup cider vinegar
1 cup toasted sesame seeds

Place sugar, paprika, mustard, salt, Worcestershire sauce and onion juice in a large mixing bowl. Beat until well blended, using medium speed on mixer. Add the oil very gradually. After all oil has been added, pour in vinegar gradually, beating constantly at medium speed. Add sesame seeds. (To toast seeds, place on a cookie sheet and bake at 300° until golden brown, not dark.) The dressing keeps indefinitely in refrigerator in a covered jar. Shake well if the dressing separates. This is good on any fruit salad.

HONEY DRESSING FOR FRUIT SALAD

Yield: 1 pint

⅓ cup sugar
1 teaspoon paprika
1 teaspoon celery seed
¼ teaspoon salt
⅓ cup honey

⅓ cup apple cider vinegar
1 tablespoon lemon juice
1 teaspoon grated onion
1 cup salad oil

Mix all ingredients except oil. Add oil while beating constantly, or mix in blender. Must be very well mixed.

AUNT JEAN'S MAYONNAISE

Yield: 1 pint

1 whole egg
1 egg yolk
Juice of large lemon
Dash of mustard
Dash of onion salt

Dash of paprika
Salt to taste
Dash of cayenne
1½ cups vegetable oil

Mix all ingredients except oil in blender; slowly add oil beating constantly until well blended.

CREAMY FRENCH DRESSING

Yield: 1¼ cups

2 teaspoons salt
1 teaspoon coarse black pepper
1 teaspoon paprika
½ teaspoon powdered sugar
½ teaspoon dry mustard

Dash cayenne
¼ cup vinegar
1 egg yolk, beaten
1 cup salad oil

Mix dry ingredients with vinegar. Add the beaten egg yolk. Add the oil. Shake or beat before using.

SOUR CREAM SALAD DRESSING

Yield: 3 cups

1½ cups sour cream
½ cup cider vinegar
¾ cup salad oil
2 tablespoons grated onion
2 tablespoons horseradish

2 tablespoons capers
1 teaspoon dill seeds
1 teaspoon paprika
1 teaspoon salt
Pepper to taste

Combine all ingredients in jar. Cover and shake well before using. Good as a dressing for marinated green beans.

SOUR CREAM FRUIT SALAD DRESSING

Yield: 2 cups

2 eggs, beaten
¾ cup sugar
½ cup pineapple juice

⅓ cup lemon juice
1 small carton sour cream

Combine eggs, sugar, pineapple juice and lemon juice in saucepan. Cook over medium heat, stirring constantly, until mixture thickens. Remove from heat and cool. Fold in sour cream and chill thoroughly before serving.

POPPY SEED DRESSING

Yield: 3 cups

½ cup sugar
2 teaspoons dry mustard
2 teaspoons salt
⅔ cup vinegar

3 tablespoons onion juice
2 cups salad oil
3 tablespoons poppy seeds

Mix sugar, salt, mustard and vinegar. Add onion juice. Stir slowly, adding oil. Beat constantly with electric beater at medium speed until thick. Add poppy seed. Serve over fruit or avocado salad.

CREAM CHEESE DRESSING

Yield: 1 cup

1 3-ounce package cream cheese
1 tablespoon lemon juice
¾ cup cream

2 tablespoons currant jelly
or raspberry jelly

Mash cream cheese with a fork and beat until smooth. Slowly beat in remaining ingredients. Chill for at least 1 hour before serving. Serve on fruit salad.

El Paso Daily Times   July 20, 1890
            Link Restaurant
            218 El Paso St.
            Short Order House and Restaurant
            Open day or night

Border Blends

SANDWICHES AND SOUPS

HINTS FOR SOUPS & SANDWICHES

Day old bread is best for sandwiches unless they are to be rolled.

When making rolled sandwiches, steam the bread slices in a colander for 1 or 2 minutes. Slightly damp bread will roll easily without cracking.

Butter or margarine should be spread on both slices of bread to keep soft fillings from soaking into the bread.

Sandwiches may be made in advance and stored in waxed paper, plastic bags, or a cloth wrung out in cold water.

Sandwiches that are to be kept overnight should be refrigerated.

Sandwiches which use jelly, mayonnaise, or salad dressing as a spread do not freeze well, as these spreads soak into the bread, making it soggy. Also, lettuce, tomatoes, celery, raw carrots, and hard-cooked eggs do not freeze well.

Brush leftover sandwiches with melted butter and sauté for a fresh and delicious flavor.

A well-washed, unpeeled yellow onion adds color to stock or soup.

Always add salt to the water in cooking meat-stock soups. Salt draws out more meat flavor.

Refrigerate broth or stock overnight for ease in removing fat the following day. Skim fat off with a metal spoon or a piece of ice wrapped in a paper towel.

Dry sherry and Madeira blend well with bland soups ($\frac{1}{4}$ cup wine to 1 quart soup). For strongly flavored soups, use dry red wine ($\frac{1}{2}$ cup wine to 1 quart soup).

Vegetables should be added to soups during the last half hour of cooking.

For strong meat broth, allow 2 cups water to each pound of meat, fat, and bone.

Soup made from fresh meat requires at least 4 hours simmering, covered, in which time the original amount will be reduced by 1/4 to 1/5.

Always roast bones in the oven before using in soup.

Simmer soups and stews; do not let them boil.

Add flavor and thickening to stews with a little oatmeal, quick-cooking oats, or grated potato.

Garnish consommé, green pea, or tomato soup with avocado slices. Other good soup garnishes include paprika, finely-chopped chives or fresh dill, grated cheese, and slivers of ham or chicken.

TUNA PUFF SANDWICH

Serves: 6

1 7-ounce can tuna, drained
 and flaked*
1½ teaspoons prepared mustard
¼ teaspoon Worcestershire sauce
¼ cup mayonnaise
1½ teaspoons grated onion
2 tablespoons chopped bell
 pepper or green chile

3 hamburger buns or split
 English muffins
6 tomato slices
½ cup mayonnaise
¼ cup finely shredded
 American cheese

Blend first six ingredients; pile onto bun halves. Top each with tomato slice. Blend ½ cup mayonnaise with cheese; spread on tomato slice. Broil four inches from heat until topping puffs and browns.

*5-ounce can lobster, 7½-ounce can crabmeat or 2 5-ounce cans shrimp may be used instead of tuna.

CURRIED TUNA SANDWICHES

Yield: 8 sandwiches

1 7-ounce can tuna
½ cup diced celery
¼ cup chopped almonds
½ cup flaked coconut
½ cup mayonnaise

¾ teaspoon curry powder
⅛ teaspoon pepper
1 tablespoon fresh lemon
 juice
8 slices toast

Mix all ingredients. Spread on toast and broil for 3 minutes or until lightly browned.

GRILLED CHEESEBURGERS ON RYE

Serves: 4

1 pound lean ground beef
4 slices Cheddar cheese
4 large slices of canned
 green chile

8 slices rye bread
¼ cup butter or margarine

Make four beef patties and cook to desired doneness. Place a slice of cheese on each and top with a chile strip. Place each patty between 2 slices of bread. Spread with butter evenly on both sides and grill in a hot iron skillet until golden brown on both sides. Serve with cold potato salad or cole slaw.

PEPITA SANDWICH

Serves: 4

4 hard rolls
1 cup refried beans
1 cup guacamole

4 pieces round steak
Green chile strips (optional)

Spread half of roll with guacamole and half with beans. Cut steaks to size of roll. Broil or pan-broil steaks (charcoal broiled is delicious). Place on roll and top with green chile strips.

BAKED ASPARAGUS-CHEESE SANDWICH

Serves: 6   Oven: 325°

6 slices bread (¾-inch thick),
   or English muffins, halved
6 slices processed Swiss cheese
4 eggs
2 cups milk

1 teaspoon salt
¼ teaspoon nutmeg
1 tablespoon chopped onion
18 cooked asparagus spears
½ cup shredded Cheddar cheese

Trim crusts from bread and arrange in bottom of greased 13x9x2-inch pan or glass dish. Top bread with slice of Swiss cheese. Beat eggs slightly; add milk, seasonings and onion. Pour over sandwiches and bake 25 minutes. Remove from oven and top each bread slice with 3 cooked asparagus spears. Sprinkle on shredded cheese. Bake 10-15 minutes. Allow to stand 5 minutes.

CHEESE-TOPPED BROILED SANDWICHES

Serves: 8

4 English muffins, halved
   (or 8 slices of toast)
8 slices turkey, ham, chicken,
   or hard cooked eggs
8 slices American, Mozzarella,
   Muenster or Cheddar cheese

8 thick slices tomatoes
1 cup mayonnaise
⅔ cup finely shredded
   American cheese
1 4-ounce can chopped
   green chile

Toast muffins under broiler. Place slice of meat on each and top with a cheese and tomato slice. Mix remaining ingredients and spread over top. Broil four inches from heat until bubbly and golden brown.

HOT HAM AND CHEESE SANDWICHES

Serves: 8   Oven: 350°

½ cup butter, softened   8 large hamburger buns
½ cup mustard   8 slices Swiss cheese
½ cup dried onion   8 slices ham
2 tablespoons poppy seed

Combine mustard, onion and poppy seed with butter; spread on buns.
Add one slice ham and one slice cheese to each. Wrap in foil. Heat 15
minutes. These sandwiches can be frozen. Place directly from freezer
into a 400° oven for approximately 30 minutes. A great quickie lunch.

Variation: Mixture may be spooned onto smaller pre-cooked dinner rolls and topped
with a piece of cheese and ham. Makes a good hot hors d'oeuvre.

TURKEY AVOCADO TOASTWICHES

Serves: 6

2 cups diced   ½ cup mayonnaise
    cooked turkey   ½ teaspoon salt
½ cup finely diced celery   12 slices bread
1 cup diced avocado   ½ cup milk
1 tablespoon lemon juice   ½ cup melted butter
½ teaspoon grated onion   2 eggs, slightly beaten
2 tablespoons diced pimento

Combine first eight ingredients. Cover and refrigerate until ready to use.
Spread mixture on 6 slices of bread and top with 6 more slices. Quickly
dip sandwiches in mixture of milk, butter and eggs. Arrange on foil over
oven rack and broil until golden brown on each side, turning with a pancake turner. Can also use electric broiler or sandwich grill.

SUPER SANDWICH

Serves: 2

2 slices bread (rye or white)   2 slices chicken or turkey
1 ripe avocado, sliced   2 lettuce leaves
6-8 slices bacon, fried   Thousand Island dressing

Toast bread. Assemble as above and top with salad dressing. Serve open-
face.

SUPREME CHICKEN SANDIE

Yield: 48 tea-sized sandwiches

1 cup chicken, diced small
¼ cup crisp bacon,
   crumbled
¼ cup chopped filberts
¼ cup finely cut dates

Mayonnaise
Salt to taste
12 thin slices bread
Butter

Combine all ingredients except bread and butter. Butter bread and spread mixture sparingly. Trim in triangles.

FROSTED SANDWICHES

Serves: 8
                                        Oven: 375°

1 loaf sandwich bread
2 5-ounce cans boned chicken
4 hard cooked eggs, chopped
⅔ cup mayonnaise

2 5-ounce jars Kraft cheese
   spread
1 egg
½ cup softened butter
   or margarine

Cut large round from each bread slice. Combine chicken, eggs and mayonnaise and mix well. Spread filling on one bread round; top with another and spread again. Close sandwich with a third bread round. Combine cheese spread, egg and butter and beat until fluffy. Frost tops and sides of sandwiches. Let stand in refrigerator at least 24 hours. Bake 15 minutes. *This is great with a fresh fruit salad and potato chips for a very informal bridge luncheon.*

TORTAS

Serves: 4

4 Mexican rolls (or any hard
   rolls)
4 tablespoons refried beans

4 slices ham
4 slices cheese
4 tablespoons guacamole

Split rolls. Layer warmed refried beans, ham and cheese on bottom half of roll. Broil until cheese melts. Spread top of roll generously with guacamole. Put together for sandwich.

CHEESE PIMENTO CHILE SANDWICH

Serves: 10-12

1 pound Longhorn cheese, grated	1 cup chopped pecans
1 4-ounce can chopped green chile (hot)	½ cup chopped ripe olives
1 2-ounce can chopped pimento	3 tablespoons salad dressing
	Sandwich bread

Mix all ingredients together. Spoon onto bread slices which can be served open-faced or covered. Mixture may be prepared ahead of time. Delicious served as finger sandwiches.

CREAM CHEESE AND CHILE SANDWICHES

1 8-ounce package cream cheese, softened	2 teaspoons minced onion (fresh or dried)
2 tablespoons mayonnaise	Dash Tabasco
1 4-ounce can chopped green chile	Dash salt
	1 loaf thinly sliced bread

Mix cream cheese and mayonnaise with fork until spreadable. (It may be necessary to add more mayonnaise.) Add remaining ingredients and spread this mixture on bread slices. Prepare a day ahead and store in airtight container in refrigerator. Or, mix cream cheese filling ahead and spread sandwiches the day of the party. Cut into fourths and serve.

ONION SANDWICH

Serves: 4 regular, or 16 tea sandwiches

1 medium white onion	White or rye bread
Kraft Miracle French dressing	Mayonnaise
Butter	Paprika

Cut onion into thin slices. Dip into boiling water (use colander or strainer) and drain immediately. Chop fine and let cool. Marinate overnight in enough dressing to cover. Butter slices of bread; spread with marinated onions combined with mayonnaise. Trim crust and cut diagonally. Dust with paprika. Serve as open-faced tea sandwiches. Save marinade for salads.

GAZPACHO

Serves: 6-8

2 stale French rolls	¼ cup canned pimentos
2 pounds ripe tomatoes	2 small sweet onions
1 large cucumber	¼ cup olive oil
2 long green chiles	¼ cup vinegar

Crumble the 2 rolls. Soak in adequate water to form a thick paste and set aside. Liquify in blender peeled and seeded tomatoes, pared and seeded cucumbers, chiles, pimentos, onions, olive oil and vinegar. Pour mixture into a wooden bowl and mix in bread paste by hand. Chill at least 6 hours. Serve ice cold with garnishes of chopped tomatoes, cucumbers, green onion, green chile and croutons passed in separate bowls.

GAZPACHO WITH SOUR CREAM

Serves: 8-10

1 cucumber	Juice of 4 limes
½ onion or 3-4 scallions	3-4 dashes Tabasco
1 avocado	1 teaspoon salt
1 tomato	½ pint sour cream
1 bell pepper	Celery
6 tablespoons salad oil	Croutons
4 tablespoons wine vinegar	Bacon bits
8 cups tomato juice	

Chop first five ingredients. Mix with next six ingredients. Refrigerate. Serve with sour cream and pass bowls of chopped celery, croutons and bacon bits.

CURRIED AVOCADO SOUP

Serves: 6

1 ripe avocado	2 tablespoons white rum
1 cup light cream	½ teaspoon curry powder
Juice of 1 lime	Freshly ground pepper to taste
2 cups chicken broth	Chopped chives
½ teaspoon salt	

Put all ingredients except cream into blender. Blend thoroughly. Then add cream, running blender momentarily. Chill thoroughly. Serve with finely chopped chives on top. Cannot be prepared ahead or frozen.

AVOCADO CHEESE SOUP

Serves: 10-12

12 potatoes
1½ cups Monterrey Jack
cheese, grated
1 large onion, sliced
½ jalapeño chile
6 cups chicken stock

1 teaspoon flour
1 teaspoon butter or
margarine
1 cup heavy cream, scalded
Salt to taste
2 avocados

Combine in large saucepan 12 peeled and sliced potatoes, cheese, onion, chile and chicken stock. Bring to a boil; simmer until potatoes are soft. Put through fine strainer into saucepan and bring to a boil. Mix flour and butter. Slowly add to soup. Simmer for 5 minutes. Stir in scalded cream; add salt to taste. Garnish with slices of avocado. *Serve as an appetizer before flank steak.*

CHEESE SOUP

Serves: 5-6

¼ cup butter
2 tablespoons minced green
onions
½ cup thinly sliced carrots
¾ cup celery, minced
2 cups chicken stock, or 2 cups
water and 2 chicken bouillon
cubes

¼ cup flour
1½ cups milk
2½ cups shredded American, or
sharp process cheese
1 tablespoon dried parsley
½ teaspoon seasoned salt

Melt butter and cook onions until golden. Stir in carrots, celery, chicken stock and salt. Simmer until vegetables are tender. Combine flour and ½ cup milk and blend into vegetable mixture stirring constantly until smooth and thick. Add cheese, parsley, and remaining milk. Stir and heat just until cheese melts. Do not boil!

SUMMER TOMATO SOUP

Serves: 6

3 10-ounce cans Heinz tomato
soup (must be Heinz)
2 pints sour cream

1 medium Bermuda onion, minced
Juice of 4 large limes
Parsley

Put all ingredients except parsley in blender. Whip until very smooth. Chill for 24 hours before serving. Garnish with parsley.

TORTILLA SOUP

Serves: 6

1 small onion, chopped	1 teaspoon ground cumin
1 4-ounce can chopped	1 teaspoon chile powder
green chile	1 teaspoon salt
2 cloves garlic, crushed	⅛ teaspoon pepper
2 tablespoons oil	2 teaspoons Worcestershire
1 cup tomatoes, peeled	sauce
and chopped	1 tablespoon bottled steak
1 can condensed beef bouillon	sauce
1 can condensed chicken broth	3 tortillas, cut in ½-inch
1½ cups water	strips
1½ cups tomato juice	¼ cup shredded Cheddar cheese

Sauté onion, chile and garlic in oil until soft. Add tomatoes, bouillon, chicken broth, water, tomato juice, cumin, chile powder, salt, pepper, Worcestershire and steak sauce. Bring soup to a boil; lower heat, simmer covered for 1 hour. Add tortillas and cheese and simmer 10 minutes longer.

JOE'S ALBONDIGA SOUP
(MEXICAN MEATBALL SOUP)

Serves: 4

3 onions	Fresh cilantro leaves, if
3 tablespoons bacon grease	available*
16-ounce can tomatoes	3 raw tortillas
1 4-ounce can chopped	1 pound extra lean ground beef
green chile	1 egg
1 quart water	1 clove garlic, crushed
3 bouillon cubes	Salt and pepper
¼ teaspoon cumin powder	

Dice onions and sauté in 3 tablespoons bacon grease. Add tomatoes, green chile, water, bouillon cubes, salt and pepper to taste, cumin powder and cut-up cilantro leaves. Cook at least 30 minutes, adding water as necessary to make a good pot of soup. Cut tortillas into tiny slivers. Work into ground meat with the egg, garlic, salt, pepper and cumin powder. Shape into tiny balls about the size of a marble. Drop into soup. When the meat balls float, soup is ready to serve.

*½ teaspoon ground coriander may be substituted.

FRIJOL CHEESE SOUP

Serves: 10

1 pound bacon
2 large onions
2½-pound can tomatoes
1 can water

6-8 stalks of celery, chopped
1 pound Cheddar cheese
2 pounds pinto beans, cooked
1-2 teaspoons vinegar

Cut bacon into small pieces and fry. Drain and sauté onions in the fat. Remove. Combine bacon and onions; add tomatoes and 1 can water. Chop celery and add to the tomato mixture along with grated Cheddar cheese. Simmer until cheese is melted and thoroughly mixed with other ingredients. Purée cooked frijoles in a blender; add to tomatoes. This will probably be very thick and can be thinned with water or tomato juice. Add vinegar; stir and season to taste.

SHERRY SOUP

Serves: 6

10½-ounce can green pea soup
10½-ounce can mushroom soup
2 cups half-and-half

10½-ounce can tomato soup
1 7-ounce can minced clams
¼ cup sherry

Mix first five ingredients together and simmer 5 minutes. Add sherry and mix well. Serve with chopped parsley sprinkled on top. Cannot be prepared ahead or frozen.

TOMATO BOUILLON

Serves: 5-6

3 cups canned tomato juice
1 thick sliced onion
1 stalk celery, sliced
1 bay leaf
4 whole cloves

10½-ounce can condensed
    consommé
½ cup California red table wine
Salt and pepper
Slices of lemon

Combine tomato juice, onion, celery, bay leaf and cloves in a saucepan. Bring to a boil. Cover and simmer for 20 minutes. Strain. Add consommé, wine, salt and pepper. Serve very hot in bouillon cups. Float slice of lemon in each cup.

POTATO SOUP WITH LEEKS

Yield: 8 cups

3 tablespoons butter
3 cups sliced leeks (white part)
3 tablespoons flour
2 quarts hot water
1 tablespoon salt

1 cup sliced leeks (green part)
4 cups peeled potatoes, chopped
½ cup heavy cream or sour cream
2-3 tablespoons minced parsley
or chives

Melt butter in a 4-quart saucepan over moderate heat; stir in white part of leeks. Cover pan and cook slowly 5 minutes without browning. Blend in flour and stir over heat for 2 minutes. Remove from heat and let cool. Gradually blend in about a cup of hot water until blended with flour; add the rest of the water, salt, green part of leeks and potatoes. Bring to boil; simmer, partially covered, 30-40 minutes until vegetables are tender. Add salt and pepper if needed. Set aside uncovered until ready to serve. Reheat to simmer just before serving and stir in cream. Garnish with parsley or chives.

CALDO DE QUESO

Serves: 6

2 cups celery, chopped
½ bell pepper, chopped
½ cup water
2 10¾-ounce cans cream of
    mushroom soup
2 cans water
½ cup tomato purée

¼ teaspoon ground coriander
½ teaspoon white pepper
¼ cup sour cream
2 cups grated Cheddar cheese
½ cup dry sherry
2 tablespoons chopped parsley
Milk

Cover and cook celery and green pepper in water until tender. Drain. Over low heat blend soup with equal parts water. Purée the soup with vegetables in a blender, or put through a fine sieve. Pour into a double-boiler over hot water. Cook and stir while adding tomato purée, ground coriander, white pepper, sour cream and Cheddar cheese until the mixture is smooth and hot. Add dry sherry and chopped parsley. Thin with milk if too thick. Soup can be prepared ahead but not frozen.

ONION SOUP WITH WHITE WINE

Serves: 6

6 tablespoons butter	Large croutons, fried in butter
4 large onions, finely chopped	½ cup Gruyere cheese
3 cups chicken broth	½ cup Parmesan cheese
1 cup dry white wine	Chopped green onion
Salt and freshly ground pepper to taste	Chopped parsley

Melt butter in skillet and add chopped onions. Cover tightly and steam over a very low flame until very soft. Add chicken broth and wine. Simmer 15 to 20 minutes. Season to taste. Sprinkle fried croutons with grated cheese and put under the broiler to melt cheese. Serve in a large heated tureen. Put croutons in each soup bowl and ladle soup over them. Serve garnished with raw onion and parsley. Cannot be prepared ahead or frozen.

CREAMY CHILLED ONION SOUP

Serves: 8

4 cups onion, chopped	2 egg yolks
¼ teaspoon leaf rosemary, crumbled	1 cup light cream
	2 teaspoons lemon juice
6 tablespoons butter	1 teaspoon salt
2 13-ounce cans chicken broth	¼ teaspoon pepper

In a large skillet sauté onion and rosemary in butter until very soft, but not brown. Remove from heat and cool. Pour half of the onion mixture into electric blender. Cover and whirl until smooth. Combine purée with chicken broth. Lower heat and simmer 5 minutes. Beat egg yolks slightly in small bowl; add cream and beat until smooth. Beat egg mixture slowly into remaining mixture in saucepan. Stirring constantly, cook 1 minute. Remove from heat and add lemon juice, salt and pepper and other mixture. Pour into large bowl. Cover and chill for 4 hours. Pour into chilled serving dishes and garnish with parsley. Serve ice cold.

El Paso Daily Times   July 20, 1890
A. Goodman
Wholesale Grocer
Opera House Building—316 El Paso St.
Mexican Beans and all kinds of White Beans specialty

BLACK BEAN SOUP

Serves: 8

3 cups black beans	1 quart beef stock
1 ham bone	1½ teaspoons garlic powder
½ pound salt pork	2 medium onions, chopped
1 bay leaf	1 large carrot, chopped
⅛ teaspoon thyme	1 tablespoon sherry
3 quarts water	Salt and pepper to taste

Cook all ingredients except sherry, salt and pepper until beans are very tender. Remove bay leaf, pork and ham bone. Pour soup, a little at a time, into blender and liquify. When smooth, return soup to stove and heat. Add salt, pepper and sherry. Cool and place in plastic containers for storing, or serve hot.

CUCUMBER DILL SOUP

Serves: 3-4

2 large cucumbers	1 tablespoon lemon juice
1 medium onion	1 teaspoon crushed dill seed
¼ cup margarine	Salt to taste
1½ cups chicken stock	½ pint sour cream

Peel cucumbers. Cut several thin slices and put in ice water. Save these cucumbers for garnish. Chop remaining cucumber and onion. Sauté in margarine until wilted but not brown. Blend in blender. Return to saucepan. Add chicken stock, lemon juice, dill seed and salt; simmer 5 minutes. Chill 6 hours. Just before serving stir in sour cream. Garnish with crisp cucumber slices and sprinkle with fresh or dried dill. If desired, add 1 or 2 drops of green food coloring.

VEGETABLE SOUP

Serves: 10

3-4 pound chuck roast	3 zucchini squash, sliced
2 onions	3 carrots, sliced
Salt and pepper	2 cups fresh cooked green
4 quarts water	beans
¼ cup Worcestershire sauce	3 large tomatoes, peeled
¾ cup catsup	3 celery stalks, sliced

Cook roast, onion, salt and pepper in water until tender. Cool; take meat apart with hands, removing fat. Put meat back in pot and add all other ingredients. Simmer most of the day. Serve a day later, as flavor is not absorbed until then.

From Rio Grande Garden

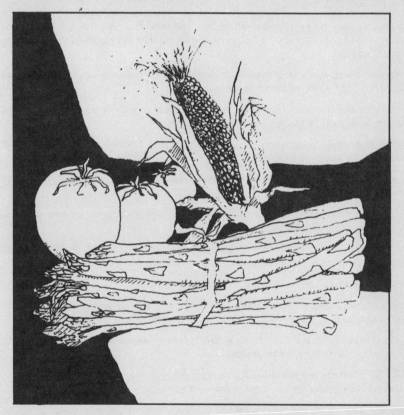

VEGETABLES

HINTS FOR VEGETABLES

When making cream sauce, melt butter over low heat; remove. Using a wide spatula, stir in flour; add milk gradually, stirring constantly. Return to heat and stir constantly. Bring to a boil and cook until sauce is thickened.

To keep green vegetables green, add ⅛ teaspoon soda to the cooking water. To keep white vegetables white, add ½ teaspoon vinegar.

Add chopped walnuts or pecans to wild rice during the last few minutes of cooking for a delicious flavor.

Mushrooms may be kept in the refrigerator for several days or in the freezer for several months. They may be frozen as purchased or parboiled for 10 minutes before freezing.

Parsley will keep for a long time in the refrigerator if, after washing, it is placed in a covered jar while still slightly damp.

To enhance the flavor of vegetables, add a bouillon cube or a teaspoon of instant bouillon or a dash of sugar to the cooking water.

Onions that have been thinly sliced, covered with boiling water, drained, and chilled will be sweet and crisp.

To enhance the color and flavor of fresh peas, add a few pods to the cooking water.

For an attractive contrast, garnish light-colored vegetables with paprika or parsley, dark vegetables with parmesan cheese.

When doubling or tripling a recipe that calls for onions, do not double or triple the onions. Cut back 1/2 for doubling and 1/3 again for tripling.

Refrigerate onions before mincing to lessen fumes.

A little butter added to the water in which greens are cooked will eliminate the need for stirring and prevent the water from boiling over.

To keep sweet potatoes from turning dark, place in salted water (5 teaspoons to the quart) immediately after peeling.

Soak raw potatoes in cold water for at least 30 minutes before frying to improve crispness. For golden-brown color, sprinkle them lightly with flour before frying.

Use hot milk when mashing potatoes to keep them from becoming heavy or soggy. Add a teaspoon baking powder to make them light and creamy.

MARINATED VEGETABLES

Serves: 8-10

3 cups chicken broth
1 cup dry white wine
1 cup olive oil
½ cup lemon juice
6 parsley sprigs
2 cloves garlic, chopped
½ teaspoon thyme
10 peppercorns
1 teaspoon salt

24 white onions (1-inch in
   diameter), peeled*
1 pound zucchini
1 pound yellow squash
3 bell peppers, seeded and
   cut into ½-inch strips
½ pound whole green beans,
   trimmed

To make marinade, place first nine ingredients in saucepan and bring to a boil; cover and simmer slowly for 45 minutes. Strain marinade, squeezing out all juices. Return to saucepan and taste for seasoning. (It should be slightly over-seasoned.) Bring marinade to a boil and add onions; cover and cook for 20-30 minutes until just tender when pierced. Remove onions to another dish. Peel zucchini and yellow squash and slice 1-inch thick; add to simmering marinade and cook 10-15 minutes until barely done. Remove to dish with onions. Add green beans and peppers to marinade and cook 8-10 minutes until barely tender. Do not overcook vegetables as they soften as they cool. Pour marinade over all vegetables. Cover tightly with foil and let marinate in refrigerator for at least 4 hours. Drain well before serving.

*8 large white onions cut in eighths may be substituted. Other vegetables may be used, such as mushrooms, celery hearts, leeks, cucumbers or artichoke hearts.

PICKLED CARROTS AND MUSHROOMS

Yield: 1 gallon marinade

1 gallon baby carrots
½ gallon baby mushrooms
2 cups corn oil
½ cup cider or wine vinegar
½ cup fresh lemon juice
2 tablespoons tarragon vinegar
1 tablespoon parsley
2 tablespoons grated onion

1 tablespoon dry mustard
1 tablespoon dill seed
1 tablespoon thyme
3 bay leaves
1 teaspoon Tabasco
2 tablespoons marjoram
1 tablespoon black peppercorns
Salt

Marinate carrots and mushrooms in mixture for 24 hours. Turn by hand. Good for buffet cocktail parties.

VEGETABLE TRIO

Serves: 4

½ pound carrots, cut into
  julienne strips
½ pound green beans,
  cut into 1-inch pieces
¼ pound mushrooms,
  sliced

1 teaspoon salt
½ teaspoon thyme leaves
3 tablespoons butter or
  margarine

Place on sheet of heavy-duty foil to charcoal grill: carrots, green beans and mushrooms with salt and thyme leaves. Dot with butter. Fold foil over vegetables and seal ends. Cook on grill over medium coals 1 hour or until vegetables are tender-crisp. Serve from foil or spoon into medium bowl.

Alternate: To cook on stove, place all ingredients in medium saucepan over medium heat. Cover and cook, stirring occasionally, 15 minutes or until vegetables are tender-crisp.

PICKLED SQUASH

Yield: 6 pints

8 cups zucchini, or yellow
  squash
3 cups yellow onions
4 green bell peppers*
1 4-ounce can pimento

3 cups white vinegar
4 cups sugar
2½ teaspoons celery seed
2½ teaspoons mustard seed
1½ teaspoons turmeric

Wash and slice vegetables; spread flat and salt generously. Let stand 1 hour; drain. In large kettle combine sugar, vinegar, celery and mustard seed and bring to a boil. Add turmeric and vegetables except pimento. Stir often and boil for 10 minutes. (Keep pot covered until vegetables cook down.) When done, add pimento. Put into sterile jars, seal and store.

*2 red and 2 green bell peppers can be used, but omit pimento.

CHILE CORN

Serves: 10-12   Oven: 350°

3 1-pound cans white shoe
    peg corn, drained
4 4-ounce cans chopped
    green chile, drained
Slightly less than 13 ounces
    evaporated milk

2 cups fine cracker crumbs
5 ounces mild Cheddar cheese,
    grated
½ cup butter, melted

Combine corn, chile, evaporated milk, 1¼ cups of the cracker crumbs, Cheddar cheese and butter. Place in 3-quart casserole. Sprinkle top with remaining ¾ cup cracker crumbs. Bake approximately 50 minutes. This recipe may be frozen uncooked.

CHILE CORN PUDDING

Serves: 4   Oven: 350°

10-ounce can whole
    green chile
1-pound can cream style corn
1 tablespoon flour
2 eggs, well beaten
¼ cup butter, melted

⅓ cup milk
½ teaspoon salt
Pepper and savory salt
    to taste
Grated cheese

Split chile and line bottom of greased pyrex baking dish. Mix other ingredients and cover chile. Cover generously with grated cheese. Bake for 30 minutes or until set.

CHILE-CHEESE GRITS

Serves: 10-12   Oven: 250°

6 cups water
1½ cups grits (uncooked)
2 teaspoons salt
3 eggs, beaten
1 pound Longhorn cheese,
    grated
3 teaspoons savory salt

Dash Tabasco
Dash paprika
½ cup butter
Dash Worcestershire sauce
1 4-ounce can chopped green
    chile

Bring water to a boil. Cook grits according to instructions on box. Add remaining ingredients. Mix well. Bake in oblong dish for 1½-2 hours. This may be prepared ahead and refrigerated. Good with barbecue beef or chicken.

CHILE HOMINY CASSEROLE

Serves: 8-10   Oven: 350°

2 20-ounce cans hominy, drained   1 4-ounce can chopped green
3 tablespoons grated onion   chile
1½ cups sour cream   Salt to taste
1½ cups shredded Jack cheese   ½ cup fine bread crumbs

Mix all together except bread crumbs. Sprinkle bread crumbs on top.
Bake for 30 minutes.

MEXICAN HOMINY

Serves: 6   Oven: 350°

2 tablespoons bacon grease   2 1-pound 15-ounce cans
2 tablespoons flour   white hominy
2 tablespoons chile powder   ¼ cup butter
16-ounce can tomatoes   ¾ cup Cheddar cheese,
2 cups water   grated
1 teaspoon salt   1 cup onion, chopped
¼ teaspoon leaf oregano,
    crumbled

Combine bacon grease, flour, chile powder, tomatoes, water, salt and
oregano in a large bowl. Toast hominy in butter until lightly browned in
a heavy skillet. Layer half the hominy, ½ cup cheese, onion and the
tomato-chile mixture in a lightly greased 6-cup baking dish; repeat with
remaining ingredients, reserving ¼ cup of cheese for the top. Bake in
oven for 25 minutes. Serve with hot Chile Sauce.

CHILE SAUCE:

1 4-ounce can hot green chile   16-ounce can tomatoes
    peppers, drained, seeded   1 teaspoon salt
    and chopped   1 small onion, quartered

Place all ingredients in blender and mix until smooth. Refrigerate until
ready to serve.

CORN BAKE

Serves: 10   Oven 350°

3 eggs, slightly beaten
1 8½-ounce package
  corn muffin mix
1 8-ounce can cream style corn
2 16-ounce cans whole kernel
  corn, drained

1 cup dairy sour cream
½ cup melted butter
1 cup shredded cheese
1 4-ounce can chopped
  green chile

Combine all ingredients except the cheese. Bake for 1 hour. Put cheese on top for the last 15 minutes.

POSOLE
(VEGETABLE)

Serves: 6   Oven: 350°

3 tablespoons butter
3 tablespoons flour
1½ cups milk
½ teaspoon garlic salt
½ teaspoon onion salt
½ teaspoon pepper

½ teaspoon dry mustard
1½ cups sharp cheese, grated
3½ cups hominy, drained
1 4-ounce can chopped green
  chile
2½ cups whole kernel corn

Make sauce by lightly browning butter and flour. Slowly stir in milk and seasonings. When thickened, add cheese. It isn't necessary for cheese to melt completely. Mix in hominy, corn and chile. Pour into buttered 1½-quart casserole. Bake 30 minutes.

CHILE QUICHE

Yield: 40 squares   Oven: 325°

3 sticks pie crust mix
2 4-ounce cans chopped
  green chile
4 tablespoons flour
1 pound Swiss cheese, grated

Salt and pepper to taste
2 tablespoons onion flakes
6 eggs
2 cups milk, heated

Prepare crust and fit into 12x15-inch cookie sheet (with sides). Drain chile; spread over crust. Mix flour with grated cheese; add salt, pepper and onion flakes. Beat eggs with milk; add to cheese mixture. Pour over crust and bake 30-40 minutes. Quiche is done when knife is inserted and comes out clean. Cut into 2-inch squares.

SCALLOPED CARROTS

Serves: 6   Oven: 350°

3 tablespoons butter
3 tablespoons flour
1½ cups milk
½ teaspoon salt
Dash of pepper

⅓ cup grated cheese
1 tablespoon finely chopped onion
4 cups cooked carrots
½ cup bread crumbs
3 slices bacon, rendered

Make a white sauce of butter, flour and milk. Add salt and pepper, grated cheese and onion. In a casserole, place a layer of carrots alternately with white sauce until dish is full. Cover with bread crumbs and bacon. Bake until bacon is crisp.

ZUCCHINI SLIPPERS

Serves: 6-8   Oven: 350°

6 zucchini squash
  (6-7 inches)
3 eggs, well beaten
2¼ cups shredded Cheddar
  cheese

¾ cup small curd cottage cheese
3 tablespoons chopped
  parsley
½ teaspoon salt
Dash of pepper

Cut off ends of zucchini, scrub well and cook whole in enough boiling salted water to cover until tender but still firm (about 12 minutes). Cut each in half lengthwise. Scoop out center pulp and discard; invert shell to drain briefly on paper towels. Meanwhile mix eggs, cheese, parsley, salt and pepper. Fill zucchini "slippers" with cheese mixture and bake in a buttered dish uncovered 15 minutes. Raise oven temperature to 450° for 5 minutes to lightly brown cheese.

CALABACITAS
(SQUASH WITH CORN)

Serves: 6-8

2 pounds summer, or
  crookneck squash
1 small onion, minced
3 ears corn, cut from cob
6 green chiles, roasted and
  peeled

1 tablespoon lard or bacon
  drippings
½ teaspoon salt
½ cup water

Thinly slice squash and chile. Sauté onion in lard and salt. Add corn and fry until golden brown. Pour water into frying pan. Add squash and chile. Cover and simmer 15-20 minutes or until corn is tender.

SQUASH-SWISS CHEESE CASSEROLE

Serves: 12   Oven: 350°

3-4 pounds fresh yellow   3 cups milk
    squash, or 4 boxes frozen   Dash salt
    crookneck squash   1 teaspoon seasoned salt
1 onion, minced   Several dashes ground nutmeg
Chopped parsley   Dash Worcestershire sauce
2 bay leaves   4 egg yolks, beaten
½ teaspoon thyme   1⅓ cups shredded Swiss cheese
6 tablespoons butter   Dash cayenne
6 tablespoons flour   Buttered bread crumbs

Put sliced squash into large saucepan with onion, bay leaf, parsley and thyme. Cover with boiling salted water and cook until barely tender. Drain and remove parsley and bay leaf. Make sauce of butter, flour and milk, stirring until thickened. Add seasoned salt, nutmeg and Worcestershire sauce. Remove from heat and gradually add egg yolks. Stir in 1 cup of cheese and cayenne. Combine squash with sauce and put into buttered baking dish 2 inches deep. Mix remaining cheese with buttered bread crumbs. Sprinkle over squash. Bake for about 35 minutes.

ZUCCHINI FRITTERS

Serves: 6-8

5 eggs, separated   ½ onion, minced
5 tablespoons flour   1 cup tomato purée
3 large zucchini squash   2 cups water or chicken stock
1 pound Monterrey or   1 teaspoon oregano
    Velveeta cheese   Salt and pepper to taste
1 cup oil

Beat egg whites very stiff, but not dry. Beat egg yolks separately and fold gradually into whites. Fold in flour. Parboil zucchini and slice into rounds. Place a slice of cheese between 2 slices of zucchini. With fingers lift zucchini and cheese carefully and dip into the batter, coating thoroughly. Fry in hot oil until golden brown. Drain on paper towel. Brown onion in ¼ cup of remaining oil. Add tomato purée and stock or water. Rub oregano between palms of hands into sauce and season with salt and pepper. Cook 20 minutes. Just before serving, drop fritters into sauce, heating thoroughly. Serve immediately.

ZUCCHINI PANCAKES

Serves: 8

3 cups zucchini, finely
    chopped
1 egg
Salt and pepper to taste

½ cup flour
1 teaspoon baking powder
Melted butter
Grated Parmesan cheese

Combine zucchini, egg and salt and pepper. Sift flour and baking powder over it. Drop the mixture by one-fourth cupfuls (or less) on a lightly buttered griddle. Brown on both sides. Be sure griddle is not too hot, as zucchini needs time to cook. Serve with melted butter and grated Parmesan cheese.

ZUCCHINI AND TOMATOES

Serves: 6
Oven: 375°

6 zucchini squash
½ cup sliced onion
4 tablespoons olive oil
2 tablespoons chopped parsley

Salt and pepper to taste
3 fresh tomatoes, sliced thin
½ cup Parmesan or Romano
    cheese

Slice zucchini and cook in boiling water until tender (approximately 5 minutes). Sauté onion in oil; add parsley and remove from heat. Drain zucchini well. Place in oblong buttered casserole in layers of zucchini, thin sliced tomatoes and onion mixture. Do not drain olive oil from onions. Sprinkle with salt and pepper and top with cheese. Bake for 30 minutes.

MEXICAN SQUASH OR GREEN BEANS

Serves: 6-8

6 zucchini squash, sliced (or
    1 pound fresh green beans)
1 onion, chopped
2 tablespoons margarine
1 3-ounce can sliced mushrooms
1 4-ounce can chopped green chile
    (more if desired)

16-ounce can tomatoes or
    4 fresh tomatoes
½ tablespoon sugar
½ teaspoon pepper
1 teaspoon salt

Cook sliced zucchini squash or green beans in a little water. Drain. Sauté onion in margarine; add to squash. Mix in mushrooms and chile. Season with salt, pepper and sugar. Simmer over low heat for 30 minutes. Best made early in the day and reheated when ready to serve.

STUFFED SQUASH

Serves: 6   Oven: 350°

6 summer squash   1 cup grated Cheddar
1 cup canned corn   cheese
1 4-ounce can green chile,   Onion salt and pepper
   chopped

Cook squash in boiling, salted water until tender. Remove and cool. Remove stem portions from each squash. Remove pulp from center of each
squash and set squash shells aside. Chop pulp and mix with corn,
chopped chile, ½ cup of cheese, and onion salt and pepper to taste.
Stuff squash shells with cheese mixture and top with remaining ½ cup
cheese. Bake 20 minutes. Recipe can be prepared ahead, but cannot be
frozen.

SURPRISINGLY SQUASH

Serves: 6   Oven: 350°

2 pounds yellow squash   1 cup heavy cream
½ teaspoon salt   ¼ cup soft bread crumbs
Dash pepper   1 cup crushed salted peanuts
2 tablespoons butter   8 slices bacon, fried crisp
1 small onion, grated   and crumbled

Dice squash. Cook in small amount of salted water until tender. Drain
and mash squash. Add salt, pepper, butter, onion and cream. Mix well.
Butter baking dish and cover bottom and sides with bread crumbs. Spoon
squash into baking dish and bake for 50 minutes. Before serving, sprinkle with peanuts and bacon.

SOUTHERN YELLOW SQUASH

Serves: 6   Oven: 350°

2 pounds yellow squash   2 eggs, slightly beaten
2 medium onions, sliced   ½ cup evaporated milk
1 teaspoon salt   1 tablespoon sugar
½ teaspoon pepper   ½ cup bread crumbs
Dash of garlic salt   ¼ cup butter
½ teaspoon nutmeg

Cook squash and onions in small amount of salted water until tender.
Drain and mash until lumpy. Add all remaining ingredients except butter
and mix well. Place in buttered casserole; top with more bread crumbs
and dot with butter. Bake about 20 minutes or until bubbly.

Variation: Add 1 4-ounce can chopped green chile and 1 cup grated Longhorn
cheese. Omit nutmeg.

SQUASH EGGPLANT CASSEROLE

Serves: 6-8   Oven: 375°

4-6 large Italian squash
1 large eggplant
1 8-ounce package cream cheese,
   softened
1 tablespoon onion
2 tablespoons Worcestershire
   sauce

1 4-ounce can chopped green
   chile
2 eggs, slightly beaten
Bread crumbs
2 tablespoons Accent
Garlic salt and pepper

Wash and thinly slice squash. Peel and dice eggplant. Boil squash and eggplant; drain well. Mix cream cheese, drained chile and eggs. Add garlic salt and pepper to taste. Mix all ingredients. Place in buttered casserole with bread crumbs on top. Bake for 30 minutes.

EGGPLANT CASSEROLE

Serves: 4-5   Oven: 350°

1½ pounds eggplant
10-ounce can chile and
   tomatoes, drained
3 slices bacon

1 onion, chopped
2 hard cooked eggs
Buttered bread crumbs

Peel, chop and cook eggplant in salted water until tender. Drain. Cook bacon until crisp; crumble. Add chile, tomatoes and bacon to drained eggplant. Fry onion in the bacon drippings until tender. Add onions and chopped eggs to eggplant mixture. Top with bread crumbs; dot with butter and bake 20 minutes.

EGGPLANT SOUFFLE

Serves: 10   Oven: 325°

2 medium eggplants
2 tablespoons butter
2 slices toasted bread, broken
   into small pieces

4 eggs, beaten until fluffy
1 medium onion, diced fine
Salt and pepper to taste
4 large tablespoons Cheese Whiz

Peel, dice and cook eggplants until soft in a small amount of salted water. Drain, mash and add remaining ingredients. Mix and turn into a greased 10-inch casserole dish. Bake about 1 hour. More Cheese Whiz may be added if desired.

GRANDMA'S RED CABBAGE

Serves: 6-8

2 tablespoons bacon drippings
4 cups red cabbage, shredded or
   chopped
¼ cup brown sugar
¼ cup vinegar
¼ cup water

1¼ teaspoons salt
2 cups cubed, unpared apple
   (optional)
½ teaspoon caraway seed
   (optional)

Heat drippings in pan; add the remaining ingredients. Cover tightly and cook over low heat, stirring occasionally. Cook 15 minutes for crisp cabbage, 30-45 minutes for tender.

BRUSSELS SPROUTS AND CELERY

Serves: 6

3 tablespoons butter
2 cups thinly sliced celery
½ cup onion, diced
3 tablespoons flour

1 teaspoon celery salt
14-ounce can chicken broth
1½ pounds Brussels sprouts
   (3 frozen packages)

Melt butter in saucepan over low heat. Stir in celery and onion. Cook until just tender. Stir in flour, celery salt and chicken broth. Cook, stirring constantly, until sauce thickens. Cook Brussels sprouts; drain and add to celery and onion. Heat and serve.

EASY CAULIFLOWER TOMATO SCALLOP

Serves: 4-6   Oven: 400°

1 head cauliflower
1 teaspoon lemon juice
2 tablespoons margarine
½ cup chopped celery
¼ cup chopped onion
¼ cup chopped bell pepper
½ teaspoon salt

Scant pepper
10½-ounce can cheese soup
⅓ cup evaporated milk
3 tomatoes, sliced and
   peeled
¼ cup bread crumbs

Break cauliflower into flowerettes. Cook with lemon juice in boiling water about 5-7 minutes or until tender-crisp; drain. Sauté onion, celery and bell pepper in margarine. Add salt, pepper, cheese soup and milk; warm. In shallow pan layer cauliflower, tomatoes and sauce and top with crumbs. Bake 20-30 minutes. Broil to brown top.

CAULIFLOWER FRITTERS

Serves: 6

1 medium cauliflower	1 egg
½ cup all-purpose flour	⅓ cup milk
1 teaspoon baking powder	½ tablespoon vegetable oil
½ teaspoon salt	6 cups vegetable oil

Cook cauliflower until just tender; cool and separate into flowerettes. Prepare fritter batter. Sift together flour, baking powder and salt. Beat egg; add milk and ½ tablespoon oil. Make a well in dry ingredients; blend in liquid and beat well until smooth. Dip cauliflower pieces in batter and fry in oil at 375° until evenly browned. Serve as is, or with cheese sauce.

GRANDMOTHER'S CAULIFLOWER

Serves: 6-8   Oven: 350°

1 large head cauliflower	4 tablespoons flour
1 cup diced celery	2 cups milk
1 4-ounce can mushrooms, drained	2 cups cheese, grated
	12 crackers, crumbled
4 tablespoons butter	Salt and pepper

Boil cauliflower and celery until tender. Melt butter; add flour. Gradually add milk and cheese and cook until smooth; season with salt and pepper. Mix with cauliflower, celery and mushrooms. Put into well-greased casserole and top with cracker crumbs and dot with butter. Bake 30 minutes.

RELISH-STUFFED TOMATOES

Serves: 20

40 cherry tomatoes	3 tablespoons wine vinegar
1 4-ounce can green chile	1 teaspoon sugar
⅔ cup celery	Salt to taste
3 tablespoons green onions	

Cut a thin slice off the top of each tomato; scoop out inside with grapefruit knife or watermelon ball scoop. Finely chop green chile, celery and green onions. Make relish by mixing all ingredients except tomatoes. Stuff tomatoes with mixture and chill. This recipe can be prepared ahead but cannot be frozen.

BAKED CHEESE STUFFED TOMATOES

Serves: 8   Oven: 350°

4 large tomatoes
2 cups grated Swiss cheese
½ cup light cream
2 egg yolks, slightly beaten
2 tablespoons snipped chives
3 tablespoons onion, grated

½ teaspoon dried marjoram
  leaves
1 teaspoon dry mustard
1½ teaspoons salt
Dry bread crumbs
Melted margarine

Grease flat baking dish. Halve tomatoes crosswise. Scoop out pulp, leaving shells intact. Chop pulp coarsely. Combine tomato pulp with cheese, cream, egg yolks, chives, onion, marjoram, mustard and salt. Mix well. Spoon cheese mixture into tomato shells. Toss bread crumbs with melted margarine. Sprinkle over cheese mixture. Arrange tomato halves in prepared dish. Bake 25 minutes or until tender.

BROILED TOMATOES BROOKHOLLOW

Serves: 8   Oven: 350°

4 large, juicy ripe tomatoes
Italian salad dressing
1 6-ounce jar marinated
  artichoke hearts

Basil
Bread or cracker crumbs
Parmesan cheese
Butter

Peel and halve tomatoes early in the morning. Pour some Italian dressing over tomatoes in an ovenproof dish. Refrigerate. One hour before serving, remove from refrigerator; slice artichoke hearts and place on tomato halves. Sprinkle with basil, bread crumbs and Parmesan cheese. Place a dab of butter on top of each and bake for 20 minutes.

CHERRY TOMATO DISH

Serves: 6   Oven: 375°

2 pints cherry tomatoes, or 6
  tomatoes, sliced
1 onion, chopped
1 bell pepper, chopped
1 teaspoon chile powder
1 teaspoon oregano

Salt and pepper to taste
1 cup bread crumbs
2 tablespoons butter
1½ cups sharp Cheddar cheese,
  grated

Wash tomatoes and let dry. Butter an 8x12-inch casserole dish. Place tomatoes evenly on bottom. Cover with onion and pepper. Mix seasonings with bread crumbs and sprinkle over vegetables. Dot with butter and cover with cheese. Bake uncovered for 30 minutes.

BARBECUE BAKED BEANS

Serves: 6   Oven: 350°

2½ cups canned pork and beans   Minced onion, celery and
¼ cup catsup   bell pepper
2 tablespoons molasses   3 drops Tabasco sauce
2 tablespoons brown sugar   1 tablespoon prepared
2 tablespoons bacon drippings   mustard
                                                      Slices of bacon

Make sauce with catsup, molasses, brown sugar, bacon drippings; add
2 tablespoons each onion, celery and pepper. Mix well with beans. Add
Tabasco sauce and mustard. Place beans in greased shallow pyrex dish.
Dice bacon slices and add to beans. Bake covered 30 minutes; uncovered
30 minutes more.

RITZY ONION CASSEROLE

Serves: 6   Oven: 350°

4 pounds onions   1 pound Old English cheese,
1 cup butter   grated
                                                  ½ box Ritz crackers, crushed

Slice onions. Put into cold water and bring to a boil. Drain. Add more
water and salt and cook until transparent. In casserole, place onions
and butter and cool. Add cheese and sprinkle crackers over top. Heat
for 1 hour to serve.

FIDEO

Serves: 8-10   Oven: 350°

1 8-ounce package vermicelli   1 pound can tomatoes
¼ cup salad oil   10-ounce can chicken broth
1 medium onion, chopped finely   Salt and pepper to taste
1 clove garlic, minced   1 tablespoon cumin powder

Sauté vermicelli in salad oil until light brown. Drain on paper towels.
Place in a casserole. Brown onion and garlic. Add can of tomatoes and
chicken broth. Add salt, pepper and cumin powder. Cover the vermicelli
with sauce. Cover casserole and cook 1 hour, adding more chicken broth
as liquid is absorbed. *This is a perfect accompaniment to roast or steak.*

PILAF VERMICELLI

Serves: 8

¼ cup butter or margarine
¼ pound vermicelli noodles, uncooked
1 cup Uncle Ben's rice, uncooked
1 teaspoon salt
¼ cup white wine
10-ounce can chicken broth

¼ teaspoon powdered saffron (optional)
1 chicken bouillon cube
1 cup hot water
½ cup onion, coarsely chopped
1 cup celery, coarsely chopped
1 6½-ounce can sliced water chestnuts

Melt butter in saucepan. Add noodles and sauté until golden brown, stirring constantly. Blend in rice, salt, wine and broth. Bring to a boil and stir in saffron. Add bouillon cube, hot water, celery and onion and bring to a boil. Cover and simmer until liquid is absorbed (about 20-25 minutes). Add water chestnuts. This recipe may be prepared ahead. Reheat slowly by adding a little broth or water.

MUSHROOMS

2-3 pounds large, fresh mushrooms
1 small onion, finely chopped
½ cup butter (no substitute)

3 tablespoons Worcestershire sauce
1 tablespoon soy sauce
¼ cup Port or red wine

Wash and clean mushrooms; slice from top to bottom in fairly thick pieces. Sauté onion and mushrooms in butter for 5 minutes, covering the mushrooms well with the butter. Add the Worcestershire sauce, soy sauce and wine. Continue cooking until most of the moisture cooks away and the liquid remaining is thickened. Turn heat to very low; cook covered for about 15 minutes. Serve over steak that has been charcoal broiled.

MUSHROOM CASSEROLE

Serves: 3   Oven: 350°

1 pound fresh mushrooms
10-ounce package crumbled Cheddar cheese
⅜-ounce package broken pecans

1 slightly beaten egg
¼ cup cream
⅛ cup butter or margarine
Salt and pepper to taste

Peel, stem and wash mushrooms. Place layer of mushrooms in heavily buttered flat casserole. Add cheese, pecans, cream, egg, butter, salt and pepper. Make only two layers. Bake uncovered for 30 minutes.

MUSHROOM PIE

Serves: 4-5   Oven: 350°

⅓ cup butter
1 medium onion, chopped
1 pound whole fresh button
    mushrooms (or large
    mushrooms, sliced)
1 tablespoon flour

½ cup light cream
1 tablespoon cognac or sherry
Salt and freshly ground pepper
    to taste
2 unbaked 8-inch pastry shells

In a skillet, heat butter and sauté onion until transparent. Wipe mushrooms with a damp cloth. Trim off ends of stems. Add to the onions and cook, stirring occasionally, 4-5 minutes. Stir in the flour, add cream and bring to a boil, continuing to stir. Add cognac, salt and pepper to taste. Cool while making pastry. Turn the cooled mushrooms into pastry-lined pan. Arrange strips of pastry over top in lattice fashion. For a glazed top, brush the pastry with milk. Bake on lower shelf of oven until crust is brown (about 20 minutes).

SPINACH MOLD

Serves: 4-6   Oven: 350°

5 tablespoons butter or margarine
2 tablespoons bread crumbs
3 tablespoons chopped onion
10-ounce package chopped frozen
    spinach (thawed and
    squeezed dry)
3 tablespoons flour

1 cup milk
3 egg yolks
¼ cup Parmesan cheese
Fresh ground pepper
Salt
3 egg whites

With 1 tablespoon butter, grease a 1-quart charlotte mold, casserole, or metal mold with cover. Dust mold with bread crumbs; tap out excess. In skillet melt 2 tablespoons butter over moderate heat. Cook onions until transparent; stir in spinach and cook 2-3 minutes or until moisture is gone and spinach sticks lightly to pan. Remove from heat. Melt 2 tablespoons butter in saucepan; stir in flour, then milk. Cook, stirring constantly until sauce is thick and smooth. Remove from heat; stir in egg yolks one at a time. Stir in cheese and spinach mixture. Season with salt and pepper to taste. Cool slightly. Beat egg whites until stiff. Stir 1 heaping tablespoon into spinach mixture. Fold in remaining egg whites. Turn into buttered mold. Place mold in larger pan with water reaching half-way up side. Cover and bake on middle shelf for about 1 hour. Should be firm to the touch.

SPINACH SURPRISE

Serves: 6   Oven: 350°

6 tablespoons flour
6 eggs, slightly beaten
1 quart small curd cottage
   cheese
8 slices American cheese,
   broken into pieces

1 package frozen spinach
   (thawed, drained and
   chopped)
½ cup margarine, cubed

Beat flour into eggs; add cottage cheese and mix well. Stir in remaining ingredients. Bake in a 9x13-inch greased pan for 1 hour.

SPINACH CASSEROLE

Serves: 6-8   Oven: 325°

3 tablespoons butter
3 tablespoons chopped onion
1 pound mushrooms, finely
   chopped
3 tablespoons flour
2 teaspoons salt
¼ teaspoon nutmeg

¼ teaspoon pepper
2 cups half-and-half
3 10-ounce packages frozen
   spinach
4 tablespoons grated
   Swiss cheese

Sauté onions and mushrooms in butter until transparent. Blend in flour, salt, pepper and nutmeg. Gradually add the half-and-half and stir until thick. In a well-buttered baking dish, spread half the uncooked spinach. Cover with half the mushroom sauce and repeat. Bake 15 minutes. Sprinkle cheese on top and return to oven; bake until cheese is melted.

TEXAS GREEN BEANS

Serves: 6-8

1 pound green beans
1 cup diced salt pork
1 small onion, chopped
1 clove garlic, chopped

2 cups tomatoes
Pinch nutmeg
1 tablespoon chile powder
Salt to taste

Snap and cut beans. Cook in enough water to prevent scorching. Fry salt pork, removing all fat except 4 tablespoons. Add onion and garlic to fat and salt pork. Cook until onion is done. Add cooked beans, tomatoes, nutmeg, chile powder and salt. Boil for 10-15 minutes.

PICANTE BEANS

Serves: 8

2-2½ tablespoons horseradish
1 pint sour cream
Vinegar
Mustard
Worcestershire sauce
Paprika

1 scant teaspoon cayenne
¼ teaspoon salt
3 16-ounce cans green beans
   (Blue Lake)
Chopped parsley

Add horseradish to sour cream until taste is sharp and add vinegar until flavor is slightly acid. Add other ingredients (except beans and parsley) to taste, and until sauce is pink. Layer ungreased casserole with beans, parsley and sauce. Refrigerate overnight. Serve cold on pieces of lettuce or cabbage. *This is so highly spiced it must be served with bland meat, roast beef being a natural.*

Alternate: To make larger quantities for a buffet, increase horseradish to 3 table-spoons for four times the recipe, and add Tabasco if a hotter flavor is desired.

GREEN BEANS SAVORY

Serves: 6

1 pound fresh green beans (or
   10-ounce package frozen
   green beans)
¼ cup water
¼ teaspoon salt
½ teaspoon sugar
Dash cayenne
⅛ teaspoon monosodium
   glutamate

¼ teaspoon soy sauce
1 medium onion, chopped
2 egg yolks
½ cup cream (sweet or sour)
Juice of 1 lemon
4 sprigs parsley, chopped

If using fresh green beans, cut into lengthwise slivers. Drop beans into mixture of boiling water, salt, sugar, cayenne, monosodium glutamate, soy sauce and chopped onion. Cover tightly and cook slowly 10-15 minutes or until tender when tested with a fork. Little liquid is left. Pour mixture of beaten egg yolks, cream, lemon juice and parsley into cooked beans. Heat slowly until sauce thickens slightly (do not boil; it will curdle). Stir constantly.

DILLED GREEN BEANS

Serves: 4

1 pound can whole or cut green beans (or 2 cups fresh cooked green beans)
1 cup liquid from beans*
2 tablespoons butter
2 tablespoons flour

1½ teaspoons dill seed
½ teaspoon instant or fresh minced onion
½ teaspoon vinegar
¼ teaspoon salt

In saucepan, melt butter and blend in flour. Stir in bean liquid. Heat and stir until sauce thickens. Add dill seed, onion, vinegar and salt. Add drained beans, heat, and mix thoroughly.

*When using canned beans, it may be necessary to add water to liquid to make 1 cup.

GREEN BEANS SUPREME

Serves: 6-8   Oven: 350°

2 pounds whole green beans (or 2 10-ounce frozen packages)
2 cups sliced mushrooms
½ cup chopped onion
1 clove garlic, crushed
2 tablespoons butter or margarine

¾ cup sour cream
1 teaspoon salt
¼ teaspoon pepper
½ cup fresh bread crumbs
¼ cup grated Parmesan cheese

Snip both ends from green beans and cook in boiling salted water until barely tender (about 5 minutes). If using frozen beans, cook half as long as directed on package. Drain well. In skillet sauté mushrooms, onion and garlic in butter until tender. Add to beans together with sour cream, salt and pepper. Put into 2-quart buttered casserole and sprinkle top with mixture of bread crumbs and cheese. Bake 20-25 minutes or until top is bubbly and golden.

PICKLED BEETS

Yield: 2 quarts

2 1-pound cans whole beets
1 cup white wine vinegar
½ cup sugar
1 teaspoon salt

3 whole cloves
4 whole black peppercorns
1 small bay leaf
2 medium onions, sliced

Drain beets, reserving 1¼ cups liquid. Place beets in 2-quart sterilized jars. Combine vinegar, sugar, salt, cloves, peppercorns, bay leaf and reserved liquid. Simmer 5 minutes. Place onions in jars. Pour hot liquid over beets and onions. Refrigerate.

LUXE PEAS AND CELERY

Serves: 4*

2 tablespoons butter or
   margarine
½ cup celery slices,
   bias-cut
1 3-ounce can mushrooms,
   broiled, sliced and drained
2 tablespoons canned, chopped
   pimento

2 tablespoons green onion,
   finely chopped
½ teaspoon salt
¼ teaspoon savory
Dash freshly ground pepper
2 cups peas, drained

Melt butter in skillet. Add all remaining ingredients except peas. Cook uncovered stirring frequently until celery is crisp-done (about 5-7 minutes). Add peas and heat until very hot.

*For 30 people, fix five times the vegetables and use three 20-ounce packages frozen peas.

SHERRIED ASPARAGUS

Serves: 6-8

2 16-ounce cans asparagus, or
   3 pounds fresh asparagus
¼ cup asparagus juice
1 tablespoon dry sherry

2 tablespoons soy sauce
1 tablespoon cornstarch
2 tablespoons vegetable oil
¼-½ cup chicken stock

Mix all ingredients except asparagus in saucepan. Heat until thick. Add cooked asparagus and serve immediately.

ASPARAGUS VINAIGRETTE

Serves: 12

3 10-ounce packages frozen
   asparagus spears (or com-
   parable amount of fresh
   asparagus), blanched
⅓ cup cider vinegar

¾ cup vegetable oil
½ teaspoon salt
⅛ teaspoon pepper
1 tablespoon finely chopped
   pimento

Cook asparagus according to directions. Drain thoroughly. Place in shallow dish. Combine remaining ingredients; blend well. Pour over asparagus. Cover and refrigerate several hours. To serve, drain vinaigrette and arrange asparagus on serving platter. Garnish with pimento.

CRUSTY ASPARAGUS CASSEROLE

Serves: 12   Oven: 350°

2 20-ounce cans asparagus,   3 eggs, beaten
   chopped   2 cups milk
2 cups cheese cracker crumbs   1 teaspoon salt
1 cup grated American cheese   Dash of pepper
   (or Longhorn)   ⅓ cup butter, melted
1-ounce jar chopped pimentos

Combine asparagus, crumbs, cheese and pimentos. Pour into 9x13-inch baking dish. Mix remaining ingredients. Pour over asparagus mixture. Bake for 35-40 minutes.

ASPARAGUS QUICHE

Serves: 6-8   Oven: 375°

1 9-inch pastry shell (homemade),   2 cups heavy cream (1 cup
   baked 5 minutes   half-and-half, 1 cup
6 slices bacon   whipping)
1 large onion, sliced thin   4 eggs
1 cup cubed Swiss cheese   ¼ teaspoon nutmeg
2 tablespoons grated Parmesan   6 stalks asparagus, partially
   cheese   cooked
                                    Salt and pepper

Sauté bacon until crisp; crumble. Sauté onion in bacon grease until transparent. Combine bacon, onion and cheeses and put in bottom of pastry shell. Mix cream, eggs and seasonings; pour into shell. Top with asparagus stalks. Bake 35-40 minutes. Do not attempt this with anything other than a homemade shell. Serve warm with a green salad and a nice wine.

RICE BROCCOLI CASSEROLE

Serves: 8   Oven: 350°

1 cup rice   10¾-ounce can cream of
1 package frozen broccoli   mushroom soup
1 8-ounce jar Cheese Whiz   10¾-ounce can cream of
½ cup chopped celery   chicken soup
½ cup chopped onion   Paprika

Cook rice according to package directions. Add all other ingredients and put in casserole. Sprinkle with paprika. Bake 30-40 minutes.

BROCCOLI SUPREME

Serves: 4-6   Oven: 350°

1 egg, slightly beaten
10-ounce package frozen broccoli,
    partially thawed
1 8½-ounce can cream style corn
1 tablespoon grated onion
¼ teaspoon salt

Dash pepper
3 tablespoons butter or
    margarine
1 cup herb seasoned stuffing
    mix

Combine egg, broccoli, corn, onion, salt and pepper in a mixing bowl. In a saucepan melt butter and add stuffing mix. Toss to coat. Stir ¾ cup of buttered stuffing and combine with vegetable mixture. Turn into ungreased 1-quart casserole dish. Sprinkle with remaining ¼ cup of stuffing. Bake uncovered 30-40 minutes.

BROCCOLI CASSEROLE

Serves: 8-10   Oven: 300°

½ cup chopped onion
¼ cup chopped celery
½ cup butter
2 10-ounce packages frozen
    chopped broccoli
1 roll Kraft Garlic Cheese

10¾-ounce can mushroom soup
¾ teaspoon Accent
1 4-ounce can mushrooms,
    drained
1 cup chopped pecans
1 cup Ritz cracker crumbs

Sauté onions and celery in ¼ cup butter. Add broccoli and simmer 20 minutes in a large skillet. Add roll of chopped garlic cheese, soup, Accent and mushrooms. Heat well and pour into a buttered 2-quart casserole. Brown chopped pecans and Ritz cracker crumbs in ¼ cup melted butter. Sprinkle mixture over top of casserole. Bake for 45 minutes.

GREEN RICE

Serves: 6   Oven: 350°

2 cups cooked rice
1 cup parsley, finely chopped
1 small can evaporated milk
1 8-ounce package pimento
    cheese, grated

4 eggs, well beaten
⅔ cup olive oil
1 small onion, chopped
Dash cayenne
Salt and pepper to taste

Mix well all ingredients and pour into a buttered 8x8-inch baking dish. Set in a larger pan with water covering the bottom. Bake 45 minutes.

CHILE CHEESE RICE

Serves: 10   Oven: 350°

¾ cup raw rice   Salt to taste
2 cups sour cream   ½ cup grated Jack cheese
½ pound Jack cheese   Butter
2 4-ounce cans chopped green
    chile

Cook rice. Combine with sour cream and season with salt. Arrange half
the mixture in buttered 2-quart casserole. Layer with Jack cheese,
cut in 1¼-inch cubes, and the chopped chile. Top with remaining
rice mixture. Sprinkle the grated cheese over the top. Dot with butter.
Bake for 30 minutes. This recipe can be prepared ahead and refrigerated, or frozen, then thawed for 1 hour and baked.

MARVELOUS RICE

Serves: 8-10   Oven: 350°

½ cup butter   2 cups beef consommé
¼ cup oil   1 4-ounce can mushrooms,
1 cup fresh, chopped green onions   drained
1 cup water (or more if needed)   ½ cup chopped almonds
2 cups uncooked rice   (optional)
1 medium bell pepper,
    chopped

Sauté onions in butter and oil. Mix all other ingredients and add to onions
and butter. Put in 2½-quart casserole and bake for 45 minutes.

EXOTIC RICE

Serves: 6   Oven: 350°

1 package Uncle Ben's Wild   3 tablespoons butter
    Rice Mix   1 cup mushrooms, drained
½ cup chopped onion   ½ cup slivered almonds
1 cup chopped celery   2 tablespoons soy sauce

Cook rice according to package directions. Sauté onion and celery in
butter and add to rice. Mix mushrooms and almonds; add soy sauce and
stir into rice. Bake in greased 2-quart casserole for 30 minutes.

WILD RICE SAUSAGE CASSEROLE

Serves: 6-8   Oven: 350°

1 package Uncle Ben's Long
   Grain and Wild Rice Mix
   (or raw wild rice)
1 pound sausage
1 pound mushrooms
2 medium onions, chopped
3 tablespoons butter
   or margarine
¼ cup flour
½ cup heavy cream

2½ cups chicken broth
1 teaspoon monosodium
   glutamate
1 teaspoon oregano
1 teaspoon thyme
1 teaspoon marjoram
Salt to taste
⅛ teaspoon black pepper
1¾-ounce package almonds,
   blanched

Fry sausage; crumble and drain on paper towel. Reserve sausage grease. Sauté mushrooms and onions in sausage grease. Drain well. In another pan, melt butter and stir in flour (as for white sauce). When slightly thickened, stir in cream and chicken broth. Simmer sauce while adding the seasonings. Add the sausage, onions and mushrooms to sauce. Add wild rice mix with package of seasonings. Stir well. Pour into greased casserole. Bake covered for 50 minutes. Sprinkle with almonds and uncover to toast.

WILD RICE CASSEROLE

Serves: 8   Oven: 325°

½ cup margarine
2 4-ounce cans sliced mushrooms
1 onion, chopped
2 tablespoons bell pepper, chopped
1 clove garlic, minced

1 cup pecans, chopped
1 cup wild rice
3 cups chicken broth
Salt and pepper to taste

Heat margarine. Add mushrooms, onion, bell pepper and garlic and cook about 5 minutes. Add pecans and cook 1 minute. Wash rice well and drain. Mix rice with margarine mixture. Add broth and season to taste with salt and pepper. Turn into greased casserole and cover. Bake about 1 hour.

THE BEST OF STUFFED POTATOES

There is nothing better than a baked potato — unless it is one that has had the pulp removed and mashed and filled with the most delicious ingredients available. Here are four Southwestern favorites:

MEXICAN BAKED POTATOES

Serves: 6   Oven: 400°

6 large baked potatoes, pulp
    removed and mashed
1 4-ounce can chopped green
    chile
3 hard cooked eggs, chopped

½ cup butter, softened
1 cup sour cream
Shredded Longhorn cheese
Salt to taste

Mix mashed potatoes, chile, chopped eggs, butter, sour cream and salt. Fill shells with this mixture. Top each potato with shredded cheese and heat in oven 15 minutes.

BLEU CHEESE-BACON POTATOES

Serves: 4   Oven: 400°

4 medium baked potatoes,
    pulp removed and mashed
½ cup dairy sour cream
¼ cup Bleu cheese,
    crumbled

¼ cup milk
4 tablespoons butter
¾ teaspoon salt
Dash of pepper
4 slices crisp cooked bacon

Mix mashed potatoes, sour cream, Bleu cheese, milk, butter, salt and pepper. Beat until fluffy. Spoon mixture into potato shells. Place on baking sheet and return to hot oven for 15 minutes or until heated. Sprinkle with crumbled bacon.

BARBECUE POTATOES

Serves: 1   Oven: 275°

1 medium potato
4 onion slices
4 slices bell pepper

⅛ cup butter
Salt and pepper

Slice potato into 4-5 slices. Assemble potato and remaining ingredients. Wrap in foil and bake 1½ hours.

WESTERN BAKED POTATOES

Serves: 6   Oven: 400°

6 baked potatoes, pulp | **1 envelope beef-flavored**
removed and mashed | mushroom soup mix
½ cup butter | **1 4-ounce can chopped**
¾ cup milk | green chile
½ cup sour cream |

Melt butter in pan over low heat. Stir in milk. Remove from heat and
add sour cream and mushroom soup mix. Add mashed potato pulp and
beat. Add green chile. Fill shells and bake until heated through. For a
different look, instead of slicing a potato in half, cut ½-inch slice from
the top and remove the pulp.

DEVILED STUFFED POTATOES

Serves: 6   Oven: 400°

6 medium baked potatoes, | **1 4½-ounce can deviled ham**
pulp removed and mashed | **¾ cup shredded Cheddar cheese**
4 tablespoons butter | **6 tablespoons chopped chives**
1 teaspoon Accent | **Paprika**
¾ cup hot milk |

Mix mashed potatoes, butter, Accent and milk; beat until fluffy. Add
remaining ingredients and season with salt and pepper. Fill potato shells
with mixture; dot with butter and sprinkle with paprika. Bake 10 minutes.

POTATOES SUPREME

Serves: 8-10   Oven: 350°

6 medium potatoes | **⅓ cup chopped green onion**
Salt | **1 pint sour cream**
½ cup butter or margarine, melted | **¼ teaspoon pepper**
2 cups shredded Cheddar cheese | **½ teaspoon salt**

Cook potatoes in boiling salted water until done; drain, cover and refrigerate overnight. The next day grate potatoes coarsely. Mix with remaining ingredients. Place in shallow 1½ or 2-quart baking dish and
bake about 35 minutes.

POTATO SOUFFLE

Serves: 6   Oven: 325°

2 cups thick mashed potatoes
½ cup light cream
1 teaspoon salt
¼ teaspoon pepper
⅛ teaspoon ground nutmeg

3 tablespoons grated Parmesan
   cheese
4 eggs, separated
¼ teaspoon cream of tartar

Add cream and seasonings to potatoes. Stir and cook over low heat until mixture is hot. Remove from heat and blend in cheese. Beat in egg yolks one at a time, beating well after each addition. Cool. Beat egg whites until foamy. Add cream of tartar and beat again until whites stand in soft stiff peaks. Carefully fold into potatoes. Butter bottom (not sides) of a 1½-quart soufflé dish and pour in mixture. Place in pan of hot water and bake in preheated oven for about 1 hour or until soufflé is well puffed and lightly browned.

SWEET POTATOES

Serves: 8-10   Oven: 375°

2 16-ounce cans sweet potatoes
1¼ cups brown sugar
   (not packed)
1½ tablespoons cornstarch
½ teaspoon salt

⅛ teaspoon cinnamon
1 teaspoon shredded orange peel
16-ounce can apricot halves
2 tablespoons butter or margarine
½ cup pecan halves

Slice potatoes in half lengthwise and place in a 10x6x1½-inch baking dish. Combine next five ingredients. Drain apricots, reserving syrup. Stir 1 cup juice into cornstarch mixture; cook and stir over medium heat. Bring to boil and cook for 2 minutes. Add apricots, butter and pecans. Pour sauce over potatoes. Bake uncovered for 25 minutes.

Variation: Mash potatoes and stir in rest of ingredients. Put into casserole and top with marshmallows. Bake at 350° until marshmallows are brown. Also, crushed pineapple may be substituted for apricots.

CANDIED PICKLES

Yield: 1 gallon

1 gallon sour pickles
1 cup tarragon vinegar
1 cup oil

1 box pickling spices
5 cloves garlic
5 pounds sugar

Drain and discard liquid from pickles. Cut pickles into slices. In large pan combine all ingredients except pickles and boil. Pour mixture over pickles and store for ten days. Wash pickles; pack in sterilized jar filling with strained liquid.

BLACKEYED PEA SAUCE

1 16-ounce can tomatoes,
   or 6 fresh tomatoes
½ bell pepper, chopped
1 medium onion, chopped
½ cup sugar

½ cup vinegar
Salt
Cinnamon
Allspice

Simmer tomatoes, bell pepper, onion, sugar, vinegar and salt for 45 minutes. The last 15 minutes add a dash each of cinnamon and allspice. Pour over cooked blackeyed peas. *A sweet and sour sauce, this may also be used for basting chicken, roast or steak.*

CUCUMBER CRISPS

Yield: 2 quarts

1 pint white vinegar
1 large clove garlic
1 tablespoon whole cloves
1 tablespoon allspice
1 bay leaf
1 stick cinnamon
1 tablespoon whole celery seed

1 tablespoon mustard seed
1 tablespoon peppercorns
1 piece dried ginger root, or
   1 teaspoon powdered ginger
1½ cups sugar
5 large cucumbers, unpared

In a large saucepan combine all ingredients except cucumbers. Boil rapidly 10-15 minutes. Cool mixture and strain. Thinly slice cucumbers and place in large bowl or gallon jar. Add cooled marinade. Cover tightly. Refrigerate at least three days, stirring once each day. Keeps well refrigerated for several weeks. *A good filler for buffet table.*

GREEN BEAN CHOW-CHOW

Yield: 5 cups

1 cup cider vinegar
½ cup sugar
1 teaspoon turmeric
1 teaspoon dry mustard
½ teaspoon salt
½ cup water
1 cucumber, chopped

1 9-ounce package frozen
   cut green beans
1 medium onion, sliced
¾ cup sliced carrots
½ cup sliced celery
½ cup chopped green bell pepper

Prepare from 1 day to 2 weeks before serving. Combine first six ingredients. Add remaining ingredients and heat to a boil. Simmer covered 10 minutes or until vegetables are tender and crisp. Refrigerate until serving time. Drain and serve as relish.

TEXAS GREEN TOMATO PICKLES

Yield: 8 quarts

8 quarts small green tomatoes
1⅓ quarts white onions,
    quartered
4 cups sugar

⅔ cup salt
1⅓ quarts vinegar
8 jalapeño peppers

Cut tomatoes in half. In large pan bring sugar, vinegar and salt almost to a boil. Add tomatoes and onions; turn off heat. Turn several times with a wooden spoon so tomatoes absorb heat. Pour tomatoes into eight sterilized wide-mouth quart jars and add liquid. Cut jalapeños in half and add two halves to each jar. Seal tightly and let stand for several days. Chill well before serving. Liquid may not fill up jars but tomatoes will settle down into liquid. Superb cocktail bites—they are crisp with a sweet/sour flavor.

GREEN TOMATO PICKLES

Yield: 15 quarts

20 pounds green tomatoes
2 cups salt
1 medium cabbage
6 large white onions
6 green chiles
6 red chiles
8 cups sugar
2 quarts vinegar

4 tablespoons celery seed
1 cup mustard seed
½ tablespoon allspice
½ tablespoon cayenne
1 tablespoon black pepper
1 tablespoon cloves
1 tablespoon cinnamon

Peel and slice tomatoes to medium thickness; soak in salt overnight. Drain salt off and rinse once. Grind cabbage, onions and chiles. Combine with tomatoes and add remaining ingredients. Boil 15 minutes. Put in sterilized jars and seal.

PICKLED PEACHES

Yield: 3 quarts

24-28 fresh peaches, peeled
2 pounds dark brown sugar
½ cup sugar
2 cups cider vinegar

1 cup water
2 sticks cinnamon
2 tablespoons whole cloves

Combine all ingredients except peaches and boil for 20 minutes. Add whole peaches, a few at a time, to syrup; cook until done. Place in sterilized jars and cover with strained syrup. Seal securely.

CRANBERRY CONSERVE

Yield: 2 quarts

3 cups cranberries
1 cup diced apple
1½ cups water

1 cup crushed pineapple
3 cups sugar

Wash cranberries and apples. Cook 10 minutes in water or until tender. Add pineapple and sugar and boil until the mixture syrups and sheets off spoon. Let stand until thickened. Put in sterilized jars and seal.

BLENDER HOLLANDAISE

Yield: 1¼ cups

1 cup butter
4 egg yolks
¼ teaspoon salt
¼ teaspoon sugar

¼ teaspoon Tabasco
¼ teaspoon dry mustard
2 tablespoons lemon juice

Heat butter until bubbling. Combine all other ingredients in blender. With blender turned on, pour in butter in a slow, steady stream until all is added. Turn blender off. Keeps well in refrigerator for several days. When reheating heat over hot (not boiling) water in double boiler.

HOLLANDAISE SAUCE

Yield: 1 cup

3 egg yolks
1 tablespoon hot water
½ cup soft butter

¼ teaspoon salt
1 teaspoon lemon juice, or
    more to taste

Combine egg yolks and water in top of double boiler and beat with wire whisk over hot (not boiling) water until fluffy. Add butter slowly, bit by bit, beating constantly. Beat until butter has melted and sauce starts to thicken. Add salt and lemon juice. Beat in 1 tablespoon hot water for lighter texture.

A Taste of Chile

MEXICAN FOOD

HINTS FOR MEXICAN FOOD

Place avocado seeds in the middle of guacamole and cover with the mixture to prevent its darkening as it stands. Lime or lemon juice may also be used to prevent discoloration of the avocado.

To keep tortillas hot for several hours, wrap tightly in foil and place in an insulated bag, or wrap the foil package in a cloth covering with 12 or 14 sheets of newspaper.

To reheat and soften tortillas, place on an ungreased surface and rub each lightly with a damp hand before heating for just a few seconds. Put them immediately into a tightly covered dish or foil packet and seal until ready to serve.

To keep tortillas hot at the table, serve between two heated plates.

Before reheating frozen tortillas, thaw by separating them, brushing off ice, and laying them flat. They will thaw in 5 minutes.

To make red chile less hot, mix with tomato sauce and use less chile than the recipe calls for.

The secret of good Mexican beans is ample use of fat, whether it be bacon drippings, butter, or lard.

Don't add cold water to beans while cooking, as it causes them to break open. And don't add salt while cooking, as it toughens the skins.

Before preparing beans, wash and pick through them thoroughly and soak in cold water overnight.

Add 1 to 3 teaspoons baking soda to beans when you first put them on to cook. When the water comes to a boil, pour it off (it will be green) and add fresh water. Cook beans until tender.

Mash avocados with a fork before putting in a blender.

To freeze chiles without loss of flavor, first blister them but leave the skins on. Skins will come off easily when chiles are thawed.

Don't rinse canned chiles (unless they are packed in vinegar), as much of the flavor will be lost.

Longhorn cheese is best for enchiladas, Monterrey Jack for chiles rellenos.

For flavor and color, add chopped green onions and diced tomatoes to the cheese used in chiles rellenos.

Don't prepare the egg mixture for chiles rellenos until ready to dip.

MEXICAN MENU

ALMUERZO

Sangrita con Tequila
Huevos Rancheros
Chorizo
Refritos
Trigo al Medio Molido con
    Chile Con Carne
Mangos Fríos

HEARTY BRUNCH

Mexican Bloody Mary
Fried Eggs with Chile
Mexican Sausage
Refried Beans
Chile-Cheese Grits

Chilled Mangos

COMIDA

Tecáte con Limón y Sal
Enchiladas con Salsa Colorada
Tacos de Pollo
Arroz Española
Chiles Fríos con Crema Agria
Flán de Naranja con Almendras

LUNCH

Tecate Beer with Lime and Salt
Red Enchiladas
Chicken Tacos
Spanish Rice
Cold Chiles Filled with Sour
    Cream
Orange Custard with Almonds

MERIENDA

Margaritas
Sangría
Ceviche
Salpicón con Tortillas
Gorditas
Pastel de Chile y Queso
Nachos
Sopaipillas
Tamales Dulces
Buñuelos
Nueces Picosas

AFTERNOON PARTY

Tequila Drink
Mexican Fruit Wine
Marinated Fish
Shredded Beef with Tortillas
Stuffed Corn Meal Pattie
Green Chile Pie
Tostadas with Chile and Cheese
Puffed Pastry
Sweet Tamales
Mexican Cookies
Hot Pepper Pecans

CENA

Copita de Tequila
Chile con Queso con Tostadas
Jícama
Caldo de Tortilla
Ensalada de Guacamole
Carne Asada
Cacerola de Chile Relleno
Moldura de Tamal
Bolillos
Empanadas
Café
Kahlua

DINNER

Tequila Cocktail
Chile-Cheese Dip with Tostadas
Exotic Vegetable Root
Tortilla Soup
Avocado Salad
Steak with Chile Strips
Chile Relleno Casserole
Tamale Ring
Mexican Rolls
Fried Pies
Coffee
Kahlua

Salud, Amor y Pesetas y el Tiempo Para Disfrutarlos

THREE CHEERS FOR CHILE!

Some Southwesterners spell it **chili** or **chilli,** in recognition of our debt to the ancient Aztecs who first gave it a name. Others prefer the later Spanish spelling, **chile.** Some Southwesterners enjoy the chile mostly as a spice, using it liberally in its dried form. Others prefer it as a vegetable, stuffed with cheese or cooked with other foods. But all Southwesterners agree that there is no other food quite like the chile — not only because it is available in so many forms, to be used in so many ways, but also because its lively flavor adds zest to almost any meal.

The chile that does so much is the long, waxy variety that may be either rich green or flaming red, depending on the season. The flavor may also vary, from mild to fiery, according to the chile's stage of development and the amount of water the plant has received. (Chile crops are usually irrigated; those grown on dry land may be so pungent as to reduce the bravest and strongest to tears. Also, a chile with a very pointed tip is hotter than one with a more rounded tip.)

There are other types of chiles, such as the popular jalapeño chile; these are described in the glossary. But it is the long green or red chiles that — with tortillas and frijoles (beans) — form the basis of Mexican cookery.

The first chile crops, picked in late summer when the pods are green and glistening, are used fresh — whole for chiles rellenos; chopped for sauces, enchiladas, and chile con queso. Fresh green chiles are also canned and frozen for out-of-season enjoyment

Chile pods left on the stalk gradually turn a sun-ripened red. These are harvested in the fall, and, while some are used fresh, most are spread on roof tops or on the ground to dry — among the most colorful sights of autumn in the Southwest. Dried red chiles may then be cooked to make sauces for enchiladas, tamales, or chile con carne. Or the the chiles may be ground to a powder for flavoring pinto beans, caldillo, or any other dish that can be enhanced by a sprinkling of spicy herbs.

Fresh green chiles must be roasted and peeled before using.

To prepare:

1. Poke a hole in the end of each chile with an ice pick.

2. Spread chiles on a cookie sheet and broil, turning until skins are blistered on all sides. If chiles begin to get too brown, lower the rack to keep them from burning. If you prefer to roast chiles on a hot griddle on top of the range, turn them often for even browning.

3. When chiles are completely roasted, place them between dish towels or in a plastic bag to steam. This aids in removing the skins.

4. Peel off the skins as soon as chiles are cool enough to handle by laying chiles on a board and slitting one side lengthwise. Open chiles carefully and remove seeds and lateral veins. Rinse under cool water and place on a towel to dry. If chiles are to be used for rellenos, try to keep the stems intact. For sauces, enchiladas, and chiles con queso, chiles will be chopped or torn into strips.

Canned green chiles, available either whole or chopped, are already roasted and peeled. If they're whole, remove seeds and lateral veins. If they're canned in vinegar, rinse under cool water.

Important: Green chiles contain volatile oils which may irritate skin and eyes. It is wise to wear rubber gloves when peeling them. Always wash hands with soap after handling chiles and avoid contact with eyes.

If you should find fresh red chiles on the market, you may wish to dry them by stringing them in bunches and hanging them outdoors. Colorful strings of chiles, called *ristras*, traditionally decorate many Southwestern doorways. However, most red chiles in the market are already dried and are prepared as follows:

1. Remove loose seeds by shaking the pods and then rinse chiles to remove dust. Use cool water, as hot water may cause irritating fumes.

2. Place chiles in a deep pot and cover with boiling water. Bring water to a second boil, cover, and boil 5 minutes. Remove from heat and allow to cool while covered. Drain.

3. Lay chiles on waxed paper, open, and remove any remaining seeds. With a dull knife, scrape the pulp from inside the chiles. Discard the tough outer skins and use the pulp to make enchilada sauce.*

*See page 228, RED ENCHILADAS.

MEXICAN FOOD GLOSSARY

Bolillo. A Mexican hard roll, similar to a French roll.

Chile ancho. A heart-shaped chile, about 3x2½ inches, of a deep mahogany color. Available dried to be soaked and used in making red chile sauce or to be ground into a powder for seasoning.

Chile jalapeño. A shiny, dark green chile, about 2½x1 inches. Among the hottest of chiles, jalapeños are available either fresh or canned. They are usually pickled, but Southwesterners often enjoy them raw, without pickling or peeling, as the chief ingredient of jalapeño relish.

Chile manzano. A yellow-green chile, similar to a jalapeño in size and apearance but somewhat milder.

Chile molido. Pure ground red chile powder, available packaged.

Chile serrano. A tapered, bright green chile, 1 to 2 inches long and fairly hot. Serranos may occasionally be found fresh, but they are usually canned, pickled or packed in oil.

Chile Sauce. As used in this book, a hot bottled catsup-type sauce. The term is a broad one, however, and can be used in reference to red or green enchilada sauce, red or green taco sauce, and salsa picante.

Chorizo. Highly seasoned Mexican sausage. Italian sausage may be substituted.

Cilantro. Leaves of the coriander plant, resembling parsley. Same as Chinese parsley.

Comino (cumin). Aromatic seed, yellow-brown or yellow-gray, used for flavoring.

Coriander. Round, pale yellow to brown seed of the coriander plant. May be used to grow fresh plants for cilantro.

Enchilada sauce. Green sauce for enchiladas is made from fresh green chiles, red sauce from dried red chiles.

Escabeche. Pickled in vinegar or marinade.

Frijoles. Pinto beans.

Jalapeño relish. A very hot relish made from finely chopped jalapeño chiles, onions, and tomatoes. Available canned.

Jícama. A large root vegetable with a gray-brown skin. The crisp white meat has the appearance of a potato, the texture of a water chestnut, and a flavor somewhat like a radish. After the skin is removed, the meat is cut into slices or strips to be served raw as an appetizer or in salads.

Mango. An oblong yellow-orange tropical fruit, available canned.

Masa Harina. Dehydrated corn flour to which water is added to make a pliable dough. It is available in most grocery stores and can be used wherever masa is called for.

Pepitas. Toasted and salted pumpkin seeds.

Picante. Sharp; hot; highly seasoned.

Refritos. Refried pinto beans.

Salsa picante. A very hot sauce made from fresh chiles and tomatoes, either chopped or puréed.

Sopaipilla. A light, puffed-up fritter, fried in deep fat. May be served as a hot bread with butter or as a dessert with honey or powdered sugar.

Tabasco. A bottled hot sauce made from red peppers and vinegar.

Taco sauce. Green taco sauce is made from fresh green chiles, red taco sauce from dried red chiles. Both are available bottled or canned and may be used to enhance the flavor of most Mexican dishes.

Tortilla. Thin, round, Mexican bread. Corn tortillas, used for tacos and enchiladas, are made from masa and measure about 6 inches in diameter. Flour tortillas, made of unleavened dough of white flour, measure 12 to 18 inches.

TEQUILA COCKTAIL

Serves: 2

Juice of 1 lemon
Juice of ½ orange

4 teaspoons of sugar dissolved
  in little water
4 jiggers tequila

Mix well. Can be put in blender with ice cubes for frosty effect.

MARGARITA

Serves: 1

1 slice lime
Coarse Kosher salt
1 4-ounce cocktail glass,
  chilled

½ ounce fresh lime juice
1½ ounces tequila
½ ounce Triple Sec
3-4 ice cubes

Rub the inside rim of the chilled glass with the slice of lime. Pour salt into a saucer and dip the glass until a thin layer of salt adheres to the moistened rim. Combine the lime juice, tequila, Triple Sec and ice cubes in a cocktail shaker. Shake well and strain into the salt-rimmed glass.

SANGRITA

Serves: 1

5 drops onion juice
5 ounces tomato juice
Worcestershire sauce to taste

5 drops jalapeño juice
1½ ounces tequila

Place all ingredients in mixer. Blend well. Pour over ice and serve.

SANGRIA

Yield: 18 cups

6 oranges, sliced
3 lemons, sliced
1 lime, sliced

1 cup sugar
½ pint brandy
1 gallon dry red wine

Arrange lemons, limes and oranges in the bottom of a large punch bowl. Sprinkle sugar over fruit. More sugar may be added if oranges are sour. Add the brandy and allow to sit at least 1 hour. Add wine, stir well, and allow to sit 30 minutes or more. Serve over ice in stemmed glasses.

FLOUR TORTILLAS

Yield. 10 tortillas

3 cups flour
3 teaspoons baking powder
1 teaspoon salt

Pinch of sugar (optional)
3 tablespoons oil (more for
    softer tortillas)
1 cup water

Mix together flour, baking powder, salt, sugar and oil. Add water and mix with hands. Form into large ball; divide into 10 smaller ones. Roll each flat with rolling pin and cook on very hot ungreased griddle, until lightly brown on each side.

SOPAIPILLAS

2 cups flour
½ teaspoon salt
2½ teaspoons baking powder

2 tablespoons shortening
¾ cup warm water
Cooking oil

Sift flour, salt and baking powder. Cut in shortening; add water and knead. Add more flour if necessary. Let dough stand 30 minutes before rolling. Do not let stand longer. Roll on slightly floured board until ¼-inch thick; cut in diamond-shaped pieces. Using a 1-quart saucepan with two inches oil, fry in deep fat, 390-400° on thermometer. Turn at once to puff evenly and brown on both sides. Because the sopaipillas brown so quickly, cook only one at a time. The high sides of the pan help to lessen the splattering. Drain. Serve hot with butter and honey on the side.

PICO DE GALLO

Yield: 2 cups

8 long green chiles, roasted, peeled
    deveined and chopped
2 small yellow chiles, roasted,
    peeled and chopped, or 2
    jalapeño chiles
5 green onions, chopped
    (including tops)

5 medium tomatoes, peeled and
    chopped
¼ cup chopped fresh cilantro
    leaves
2 tablespoons salad oil
1 teaspoon vinegar
Salt to taste

Combine all ingredients; chill. Will keep at least two weeks in refrigerator. Serve with meats, chicken, hamburgers, etc.

GREEN CHILE SAUCE

Yield: 1 cup

1 8-ounce can tomato sauce
1 4-ounce can chopped green
    chile
½ medium onion, chopped (if de-
    sired, onion may be sautéed)

1 clove garlic, minced
½ teaspoon crushed red pepper
Dash of salt
Pinch of oregano

Mix all ingredients and store in refrigerator. Good with tacos, tostados for dip, or on Huevos Rancheros (see Index).

JALAPEÑO CHILE SALSA

Yield: 1 cup

4 small fresh jalapeño chiles,
    chopped
2 large tomatoes, peeled and
    chopped

1 onion, minced
½ teaspoon garlic powder
Dash of salt

Mix all ingredients thoroughly. This is delicious served with crackers, or as a chile sauce for tacos or any Mexican dish. Good served with meat.

MEXICAN SAUCE

2 cloves garlic
1 tablespoon salt
1 medium onion, chopped
    fine
4 tablespoons olive oil
6 8-ounce cans tomato
    sauce

1 4-ounce can chopped
    green chile
2 10-ounce cans beef
    bouillon
1 teaspoon cumin

Mash garlic with salt. Combine with onion and olive oil in heavy skillet and sauté until onions are transparent. Add tomato sauce, chile bouillon and cumin. Bring to a slow boil. Reduce heat and simmer for 30 minutes. For best results prepare a day ahead. Good over Chiles Rellenos or Huevos Rancheros (see Index), Can be frozen.

Refritos (Refried Beans) may be prepared by using left over frijoles which have been mashed and fried in butter, bacon drippings or lard. Delicious for breakfast, lunch or dinner and a cocktail party treat as a dip or on tostados for Nachos.

CHILE SALSA

Yield: 2 cups

½ onion, finely chopped
1 clove garlic, minced
Olive oil or bacon drippings
2 jalapeño chiles, chopped

8-10 long green chiles, chopped
3 small tomatoes, peeled and
    chopped
Salt

Sauté onion and garlic over very low heat in oil. Add chiles and simmer for about 5 minutes. Add tomatoes and salt. Cook 10 more minutes. Cool and serve as a garnish.

GREEN CHILE RAJAS

Fresh green chile
Salt and pepper

1 minced clove garlic, or more
    if desired

Prepare chile. Cut into ¼-inch strips. Place in bowl. Season with minced fresh garlic, salt and pepper. Refrigerate for several hours. This is an excellent accompaniment with grilled steaks or barbecued meats. Keeps in refrigerator a week.

QUESADILLAS
(HOT CHILE AND CHEESE TORTILLAS)

Serves: 10   Oven: 350°

1 dozen corn tortillas
Shredded or crumbled Longhorn,
    Jack, or Asadero cheese

1 4-ounce can chopped green
    chile
Salt

Soften corn tortillas in hot oil (not crisp). Cover one tortilla with cheese and green chile; sprinkle with salt. Place second tortilla on top. Continue procedure until six individual quesadillas are made. Place on cookie sheet in oven until cheese melts. Serve cut into four sections.

TACOS

The word "taco" originally meant a snack, but has come to mean a Mexican sandwich which is made by using a corn tortilla with any one of a variety of fillings. Tacos may be folded or rolled, fried very crisp or fairly soft.

FOLDED TACOS

To prepare a taco shell, fry one corn tortilla at a time in ½-inch of hot oil over high heat until it begins to blister and becomes limp. Fold in half and hold open with tongs so there is a space between for filling. Fry until crisp and light brown, turning as necessary. Drain well on paper towels. To keep shells warm until ready to fill, place on a paper towel lined pan in a 200° oven.

ROLLED TACOS

A rolled taco is prepared by softening a corn tortilla in hot oil, as for a folded taco. Drain on paper towels. Place 3 or 4 teaspoonfuls of filling in the center of soft tortilla and roll to resemble a fat cigar. Place tacos in pan and bake at 350° for 10-15 minutes until crisp. Do not leave in oven too long as they may become too crisp. Rolled tacos may also be fried in hot oil but the oven method is cleaner and easier.

FLAUTAS

The word "flauta", meaning flute in Spanish, describes the tubular shape of this Mexican dish.

Traditionally, shredded meat or chicken is used to fill flautas, but any taco filling may be used. For each flauta, soften 2 tortillas as for folded tacos; lay tortillas flat and overlapping. Spoon filling across the greatest length of the overlapped tortillas and roll. Cook until crisp.

FILLINGS:

The following are three basic fillings for all varieties of tacos. Usually three tacos are a sufficient meal for one person. Each of the following recipes fills 12 taco shells.

CHEESE FILLING:

6-8 fresh green chiles, roasted and peeled, or 10-ounce can whole green chile

1 pound Cheddar cheese
1 pound Monterrey Jack cheese

Remove seeds from chile. Cut 12 slices of each cheese. Into hot prepared taco shells, put 1 slice Jack cheese, half a chile strip and 1 slice Cheddar cheese. Place in 300° oven until cheese melts. Serve at once.

CHICKEN FILLING:

1 onion, finely chopped
1 small clove garlic, minced
6 tablespoons oil
1 4-ounce can chopped green
   chile
1 teaspoon salt
Dash monosodium glutamate
½ teaspoon marjoram

14½-ounce can whole tomatoes
2 cups cooked chicken, diced
½ pint sour cream
1 can frozen guacamole
1½ cups Monterrey Jack cheese,
   grated
Shredded lettuce

Sauté onion and garlic in oil until soft. Add chile, salt, MSG, marjoram and drained tomatoes. Cut up tomatoes and cook mixture gently for 10 minutes. Add chicken and cook slowly until chicken is heated thoroughly (about 10 minutes). Before filling prepared taco shells, drain chicken mixture. To assemble tacos, place 2 teaspoons chicken mixture, 2 teaspoons sour cream, and 2 teaspoons guacamole. Top with cheese and shredded lettuce. Serve at once.

BEEF FILLING:

1-1½ pounds ground meat
½ cup chopped onion
¼ teaspoon cumin
1 teaspoon salt
10-ounce can tomato and
   green chile (optional)

Shredded lettuce
Chopped tomatoes
Grated cheese
1 4-ounce can taco sauce

Brown meat and onion; drain. Add salt, cumin and tomato and chile. Simmer approximately 15 minutes. Fill each prepared taco shell with meat. Shells may be kept warm in oven at 200° for a few minutes. Just before serving, add lettuce, tomatoes and cheese. Taco sauce should be served at table for individual taste.

TAPATIAS
Tapatías are flat fried corn tortillas with a variety of toppings.

To prepare tapatías, fry corn tortilla in hot oil until crisp. Drain on paper towels. Prepare toppings and spread over hot tortillas. The different ingredients for toppings are guacamole, refried beans, Spanish rice, or chicken. Garnish with shredded lettuce, diced tomato, chopped onion, grated cheese and chopped green chile. Picante or taco sauce can be served with tapatías.

BEAN TAPATIAS

Serves: 6

12 corn tortillas	1 onion, minced
3 cups pinto beans	1 tablespoon vinegar
2 tablespoons oil	1 teaspoon oregano
4 cups Longhorn, or	2 tablespoons oil
sharp Cheddar cheese	1½ teaspoon salt
1 head lettuce, shredded	4-6 peeled green chiles
1 can tomato purée	

Fry and mash cooked pinto beans in oil. Put a layer of mashed beans on top of each tortilla and top with cheese and lettuce. Serve warm with a sauce made of tomato purée, onion, oregano, vinegar, oil, salt and chile.

CHICKEN GUACAMOLE TAPATIAS

Serves: 6

12 corn tortillas, fried crisp	½ onion, chopped
Cooked meat of 1 chicken, or	1 tomato, chopped
3 whole breasts	¾ cup sour cream
2 cups guacamole (or large can	Grated Longhorn cheese
of refried beans or both)	Picante sauce
2 cups shredded lettuce	

Spread fried tortillas with guacamole (or refried beans heated in 3 table-spoons bacon grease). Top with chicken, lettuce, onions, tomato, cheese, sour cream. Accompany with picante sauce.

CHICKEN TAPATIAS

Serves: 4-6

2 chicken breasts	Garlic to taste
1 medium onion	Pepper to taste
1 medium tomato	6 corn tortillas
Pinch of oregano	1 medium can refried beans
Bacon drippings	

Boil chicken breasts in water for 2 hours. Bone and cut into strips. Using half the chicken stock, bring to a boil and add chopped tomato, onion, oregano, salt, pepper and garlic. Cook liquid down to half; add chicken and simmer until all liquid is absorbed. Heat beans in 3 table-spoons bacon grease until hot. Cover fried tortilla with chicken and beans and top with lettuce, tomato and onion. Top with sour cream.

BURRITOS

Burritos are flour tortillas with a variety of fillings.

To prepare a burrito, heat a flour tortilla briefly on a hot griddle, or in the oven. Remove and lay tortilla flat. Spread with desired filling and fold sides over until tortilla is shaped like a tube. Hold together with a toothpick. Burritos may be served with picante sauce or taco sauce. Two burritos are usually served each person. They may be eaten with a fork or with fingers.

Any one or a combination of the following fillings is a delicious Mexican treat: chile con carne, refritos, chile con queso, guacamole, scrambled eggs with green chile, or leftover roast (either diced or shredded) fried with onions, potatoes and green chile. Burritos de Gallina is a very special dish.

BURRITOS DE GALLINA
Yield: 1 dozen   Oven: 300°

2-3 pound fryer, cooked and boned	1 4-ounce can chopped green chile
10-ounce can tomatoes	1 pound Monterrey Jack cheese, grated
1 medium onion	1 dozen flour tortillas
1 clove garlic, minced	Salt and pepper to taste

In saucepan sauté onion and garlic in small amount of oil (about 1 tablespoon) until glazed. Add green chile and tomatoes and bring to a boil. Lower heat and simmer for 1 hour. Add chicken and mix until meat is shredded. Season with salt and pepper. Place about 1½-2 tablespoons mixture in each flour tortilla with a generous amount of cheese. Roll tortilla. Place in greased 12x9x2-inch baking pan and cover with foil. Heat about 30 minutes. Burritos may be frozen (individually). Warm 1 hour. *Put in children's lunches frozen—by noon they're ready to eat!*

BACON AND EGG BURRITO

Serves: 1   Oven: 350°

2 slices bacon	Grated cheese
1 teaspoon chopped onion	2 tablespoons chopped green chile, or taco sauce
1 egg	
1 flour tortilla	Salt and pepper

Fry bacon and set aside to drain. Into bacon grease, break egg as if to fry. Break yolk with fork, and stir slightly. Sprinkle with onion, salt and pepper. Flip egg; fry until firm. Line center of a flour tortilla with grated cheese. Place hot fried egg on top of cheese. Spoon chile onto egg and top with bacon. Fold tortilla sides over; wrap in foil and warm in oven.

BREAKFAST TORTILLAS

Serves: 4-6

4 eggs	Bacon
1 teaspoon salt	Grated cheese
1 tablespoon milk	Diced avocado
3 tablespoons butter	Taco sauce
8 flour tortillas	Chopped green chile (canned)

Beat together eggs, salt and milk. In large frying pan, melt butter over medium heat. Dip tortillas, one at a time, in egg mixture; drain briefly and fry in butter until golden brown. Serve hot. Pass the condiments and allow each person to create his own dish.

HUEVOS RANCHEROS

Serves: 1   Oven: Broil

1 egg	2 tablespocns taco sauce
1 tortilla	Grated cheese

Fry tortilla slightly in hot oil and drain. Fry egg and place on tortilla. Spoon taco sauce over egg and top with grated cheese. Put under broiler for a few seconds to melt cheese. Serve with bacon or ham for breakfast.

Alternate: Serve with Spanish rice, refritos and guacamole for luncheon or Sunday night supper.

RAPIDO MEXICAN DISH

Serves: 4

1 pound hot sausage	1 cup dairy sour cream
1 onion, chopped	1 cup milk
1 bell pepper, chopped	2 tablespoons sugar
16-ounce can tomatoes	1 teaspoon salt
1 8-ounce package elbow macaroni, uncooked	1 tablespoon chile powder

Brown sausage, onion and bell pepper. Add all other ingredients. Cover and simmer 20-25 minutes or until macaroni is tender.

MENUDO

Serves: 20

4 pounds tripe, cut into
   1-inch squares
1 meaty marrowbone
1 large onion, chopped
2 pounds oxtail
8 cloves garlic
3 cups canned tomatoes
6 cups yellow hominy
2 onions, chopped

1 teaspoon thyme
2 cups green chile sauce
12 long green chiles
20 dried red chiles
8 cloves garlic
4 cups water
½ cup fresh mint
1 cup parsley
½ cup fresh cilantro

Cover first five ingredients with water and simmer 6-8 hours. Refrigerate overnight. Remove fat and bone. Add the next five ingredients to meat and simmer 3 hours. Remove seeds from chiles, cover with water and simmer 30 minutes. Remove and blend in blender with garlic cloves and water. Add to soup. The last hour of cooking, chop mint, parsley and cilantro and cook with soup.

CALDILLO
(MEXICAN STEW)

Yield: 1 gallon

3 pounds cubed beef
1½ cups diced onion
Bacon fat
3 cups tomatoes, diced
1½ cups green chile strips
½ cup beef stock

½ cup chicken stock
2 teaspoons salt
2 teaspoons pepper
2 teaspoons garlic salt
2 teaspoons cumin
2 pounds cubed potatoes

Sauté beef and onions in bacon fat. Add tomatoes, chile strips, stocks and seasonings. Cook over low heat until meat is tender. Add cubed potatoes during the last 30 minutes. Caldillo may be frozen after preparation.

CHILE VERDE CON CARNE

Serves: 4-6

2 pounds round or Swiss steak, cut in 1-inch cubes
2 tablespoons oil
1 medium onion, chopped

2 large tomatoes, peeled and chopped, or 1 cup canned tomatoes
8 fresh green chiles*
2 cloves garlic, chopped

Brown meat lightly in hot oil and salt to taste. Add onions; cook until clear. Add tomatoes and water to cover. Add garlic and chiles. (Two diced potatoes may be added, if heartier dish is desired.) Simmer 45 minutes to 1 hour.

*2 4-ounce cans chopped green chile can be used.

HOMEMADE CHILE

Serves: 10 without beans
       14 with beans

3 pounds chuck roast (fat removed), coarsely ground
2 pounds lean ground meat
2 large onions, diced
5 cloves garlic, finely chopped
3 tablespoons whole cumin seed
1 tablespoon salt
2 teaspoons black pepper

½ teaspoon cayenne pepper
3 tablespoons chile powder
2 28-ounce cans peeled whole tomatoes
2 15-ounce cans tomato sauce
14-ounce can red enchilada sauce
1½ cups water

Brown meat, onions and garlic in a large roaster. When meat is brown, add seasonings and stir. Over meat and onions, shred tomatoes by hand so that both tomatoes and juice will fall into pan. Stir in tomato and enchilada sauce. Cook over low heat for 1½ hours. Add 1½ cups water and cook 1½ hours longer. Cool and skim off grease. Serve hot with crackers or hard rolls. A light mango mold salad or an avocado salad adds the perfect cool touch. This recipe may be frozen after it is cooked. To defrost, remove from freezer and thaw at room temperature or place frozen container in hot water to loosen from sides and place frozen chile in a roaster. Heat slowly.

Variation: Add 3-4 cups cooked pinto beans the last 10 mintes of cooking time.

WINTER CHILE CON CARNE

Serves: 8 without frijoles,
      12 with frijoles

5 pounds beef chuck, cut into
      1½-inch cubes
½ cup olive oil
1 cup flour
½ cup Gebhardt's chile powder
¼ cup chile molido
2 teaspoons cumin

2 teaspoons oregano
3 cloves garlic, chopped
1 quart beef broth
1 teaspoon salt
¼ teaspoon freshly ground
      black pepper
4 cups cooked frijoles
      (see Index)

Brown meat in oil in a large heavy saucepan. Sprinkle with flour and both chiles. Cook, stirring, 3-5 minutes, until meat is coated with flour and chile powder. Place cumin and oregano in the palm of one hand; rub the spices in the hand, letting fall over the meat. Add garlic, beef broth, salt and pepper. Bring mixture to boil. Cover and simmer very slowly (at least 4 hours). The chile may be cooked over low heat so that it barely simmers for as long as 24 hours. More beef broth may be added during cooking. This may be served with or without frijoles (pinto beans) but is much better if beans are added during last 15 minutes of cooking time. If frozen, let stand in refrigerator one day and heat slowly for 2 hours before serving. Check chile, as this seasoning seems to evaporate. Add more chile molido if necessary.

MAMA'S CHILE CON CARNE

Serves: 4 without beans, 6 with beans

1 pound coarsely ground pork
2 pounds coarsely ground beef
1 large onion, cut up
1 3-ounce bottle Gebhardt's
      chile powder
2-3 tablespoons cumin

¼ cup chile molido
1 teaspoon oregano
16-ounce can small tomatoes
1 large clove garlic, minced
1 can beef broth
2 cups cooked frijoles
      (see Index)

Brown pork, beef and onion at same time; drain. Add both chiles, cumin and oregano; continue to cook. Add tomatoes and break them as they stew. Add beef broth as needed, cooking at least 30 minutes. This may be served in bowls with or without frijoles, but is much better if beans are added during last 15 minutes of cooking time. *Chile Con Carne is even better warmed the next day.*

CHILAQUILES

Serves: 6   Oven: 350°

1 dozen tortillas*
Cooking oil
2 medium onions, diced
2 large cloves garlic, minced
1 large bell pepper, diced
2 tablespoons salad oil
1 pound ground meat

2 8-ounce cans tomato sauce
   (or 2½ cups canned
   tomatoes)
1 teaspoon salt
2 tablespoons red chile powder
Grated cheese
Ripe olives, sliced

Cut tortillas into 1-inch squares; fry in oil until light brown; drain. Sauté onions, garlic and bell pepper in 2 tablespoons oil, stirring often. Add ground meat, stirring until meat is well done. Add tomato sauce, tortillas, salt and chile powder. Simmer 30 minutes, stirring occasionally Pour into 2-quart casserole and sprinkle with grated cheese. Top with sliced olives after cheese has melted in oven (about 20 minutes). This recipe may be frozen. Thaw at room temperature and heat.

*In some areas where tortillas are unavailable, use packaged tostadas and ½ teaspoon salt.

GORDITAS

Serves: 4   Shell:

1 pound ground beef
1 small onion, chopped
2 teaspoons salt
¼ teaspoon pepper
1 teaspoon garlic salt
¼ teaspoon chile powder

2 cups Masa Harina
1 teaspoon baking powder
2 teaspoons salt
1 cup water
2 pieces fried bacon, crumbled
2 tablespoons Longhorn cheese
Shredded lettuce
Sliced or diced tomatoes
Grated cheese

Fry beef and onion together. Season with salt, pepper, garlic salt and chile powder. While meat is cooking, mix with hands all ingredients for shells. Pinch off small portion of dough and roll into 2-inch ball. With quick patting motion, flatten out to ½-inch thickness about three inches in diameter. Fry in hot grease until golden brown, turning once. Drain. Make a slit through middle; open slightly (like a taco shell) and stuff with meat mixture, lettuce, tomatoes and cheese. Serve with favorite chile or taco sauce.

SALPICON
(MEXICAN SHREDDED BEEF)

Serves: 16-20

8 pounds top sirloin or
    eye of round
2 cloves garlic
1 bay leaf
12-ounce can tomatoes
1/4 cup fresh cilantro*
Salt and pepper to taste
1 bottle Wishbone Italian salad
    dressing

1 cup chopped green chiles
    (fresh or canned)
1 cup cooked garbanzo beans
1/2 pound Monterrey Jack cheese
    cut in 1/2-inch squares
2 avocados, cut in strips
1 bunch parsley

Place beef in heavy pot; cover with water and add garlic, bay leaf, tomatoes, cilantro, salt and pepper. Cook over medium heat about 5 hours. Remove broth, cool meat and cut into 2-inch squares. Shred and arrange in a 9x11-inch pyrex dish. Cover beef with salad dressing and allow to marinate overnight in refrigerator. Before serving, arrange the following in layers over beef: beans, cheese, chiles, avocados. Decorate with parsley. *This is a perfect dish for a buffet table.*

*Cilantro is fresh coriander.

CHIMICHONGAS

3 pounds beef, cut in small cubes
Lard
6 green chiles,
    roasted and peeled
1-2 serrano chiles
1 large onion, diced
1 clove garlic

2-3 tomatoes, quartered
2 cups beef stock
1/2 teaspoon oregano
Salt and pepper
Flour tortillas
Longhorn or Monterrey Jack
    cheese

Brown meat in lard. Place chiles including seeds in blender with onion, garlic and tomatoes. Purée and add to browned meat with stock and seasonings. Cover and simmer 2-3 hours. Cook until thick, being careful not to burn during last part of cooking. Fill flour tortillas as for burritos, using toothpicks if necessary to keep filling inside. Deep fat fry until golden brown; drain and put on broiler rack. Sprinkle with grated cheese and melt under broiler until bubbly. Serve immediately.

Variation: After cooking, spread one side with a layer of guacamole, then serve!

CARNE ASADA

Serves: 4-6   Oven: 375°

4-6 sandwich steaks
Cooking oil
1 medium onion, finely diced

10-ounce can green chile,
    cut in strips (or fresh
    chiles, roasted and peeled)
Monterrey Jack cheese, grated

Sauté onion and chile strips in a small amount of oil. Drain and set aside. Fry steaks in oil adding more when necessary; place steaks on a cookie sheet. Top each with portions of chile, onion and grated cheese. Bake until cheese melts.

CHORIZO
(MEXICAN SAUSAGE)

1 clove garlic
3 teaspoons oregano
½ cup vinegar

½ cup or less red chile powder
Water
2½ pounds ground pork or
    hamburger

Place all ingredients except meat into blender and mix well. Pour mixture over meat; cover with a plate and marinate at room temperature all day. Pour off any water which accumulates. The flavor will ripen and the chile will prevent spoiling. Refrigerate or freeze. To cook, crumble in skillet and fry. Serve with scrambled eggs.

MEXICAN MEAL-IN-A-DISH

Serves: 4-6   Oven: 350°

3 cups cooked roast beef,
    cubed
1 egg
1½ teaspoons salt
¾ teaspoon baking soda
1 cup buttermilk

1 cup yellow corn meal
16-ounce can creamed corn
1 large onion, chopped
2 4-ounce cans chopped green
    chile
3 cups grated Longhorn cheese

Mix together all ingredients except cheese. Layer mixture and cheese in a baking dish, ending with a layer of cheese. Bake 30-40 minutes.

ENCHILADA CASSEROLE CON ESPINACAS

Serves: 12   Oven: 325°

2 pounds ground chuck
1 large onion, peeled and
      finely chopped
16-ounce can tomatoes, or
      10-ounce can tomatoes
      and green chiles
12-ounce package frozen
      spinach cooked according
      to directions, squeezed
      dry
Salt to taste
Freshly ground pepper to taste

10¾-ounce can golden
      mushroom soup
10¾-ounce can cream of
      mushroom soup
1 8-ounce carton sour cream
¼ cup milk
¼ teaspoon garlic powder
½ cup butter
12-16 tortillas
2 4-ounce cans chopped
      green chile
½ pound Longhorn or mild
      Cheddar cheese, grated

Place meat in heavy skillet; cook over medium heat until it loses all its color. Drain off any fat or liquid. Stir in next five ingredients. In a bowl combine the next five ingredients and mix well. Dip half the tortillas in melted butter. Arrange on bottom and sides of a large shallow casserole. Spoon in meat mixture. Do not disarrange tortillas. Spread chopped chile over mixture with all but ½ cup of cheese. Cover with remaining tortillas dipped in butter; add sauce, smoothing over whole surface. Cover with plastic wrap. Refrigerate overnight. Sprinkle casserole with reserved cheese before placing in oven. Bake 35-45 minutes.

CREAM CHICKEN ENCHILADAS

Serves: 6   Oven: 350°

1 onion, chopped
2 tablespoons oil
1 clove garlic, crushed
2 cups tomato purée
2 cups cooked, chopped chicken
3-4 chiles, chopped

1 dozen tortillas
6 chicken bouillon cubes
3 cups hot cream (½ pint
      cream and 1 pint
      half-and-half)
¾ pound Monterrey Jack
      cheese, grated

Sauté onion in oil; add garlic and tomato purée. Add chicken and chiles and simmer 10 minutes. Soften tortillas in about 1 inch of hot oil. Do not overcook. Dissolve bouillon cubes in hot cream. Dip each tortilla in this mixture and cover generously with chicken filling. Roll up tortillas and arrange in baking dish. Pour remaining cream over all and top with cheese. Bake for 30 minutes.

CRABMEAT ENCHILADAS

Serves: 4   Oven: 250°

1 chopped onion
2 tablespoons oil
2 tablespoons flour
2-2½ cups milk
1 4-ounce can chopped green
   chile

½ pound Monterrey Jack cheese,
   grated
1 dozen tortillas
Oil
1 7½-ounce can crabmeat
Salt and pepper to taste

Sauté onion in oil. Add flour, milk, chile and a little cheese. Cook until medium thick. Dip each tortilla in hot oil for a few seconds until limp. Put 1 tablespoon each of cheese, crabmeat and sauce in a tortilla and roll up. Place in shallow baking dish and pour remaining sauce on top. Bake 10-15 minutes.

BEEF ENCHILADA CASSEROLE

Serves: 6   Oven: 350°

1 pound ground meat
1 onion, chopped
1 4-ounce can chopped green
   chile, drained
14-ounce can enchilada sauce

13-ounce can evaporated milk
10¾-ounce can cream of
   chicken soup, undiluted
12 tortillas, fried and broken
   into pieces
¾ cup grated cheese

Brown meat and onion; add green chile. Mix and heat enchilada sauce, milk and cream of chicken soup. Place half the tortillas, half the meat mixture and half the sauce in a baking dish. Repeat. Sprinkle cheese on top and bake 15-20 minutes. If dish is prepared and refrigerated ahead of time, bake 45 minutes.

COTTAGE CHEESE ENCHILADAS

Serves: 10-12   Oven: 350°

1 large onion, minced
16-ounce carton cottage cheese
2 14-ounce cans red enchilada
   sauce
2 dozen tortillas
2 tomatoes, sliced thin

1 4-ounce can chopped green
   chile
¾ pound Longhorn cheese,
   grated
Butter

Add minced onion to cottage cheese. Sauté tortillas in butter and dip in heated enchilada sauce. Fill each tortilla with cottage cheese and roll. Place tomato slices and chile over the platter of enchiladas and pour over remaining red sauce. Sprinkle grated cheese liberally over the whole dish. Bake 25 minutes.

CHICKEN-GREEN CHILE ENCHILADAS

Serves: 5

1 small onion, chopped
1 carrot, sliced
4 cups water
2 whole chicken breasts
4 long green chiles, roasted,
    peeled and deveined
3 tablespoons flour
3 tablespoons butter

1 cup milk
1 ripe avocado
1 medium onion, chopped fine
¾ pound Monterrey Jack cheese,
    grated
10 corn tortillas
1 cup sour cream

Cook onion and carrot in 4 cups of water until tender. Add chicken breasts and poach until tender (about 10 minutes). Don't overcook. Cool meat in broth; remove, reserving broth. Skin, dice and salt chicken lightly. Blend broth, carrots, onions and chiles in blender. In sauce-pan, slightly cook flour in melted butter. Add 3 cups of blended broth (leaving 1 cup in blender) and milk; cook and stir until thickened. Add pulp of avocado to broth in blender and blend until smooth. Add avocado mixture to sauce in pan and stir until mixed. Keep sauce warm. Cook each tortilla separately in hot oil until soft. Fill and roll each with chicken, onion and cheese. Put filled and rolled tortillas in a greased flat cas-serole. Cover with sauce and top with remaining grated cheese and sour cream. Keep hot until ready to serve. *This is very rich and too much trouble for quantity cooking, but good for a small dinner party.*

RED ENCHILADAS

Serves: 4   Oven: 350°

10 dried red New Mexico chiles*
½ cup water
½ teaspoon ground cumin
½ teaspoon ground oregano
1 tablespoon oil

1 dozen fresh tortillas
Oil
1½ cups grated Cheddar cheese
Grated raw onion (optional)

Place prepared chiles in blender; run at high speed. Add spices. Strain mixture through a sieve or strainer and place in frying pan. Add oil to sauce and water if needed. Cook 15 minutes over medium heat. Fry tortillas just slightly in hot oil and drain on paper towels. Dip tortillas in sauce. Fill with cheese (and chopped onions, if desired). Place rolled tortillas in a shallow baking dish. Pour over remaining sauce and sprinkle with remaining cheese. Bake approximately 20 minutes. Can be served with a fried egg on top and grated lettuce on the side.

*See page 209 for how to prepare dried red chiles.

CORN ENCHILADAS

Serves: 8   Oven: 375°

3 onions, chopped
3 tablespoons butter
2 12-ounce cans whole kernel corn
½ teaspoon whole cumin seed
¼ cup water
1 cup sour cream
2 cups grated Monterrey Jack
     cheese

2 4-ounce cans chopped green
     chile
12 tortillas
Oil
2 10-ounce cans red enchilada
     sauce (hot or mild)

Sauté onion in butter. Add corn, cumin seed and water. Cover and simmer until all liquid is gone (approximately 5 minutes). Stir in sour cream, 1 cup cheese and chile. Keep warm. Fry tortillas until soft; drain and roll each tortilla with corn mixture inside. Pour 1 can enchilada sauce into a baking dish. Add rolled tortillas and cover with other can of sauce. Sprinkle with remaining cup of cheese and bake covered 15 minutes and uncovered 15 minutes more. This recipe can be prepared ahead and heated when ready to serve.

MONTERREY ENCHILADAS

Serves: 6   Oven: 375°

3 tablespoons oil
2 large onions, thinly sliced
2 fresh green chiles, seeded
     and chopped
Salt to taste
2 cups sour cream

2 10-ounce cans red
     enchilada sauce
1 dozen corn tortillas
1 pound soft Monterrey Jack
     cheese, cut in strips
2 cups shredded Cheddar cheese

Heat oil in wide frying pan; add onions and chile and cook until soft. Season with salt. Turn mixture into a smaller container and set aside. In frying pan blend sour cream and enchilada sauce; heat and stir until bubbly. Remove from heat. Dip a tortilla in sauce and let stand a few seconds to soften; place in a shallow baking dish and spoon a part of the onion mixture across the center and top with cheese. Fold tortilla around filling. Repeat this procedure until all tortillas are filled and arranged close together in a baking dish. Ladle remaining sauce over casserole and sprinkle the tortillas evenly with cheese. Bake 20-25 minutes. Serve very hot.

CREAM ENCHILADAS

Serves: 4

2 large chopped onions	16-ounce can tomatoes, drained
Oil	2 cups grated Velveeta
2 large cloves garlic, chopped	cheese
1 4-ounce can chopped green	1 cup heavy cream
chile	12 tortillas

Fry onions in small amount of oil. Add garlic, green chile (juice included) and tomatoes. Simmer until thoroughly blended. Fifteen minutes before serving, add cheese and cream. Add more cream if mixture is too thick. Immerse tortillas in hot grease until heated thoroughly, then dip into chile mixture. Place on heated plates. Repeat process, serving 3 tortillas to each person. Spoon small amount of chile sauce on top of tortillas and garnish with shredded lettuce. The sauce may be made ahead and frozen.

GREEN ENCHILADA CASSEROLE

Serves: 4   Oven: 325°

1 onion, chopped	1 pound Longhorn or Monterrey
1 clove garlic, chopped	Jack cheese, or combi-
16-ounce can tomatoes	nation of both
2 4-ounce cans chopped	12 tortillas
green chiles	½ cup sour cream
1 cup sour cream	

Brown onions and garlic in bacon drippings. Add tomatoes and green chiles and cook until thick. Add 1 cup sour cream and grated cheese and stir until cheese is melted. Soften tortillas for a few seconds in hot oil and drain. In a casserole dish, alternate tortillas and sauce. Bake 30 minutes. Garnish with dabs of sour cream before serving.

HINTS ON MAKING TAMALES

One pound masa to 1 pound meat makes approximately 1 dozen tamales. The yield is determined by size of tamale. Filling may be prepared the day before and refrigerated. Beef as well as chicken or pork may be used if desired. Masa harina may be purchased at most stores. Canned red chile sauce may be substituted for fresh chile sauce but the same rich flavor is not obtained. Finger tamales may be made for appetizers. In making tamales, the cut end of the corn husk is used as the top and the slim, pointed end as the bottom. Dried red chile may be purchased as mild or hot, whichever the buyer prefers.

MRS. MITCHELL'S HOT TAMALES

Yield: 60

3½ pounds chicken
3½ pounds pork roast (if boneless, 2 pounds)
2½ pounds corn husks
24 pods dried red chile
4 cups water
2 teaspoons salt
1 large onion, chopped
3 cloves garlic, chopped
7 tablespoons salt

4 cups red chile sauce
2 tablespoons melted lard
5 pounds masa harina (ground corn for tamales bought at tortilla factory)
1½ pounds lard (not shortening)
5 tablespoons baking powder
3 cups meat broth (from meat cooked for filling)

Boil chicken and pork roast together and cook until meat falls off bones. Remove from stove and let cool. Discard fat. Drain meat and save broth. Then shred meats. Clean and dry corn husks. (Corn silks brush off easier when husk is dry.) Wash in warm water and leave to soak until ready to use. Wash red chile pods and remove stems and seeds. Bring chile and water to a boil; reduce heat and steam 10 minutes or longer. Pour liquid into blender; strain sauce through colander or seive if there are chile skins remaining after blending. The yield should be approximately 4 cups red chile sauce. Add 2 teaspoons salt. Sauté onions and garlic in 2 tablespoons lard; add 1 cup broth, 2 cups red chile sauce, 2 tablespoons salt and shredded meats to make filling. Let simmer 20 minutes, adding more broth if needed. Whip lard to consistency of whipped cream. Mix with masa, adding baking powder and 5 tablespoons salt. Beat until mixture is very fluffy (masa will float on top when dropped into a cup of cold water). Add 2 cups chile sauce and 2 cups broth; mix well. More broth can be added if masa seems too thick to spread easily. Spread husks with masa and filling by placing 1 heaping tablespoon masa in middle of husk and spreading toward outside edges, top and bottom. Spread closer to top of husk than bottom. Spread 2 tablespoons filling in middle of masa lengthwise. Overlap husk in a roll and fold bottom of husk up 1½-inches. Place on flat surface with fold underneath. Repeat until all masa and filling has been used.

Steam cook tamales by placing them upright on folded end in steamer. Place husks or foil on top; cover tightly and steam 2-3 hours. If no steamer is available, use a large cooking vessel such as a cold-pack canner. Line bottom with foil, as the husks scorch easily. Place tamales on rack or pan inside of cooker and put a tin can, which has had both ends opened, in the center. Stack tamales around can and pour four or five inches of water in cooker. Steam 2-3 hours tightly covered. Tamales are done when one can be rolled clear and free of the husk.

SWEET TAMALES

Yield: 3 dozen

1 pound masa harina
½ pound lard
1 teaspoon baking powder
1 tablespoon salt
1 cup chicken or pork broth
1 cup brown sugar

1 cup raisins
1 teaspoon cinnamon
½ teaspoon cloves
½ teaspoon allspice
½ cup chopped pecans

Mix masa, lard and baking powder together until a small portion (the size of a pea) floats in a glass of cold water. Add rest of ingredients to dough and mix thoroughly. Place 2 tablespoons dough in middle of corn husk, spreading towards top end and fold over bottom end. Proceed with same cooking instructions as for Hot Tamales.

TAMALE PIE

Serves: 6   Oven: 375°

1 4-ounce bag Fritos
1 cup grated American cheese

½ cup chopped onion
1 20-ounce can chile con
    carne without beans

Place layer of Fritos in bottom of buttered casserole. Spread half the chile, onion and cheese over Fritos. Repeat. Bake 25 minutes.

TAMALE RING

Serves: 8-12   Oven: 350°

1 cup yellow corn meal
1 cup milk
4 whole eggs, beaten
2 8-ounce cans tomato sauce
16-ounce can whole kernel corn

½ cup pitted black olives,
    sliced
1 teaspoon salt
1 tablespoon chile powder
1 20-ounce can chile con carne

Soak corn meal in 1 cup milk for 1 hour. Combine beaten eggs with tomato sauce; add other ingredients except chile con carne. Bake in buttered ring mold, setting mold in pan of water in oven for 1 hour or until knife inserted comes out clean. Unmold. Fill ring with heated chile con carne.

Very manly dinner!

INDIAN PIE

Serves: 6   Oven: 350°

1½ large onions, chopped	1 teaspoon sugar
Butter	2 dozen corn tortillas
3 14-ounce cans red	3 cups Velveeta cheese, grated
enchilada sauce	1 pint heavy cream
Salt	3 eggs, beaten

Cook onions in butter; add red enchilada sauce. Bring to a boil; add sugar and pinch of salt. Arrange tortillas, cheese, heavy cream and sauce in layers. Repeat several times. Pour eggs over last layer and bake 1 hour. Serve immediately.

PAELLA

Serves: 6   Oven: 325°

2 chickens, cut up	4 tablespoons oil
2 teaspoons salt	3 cups rice (Italian rice
1 teaspoon paprika	is excellent)
1 cup flour	½ teaspoon saffron
½ cup oil	2 teaspoons Tabasco
½ cup water	Salt to taste
1 pound cooked ham, cut into	2 16-ounce cans drained peas
bite-sized pieces	(liquid reserved)
1 medium onion, chopped	1 pound cooked seafood*
1 cup bell pepper, chopped	1 2-ounce jar sliced pimento
2 medium tomatoes, cut in pieces	

Early in the day, shake chicken in a bag containing mixture of salt, paprika and flour. Brown floured chicken well in two skillets with ¼ cup oil in each. Add ¼ cup water to each skillet and cook chicken 30 minutes. Remove chicken and brown the ham in the remaining oil; set aside. Later in day in a clean skillet, sauté the onion, bell pepper and tomatoes in 4 tablespoons oil until onion is yellow. Remove and brown rice in the remaining oil, adding more oil if necessary. When brown, add onion mixture, 6 cups liquid (liquid from peas plus broth or water), saffron, Tabasco and salt. Cook the rice until just underdone. Put rice mixture, chicken and ham in a large container; cover and cook in oven for about 30 minutes, watching the rice. Uncover and add peas, seafood and pimento. Heat throughout and serve.

*Shrimp, clams, mussels or scallops.

CHICKEN OR TURKEY MOLE

Serves: 6

1 turkey or 2 3-pound chickens,
    cut into pieces
2 tablespoons bacon grease
2 cups mole sauce (home pre-
    pared recipe below, or 1
    jar commercial sauce*)
1½ cups broth
½ teaspoon salt
Dash coriander

Dash cumin
Dash garlic powder
Dash ground cinnamon
1 rounded teaspoon peanut
    butter
⅛ round of Mexican
    chocolate
2 teaspoons sugar
1 heaping teaspoon raisins

Simmer the cut up turkey or chicken in water to cover until tender, add-ing salt to taste. Heat oil and add mole sauce. Fry a few minutes; add remaining ingredients and simmer 30 minutes. Add broth if it gets too thick. Place boned turkey or chicken into sauce and heat thoroughly. Serve with hot buttered tortillas.

MOLE SAUCE:

Yield: 8 cups

30 chiles mulattos
20 chiles anchos
10 chiles pasillas
1 tablespoon mixed seeds from
    chiles
½ cup almonds (not blanched)
1 corn tortilla
2 French rolls
1 onion, peeled
2 peppercorns
1 clove garlic, peeled
1 tablespoon sesame seeds

Pinch anise seed
Pinch coriander
1 quarter Mexican chocolate
    (comes in rounds, marked
    in quarters)
4-6 cups hot turkey or chicken
    broth
½ cup oil
1 teaspoon sugar
Pinch cumin powder
Salt to taste
Pinch powdered cloves (optional)

Wash and dry the three kinds of chiles (all can be bought at Mexican food stores). Place chiles in a dry, heavy skillet and toast lightly. Remove seeds. Soak chiles in water to cover. Toast the tablespoon of chile seeds with the almonds in a dry skillet until brown. Fry the tortilla crisp in a little oil. Cut rolls in half and fry until brown. Grind all ingredients to the consistency of paste. Add a cup or more of broth to the ground chile (enough to strain the chile). Stir through sieve; add broth if needed. Sauce can be frozen in 2 cup amounts.

*8¼ ounces of Pipian Doña Maria Red Mole sauce can be used. Directions are on bottle. Use shaved milk chocolate in place of Mexican chocolate.

CHILES RELLENOS CON CARNE

Serves: 6

STUFFED CHILES:

1 pound boiling meat (or
    ground beef)
4 cups water
1 beef bouillon cube*
1 teaspoon salt
1 cup raisins

½ teaspoon cloves
1 teaspoon ground coriander seed
2 cloves garlic, chopped
2 tablespoons onion, chopped
12 long green chiles, roasted
    and peeled

If using boiling meat, cook in water until done. Reserve meat stock. Grind meat and add salt, raisins, spices, garlic and onion. Add enough of the stock to moisten; cook until thick. Prepare chiles for use. Slit each chile down the center; remove as many seeds as possible and fill with meat.

*If using ground meat, steam fry and use bouillon cube for stock.

BATTER:

6 eggs, separated
6 tablespoons flour

Salt to taste

Beat egg whites until stiff; beat yolks until thick and fold into whites. Add flour and mix well; add salt. Using a large spoon, dip stuffed chiles into batter. Drop into ½-inch hot oil and fry until brown on both sides. (In electric skillet fry with oil at 350°.) Remove chiles from skillet and drain on paper towels.

SAUCE:

4 tablespoons shortening
2 tablespoons flour

1 cup meat stock
1 cup tomato sauce

Brown flour in shortening; add meat stock and tomato sauce and cook for 5 minutes. Pour sauce over stuffed chiles and serve.

CHILES RELLENOS CON QUESO

Serves: 4

8 fresh long green chiles
½ pound sharp Cheddar cheese,
    grated
1 tablespoon onion, finely chopped

8 eggs
1 cup flour
Salt and pepper

Prepare chiles, being careful to make only one slit down the chile. Mix cheese and onion and fill chiles. Separate eggs; beat whites until stiff. Beat yolks until very light. Add yolks to whites, beating constantly. Season flour with salt and pepper. Dip chiles into flour and then into the egg mixture. Fry two at a time in skillet in ½-inch hot oil until golden. Turn once, browning both sides. Serve hot.

CHILE RELLENO CASSEROLE

Serves: 8   Oven: 350°

1 pound lean ground beef
½ cup chopped onion
½ teaspoon salt
¼ teaspoon pepper
2 4-ounce cans green chiles,
   seeded and halved crosswise
1½ cups grated sharp Cheddar
   cheese

1½ cups milk
¼ cup flour
4 beaten eggs
Dash Tabasco
½ teaspoon salt
¼ teaspoon pepper

In skillet, brown beef and onion in a little oil; drain off excess fat. Sprinkle with salt and pepper. Place half the chiles in 10x6x1½-inch casserole, sprinkle with cheese. Add meat mixture and another layer of chiles. Combine remaining ingredients and beat until smooth. Pour over meat mixture and bake until knife comes out clean (45-50 minutes). Cool 5 minutes and cut into 6-8 squares.

COLD CHILES RELLENOS

Serves: 4

8 fresh green chiles, roasted
   peeled and deveined
⅓ cup vinegar
⅔ cup salad oil
½ teaspoon salt
¼ teaspoon pepper

1 teaspoon dried oregano
1 6½-ounce can tuna
½ cup bell pepper, finely chopped
4 tablespoons mayonnaise
1 cup sour cream
Lettuce leaves

Prepare chiles. Make a marinade of the vinegar, oil, salt, pepper and oregano and marinate chiles for at least 1 hour. Drain tuna; mix with bell pepper and mayonnaise. Drain chiles and stuff with tuna mixture. Serve the stuffed chiles on lettuce leaves with sour cream on top of each chile. Serve with hot, buttered flour tortillas and corn on the cob.

Variation: For a salad, marinate chiles and stuff them with sour cream only.

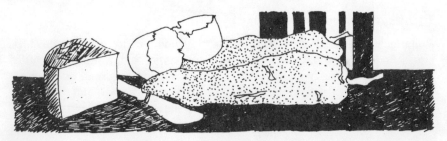

CHILES FRIOS

Serves: 6-10

2 ripe avocados
Salt to taste
Few drops lemon juice
10 fresh green chiles, roasted
    and peeled

1 large onion, sliced
1 bottle Kraft Miracle
    French dressing

Mash avocados and season to taste with salt. Add a few drops of fresh lemon juice to prevent avocados turning dark. Remove seeds from chiles. Salt insides; fill with mashed avocado and place in a pyrex dish. Thinly slice onion and arrange in circles on top of chiles. Pour dressing over all. Cover with aluminum foil and refrigerate at least overnight. This can be kept for two days. A good accompaniment for a Mexican dinner served as a salad.

Variation: Drain dressing from chiles; serve on lettuce leaves and top with sour cream.

GREEN CHILE PIE

Serves: 4   Oven: 325°

10 long fresh green chiles,
    roasted, peeled, halved
    and deveined
10 slices bacon
1 pound Cheddar cheese, grated

⅓ pound Swiss cheese, grated
6 eggs, beaten
Salt and pepper to taste
Slices of Muenster cheese

Line bottom and sides of a 9-inch pie pan with prepared chiles. Cook bacon. Drain and crumble over chiles. Mix Cheddar and Swiss cheeses; beat in eggs, salt and pepper. Pour mixture into pie pan. Top generously with slices of Muenster cheese. Bake 45-50 minutes.

BAKED CHILES

Serves: 4-6

1 26-ounce can green chiles, or
    8 fresh prepared chiles
¾ pound Monterrey Jack cheese
1 onion, chopped

1 tablespoon margarine
16-ounce can stewed tomatoes
2 eggs

Stuff chiles with grated Jack cheese and place in buttered casserole. Sauté onion in margarine. Add chopped stewed tomatoes and simmer 10 minutes. Pour sauce over chiles. Beat egg whites until stiff. Fold into beaten yolks and place over sauce and chiles. Bake 45-60 minutes. This casserole can be prepared ahead and frozen before the addition of the eggs.

BAKED CHILE CON QUESO

Serves: 6   Oven: 350°

1 small onion, chopped
Margarine
16-ounce can stewed tomatoes
3 4-ounce cans chopped green
    chile

¾ pound Package Monterrey
    Jack cheese, grated
12 corn tortillas
Salt to taste
1 cup sour cream

Sauté onion in margarine in skillet. Salt chopped onions. Place colander inside a mixing bowl. Add tomatoes to the colander. With a pastry cutter chop the tomatoes, letting the juice fall into bowl. Add chile to the tomatoes and stir. Remove colander with chile and tomatoes from the bowl. Place chile and tomatoes in 1½-quart baking dish; add onions and cheese. Bake until cheese melts (about 1 hour). Butter tortillas. Wrap tightly in foil and bake 30 minutes in same oven with chile. Spoon chile onto tortilla, top with sour cream and fold like a taco.

POSOLE CON PUERCO

Serves: 10-12

2 or 3 pound pork loin roast
2 tablespoons chile powder
1 8-ounce can tomato sauce
Dash garlic salt

Dash onion salt
1 slice white bread
1 29-ounce can hominy,
    drained

Boil roast in salted water until tender enough to fall apart. Cool the meat and cut into bite-sized pieces. Skim the fat from the cooled broth. (Ice cubes pick it up easily.) Mix chile powder with enough cold water to make a paste; put into broth. Add tomato sauce, garlic and onion salts. Soak bread in water and mash with a fork; add to broth. Add hominy. Simmer 30 minutes.

TURKEY OR CHICKEN SOPA

Serves: 8   Oven: 325°

1 pint sour cream
3 10-ounce cans tomato
    and green chile
1 onion, finely chopped
1 cup Monterrey Jack
    cheese, grated

4 cups diced cooked turkey, or
    6 chicken breasts, cooked
    and cut in pieces
8-10 tortillas, softened in
    hot oil and cut in half

Lightly grease a 3-quart casserole. Mix sour cream, tomato and chile, onion and chicken. Line casserole with tortillas, slightly overlapping. Cover with chicken mixture. Add another layer of tortillas and chicken and top with grated cheese. Bake 1 hour. May be prepared ahead and frozen. Allow the uncooked casserole to defrost at room temperature for 2 hours and proceed to bake for 1 hour.

BAKED MEXICAN RICE

Serves: 4   Oven: 350°

1 onion, finely chopped
1 clove garlic, chopped
⅓ cup olive oil
1 cup rice
1 teaspoon salt
1 teaspoon freshly ground black
    pepper

2 tablespoons chile powder
1 4-ounce can drained button
    mushrooms
10-12 slices chorizo
1½ cups beef or chicken stock
Parmesan or Longhorn cheese,
    grated

In a heavy casserole, sauté chopped onion and garlic in olive oil until just soft. Add rice, salt, pepper and chile powder; brown slightly. Add mushrooms, chorizo and beef or chicken stock (enough to come 1-inch above the rice), which has been heated until boiling. Cover with a tight lid and bake 30-35 minutes or until liquid is completely absorbed. Sprinkle with grated Parmesan or Longhorn cheese.

SPANISH RICE

Serves: 4-6

1 cup rice
2 tablespoons bacon grease
16-ounce can stewed tomatoes
2 cloves garlic, finely chopped

1 teaspoon black pepper
1 medium onion, chopped
1 teaspoon salt
1½ cups water

Fry rice in bacon grease until browned; add onion and garlic and sauté with rice for 1 minute. Add remaining ingredients, cover and simmer until tender (approximately 20 minutes).

SOPA SECA (SPANISH RICE)

Serves: 6

1 onion, chopped
1 clove garlic, finely chopped
1 4-ounce can chopped green
    chile
3 tablespoons bacon fat
1 cup long grain rice

1 cup canned Italian plum
    tomatoes
1 cup juice (drained from
    Italian tomatoes)
¾ cup canned garbanzo
    beans, drained
Salt to taste

Sauté onion, garlic and chile in fat until transparent. Add rice and cook over low heat, stirring occasionly, until rice is golden. Break up tomatoes and add to rice mixture. Pour in juice and bring to a boil. Cover and simmer about 20 minutes. Add garbanzos and cook 5 minutes or until rice is tender and has absorbed juice.

FRIJOLES

Serves: 6-8

1 cup pinto beans	1 teaspoon sugar
5 cups water	½ cup diced salt pork
1 clove garlic	Salt to taste

Wash and soak beans overnight. Cook in boiling water, adding the garlic, sugar and salt pork. If beans dry, add water whenever necessary. Cook beans until tender (3-6 hours, depending on the altitude). May be cooked in pressure cooker for 1 hour at 15 pounds pressure.

Variation: Chile powder or chopped green chile, sliced onion, ham hock—all or any of these may be cooked with beans.

RANCHERO BEANS

Serves: 8-10

2 cups pinto beans	1 fresh tomato, peeled and
Water	chopped
1 cup diced bacon ends	Salt
2 tablespoons chopped onion	Pepper
1 yellow (hot) chile, roasted and	Garlic powder
peeled	Chile powder

Sort beans; wash and soak overnight. Drain and in fresh water to cover, cook beans until done (at least 2 hours). Partially fry bacon; sauté onions, pepper and tomato in bacon grease. Add all to beans with seasonings and simmer for at least 15 minutes.

CHILE BEEF CASSEROLE

Serves: 8-10   Oven: 350°

½ cup raw rice	2 4-ounce cans whole
4 tablespoons cooking oil	green chiles
1 pound ground beef	2 cups bouillon
1 clove garlic, minced	1 cup tomato juice
2 onions, thinly sliced	1 small can tomato paste
¾ pound Monterrey Jack and	¾ teaspoon oregano
Old English cheese	¾ teaspoon cumin seed

Cook rice in oil about 5 minutes; remove rice. Add meat and garlic and cook until meat loses red color; drain. Cut chiles and cheese (or grate) into strips. Layer rice, meat, onion, chile and cheese in 2-quart casserole. Bring bouillon, tomato juice, tomato paste, oregano and cumin seed to a boil and pour over mixture. Cover tightly and bake 1 hour. Add more tomato juice if too dry.

INDEX

Soups

MEXICAN INDEX

TABLE OF MEASUREMENTS

1 dash = 2-3 drops
3 teaspoons = 1 tablespoon = ½ fluid ounce
2 liquid tablespoons = 1 ounce
4 tablespoons = ¼ cup
16 tablespoons = 1 cup
1 cup = 8 ounces = ½ pint
2 cups = 1 pint
4 cups = 2 pints = 1 quart
4 quarts = 1 gallon
16 ounces = 1 pound

EQUIVALENCIES

2 tablespoons butter = 1 ounce
1 stick butter = ½ cup
½ pound butter = 1 cup
1 pound granulated sugar = 2 cups
1 pound brown sugar, packed = 2½ cups
1 pound confectioners sugar, sifted = 4¾ cups
1 pound flour, sifted = 4 cups
1 pound cheese, grated = 4 cups
16 marshmallows = ¼ pound
½ pint cream = 2 cups, whipped
1 square chocolate = 1 ounce
1 pound diced cooked chicken = 3 cups

The active members of the Junior League of El Paso wish to express their appreciation and thanks to the many contributors who have made our book possible. We are most grateful to the sustaining members who gave so generously of their time in compiling the material in this book and to the editors Carolyn Ponsford and Jan McNutt. Thanks also to our technical advisors, Mr. and Mrs. Howell Zinn, Mr. Morgan Broaddus, Mr. Russell Waterhouse, and Mrs. Sandra Martin.

COOKBOOK ORDER FORM

JUNIOR LEAGUE OF EL PASO, INC.
520 THUNDERBIRD
EL PASO, TEXAS 79912

Please send me_____copies at $9.95 per copy plus $1.50 for postage

and handling. Enclosed is my check or money order for _____

Name _____

Address _____

City and State _____

Zip Code _____

☐ Check if gift.

Texas residents add 50¢ for state sales tax.
Make checks payable to: The Junior League of El Paso, Inc.

COOKBOOK ORDER FORM

JUNIOR LEAGUE OF EL PASO, INC.
520 THUNDERBIRD
EL PASO, TEXAS 79912

Please send me_____copies at $9.95 per copy plus $1.50 for postage

and handling. Enclosed is my check or money order for _____

Name _____

Address _____

City and State _____

Zip Code _____

☐ Check if gift.

Texas residents add 50¢ for state sales tax.
Make checks payable to: The Junior League of El Paso, Inc.

COOKBOOK ORDER FORM

JUNIOR LEAGUE OF EL PASO, INC.
520 THUNDERBIRD
EL PASO, TEXAS 79912

Please send me_____copies at $9.95 per copy plus $1.50 for postage

and handling. Enclosed is my check or money order for _____

Name _____

Address _____

City and State _____

Zip Code _____

☐ Check if gift.

Texas residents add 50¢ for state sales tax.
Make checks payable to: The Junior League of El Paso, Inc.

COOKBOOK ORDER FORM

JUNIOR LEAGUE OF EL PASO, INC.
520 THUNDERBIRD
EL PASO, TEXAS 79912

Please send me_____copies at $9.95 per copy plus $1.50 for postage

and handling. Enclosed is my check or money order for _____

Name _____

Address _____

City and State _____

Zip Code _____

☐ Check if gift.

Texas residents add 50¢ for state sales tax.
Make checks payable to: The Junior League of El Paso, Inc.

COOKBOOK ORDER FORM

JUNIOR LEAGUE OF EL PASO, INC.
520 THUNDERBIRD
EL PASO, TEXAS 79912

Please send me_____copies at $9.95 per copy plus $1.50 for postage

and handling. Enclosed is my check or money order for _____

Name _____

Address _____

City and State _____

Zip Code _____

☐ Check if gift.

Texas residents add 50¢ for state sales tax.
Make checks payable to: The Junior League of El Paso, Inc.

COOKBOOK ORDER FORM

JUNIOR LEAGUE OF EL PASO, INC.
520 THUNDERBIRD
EL PASO, TEXAS 79912

Please send me_____copies at $9.95 per copy plus $1.50 for postage

and handling. Enclosed is my check or money order for _____

Name _____

Address _____

City and State _____

Zip Code _____

☐ Check if gift.

Texas residents add 50¢ for state sales tax.
Make checks payable to: The Junior League of El Paso, Inc.